Fortuna and the Immortality Garden (Machine)

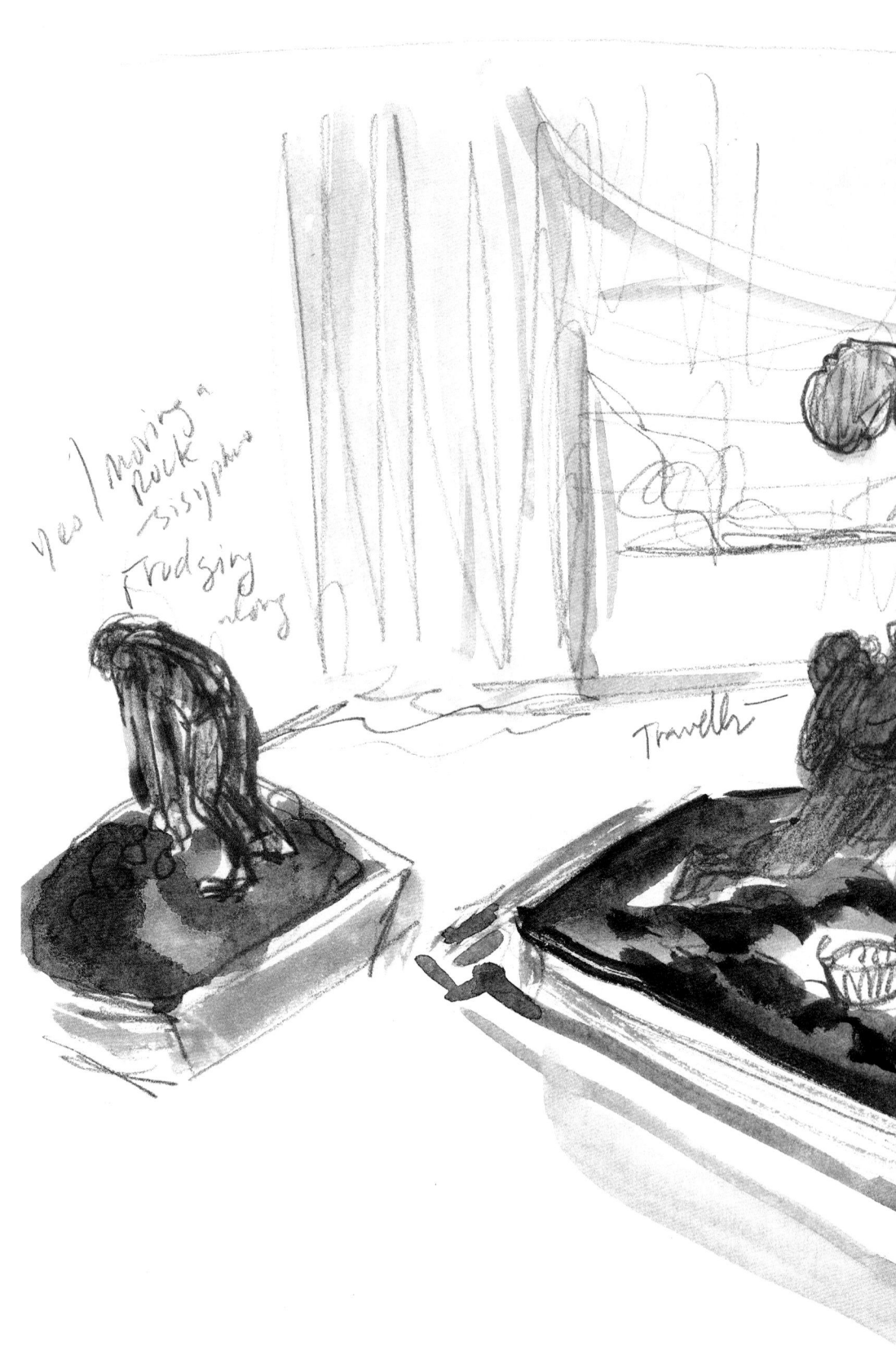

varous posting

Background
Cutouts or
wall print
Landscape of
NorCal
Village

Portuna

gold Mining
Baby girl room

The Immortality Garden (Machine) *remembers:*
my dad, Larry M. Walker, who nurtured me,
Brent Sikkema, who encouraged me,
June Leaf, who danced with me,
and Pearl, whom I held.

—KW

Fortuna and the Immortality Garden (Machine)
A Respite for the Weary Time-Traveler.
Featuring a Rite of Ancient Intelligence
Carried out by The Gardeners
Toward the Continued Improvement
of the Human Specious
by
Kara E-Walker

Edited by Eungie Joo
San Francisco Museum of Modern Art in association
with Princeton University Press, Princeton and Oxford

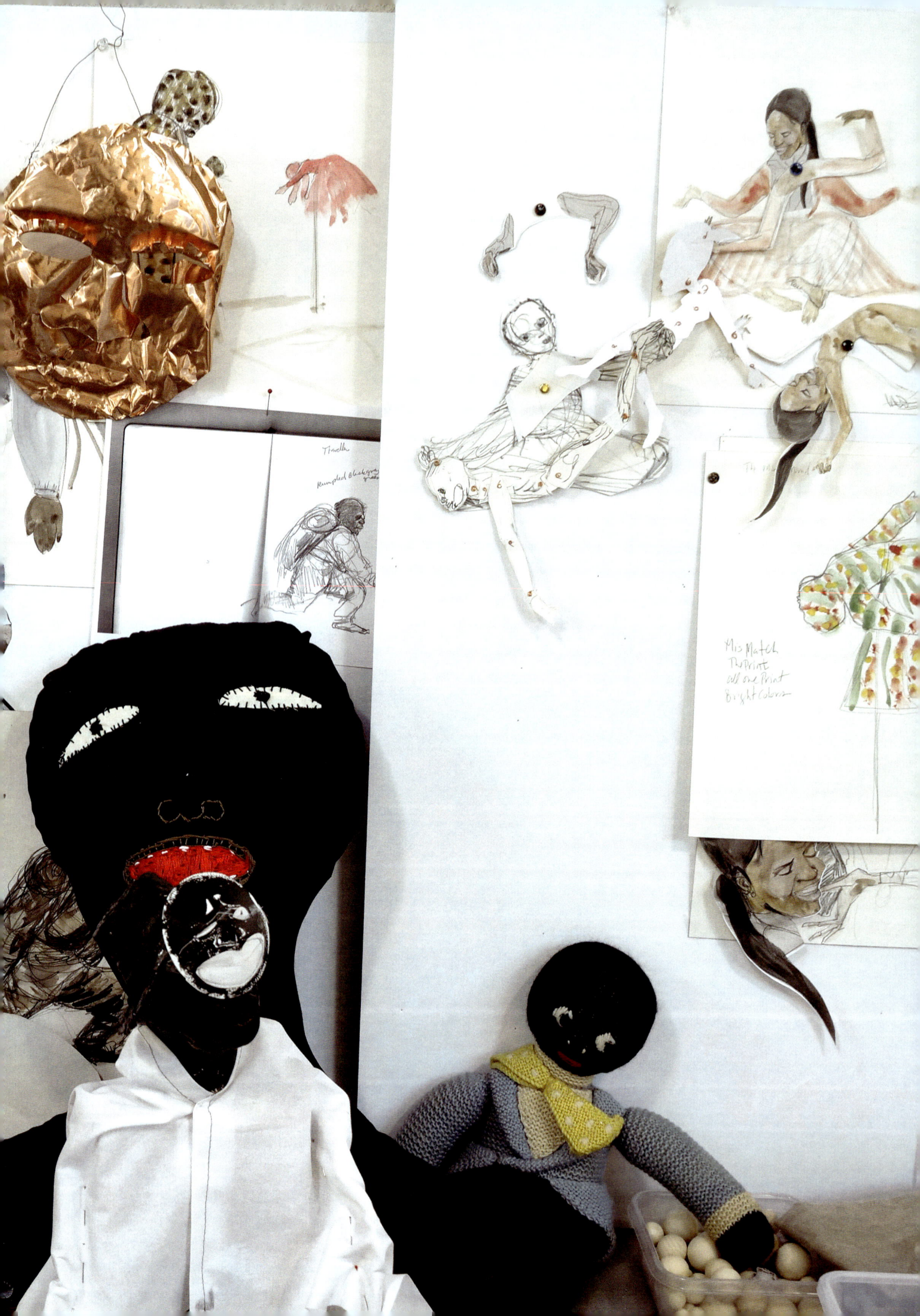

CONTENTS

INTRODUCTION   8
Eungie Joo

I AM NOT YOUR ROBOT   12
Kara Walker

IN CONVERSATION   18
Kara Walker and Eungie Joo

GENERAL STRIKE … WHAT SHAPES REMAIN   34
Damani McNeil

CYBORGS: A MYTH OF POLITICAL IDENTITY   50
Donna Haraway

SELECTIONS FROM THE NOTEBOOKS   58
OF GARY GRAHAM

RACE AND THE UNCANNY VALLEY: 74
NIGGERS, SLAVES, AND MACHINES
David A. M. Goldberg

AFTERWORD   121
Christopher Bedford

ACKNOWLEDGMENTS   123
Eungie Joo

CONTRIBUTORS   126

IMAGE CREDITS   127

INTRODUCTION
Eungie Joo

This publication documents the mesmerizing new installation *Fortuna and the Immortality Garden (Machine) / A Respite for the Weary Time-Traveler. / Featuring a Rite of Ancient Intelligence Carried out by The Gardeners / Toward the Continued Improvement of the Human Specious / by / Kara E-Walker*, commissioned by the San Francisco Museum of Modern Art. In 2018, when Walker was presented with SFMOMA's Contemporary Vision Award, she and I began discussing an exhibition of her work in San Francisco, her hometown and childhood inspiration. We landed on the idea of activating the amazing Roberts Family Gallery with its first site-specific commission. The final project refused to take shape for many months, until, by the artist's own admission, a COVID-induced fever dream propelled her many ideas into form.

By the time this project emerged in full, Walker had already begun to assemble an array of research materials on transhumanism, Afropessimism, medieval robotics, and body autonomy. As she began to imagine each automaton and its movement, Walker sewed, drew, stuffed, cut, glued, and crawled. She envisioned a field of obsidian to absorb negative energy and offer a new start; she pulled out images of the orange sky that loomed over us during California wildfires on September 9, 2020; she remembered a man slumping on the streets of San Francisco; she thought about the public and what the work could offer them. For the publication, we wanted to remember these sources and fleeting thoughts through rich documentation and a combination of meaningful texts to guide our thinking beyond the work itself. Assembled here are pieces of fiction, theory, conversation, and critique set amid a visual story of imagination, experimentation, and production.

In her text that opens this volume, "I Am Not Your Robot," Walker explains the work in profound terms related to body, soul, and machine, situating it as a reflection of numerous personal associations, including her "obsession with obscure and outmoded premodern forms of popular expression," and describing it as both mechanism and memorial.[1] Walker's captivating words continue in our conversation—one between artist and curator—in which we discuss her inspirations, sources, and ideas surrounding the development of *Fortuna and the Immortality Garden (Machine)*. At the heart of the work, she says, is the question "What is to become of us?" She goes on to explain the pleasure of studio work; how her attempt to use ChatGPT to help generate fortunes failed; her love of the California Academy of Sciences; and this exhibition's goals of access, acceptance, and the affirmation of humanity. Contextualizing her exploration of technology, she admits, "My automatons reference an eternally retrospective Blackness—archetypes rather than stereotypes. Their fantastical costuming contains signifiers of oppression and destruction and mortality.... Therein comes the question of the ethics of robotics and what they want robots to do, and how different is that from slavery?"[2]

Walker's thinking about human, machine, and feminist possibilities was influenced by Donna Haraway's seminal 1985 essay "A Cyborg Manifesto." As Walker and I researched new ideas around feminism, technology, and freedom, it became clear that this early source of inspiration remained the most relevant. In the final section, which is reprinted here, Haraway writes, "Cyborg politics are the struggle for language and the struggle against perfect communication, against the one code that translates all meaning perfectly, the central dogma of phallogocentrism. That is why cyborg politics insist on noise and advocate pollution, rejoicing in the illegitimate fusions of animal and machine."[3] We hope younger imaginations might find new fruit in her provocative transgressions.

Intrigued by an emergent generation's take on history, labor, and the goals of innovation, we commissioned a text by writer Damani McNeil, in which he positions the intersection of technology, labor, and race—concepts central to Walker's work—in a fictional Bay Area of the near future. In "General Strike... What Shapes Remain," the narrator remembers a funerary procession for two slain union members during the West Coast waterfront strike in 1934, which led to the formation of the International Longshore and Warehouse Union, one of the first integrated unions. By the mid-twenty-first century, owners are done with labor's demands: "It became clear that the human element was detrimental to the human experience, and no one felt like those folks who served others or built the nation were all that important to keep around." In this dystopia, where everything appears clean and efficient, all that was forgotten blows back in with the return of an enigmatic fog. As McNeil's narrator describes, "In a place where so much has been lost to time and so much has been sacrificed in the name of progress, the fog has quite a laundry list of grievances and people to remember."[4]

Extrapolating on related concepts in his essay "Race and the Uncanny Valley: Niggers, Slaves, and Machines," David A. M. Goldberg calls upon his decades-long research on race and technology to explore inextricable connections between chattel slavery and technology-based "innovation" and automation through Walker's *Fortuna and the Immortality Garden (Machine)*. He notes that "escape from anti-Blackness remains impossible, but using twenty-first-century tactics [Walker] takes advantage of the brief and narrow window of opportunity for self-definition that opens when Black folks gain representational control of a medium."[5] Dissecting the fetishization of Black automatons by the likes of Harriet Beecher Stowe, the robotics theory of Masahiro Mori, the techno-utopian ideas of Theodor H. Nelson, and the racialized performances of robots in demonstration videos by Boston Dynamics, Goldberg recognizes Walker's deployment of technology as masterfully anachronistic and powerfully intentional.

Finally, this publication lingers on many aspects of the production and development of *Fortuna and the Immortality Garden (Machine)*, thanks in large part to its active documentation by Ari Marcopoulos. His understanding of the artist and the work adds immeasurable dimension to this photography, which tells its own visual story in these pages. Interspersed among these pages are historical photographs by Arnold Genthe and John Gutmann that document, respectively, the fires caused by the 1906 San Francisco earthquake and the 1934 waterfront strike. The Genthe photograph reproduced at the end of this book served as source material for the custom fabrics designed by Gary Graham for the automatons Belltoller and Waterbearer. Images of these fabrics and a text on the collaboration between Graham and Walker on the costuming of the automatons can be found on pages 58–63. Many years ago, Walker encountered Eugene Richards's photograph *Broken Doll* (1970), in which a young girl conspiratorially touches heads with her doll (page 80)—a confidence echoed in Walker's automaton Whisperer. The completed commission as installed at SFMOMA is richly documented here by Fredrik Nilsen as well as Marcopoulos. We hope this book not only serves as a keepsake but also inspires further thinking on the work.

1. Walker, page 16 in this publication.
2. Walker, page 28 in this publication.
3. Haraway, page 52 in this publication.
4. McNeil, pages 37 and 40 in this publication.
5. Goldberg, page 76 in this publication.

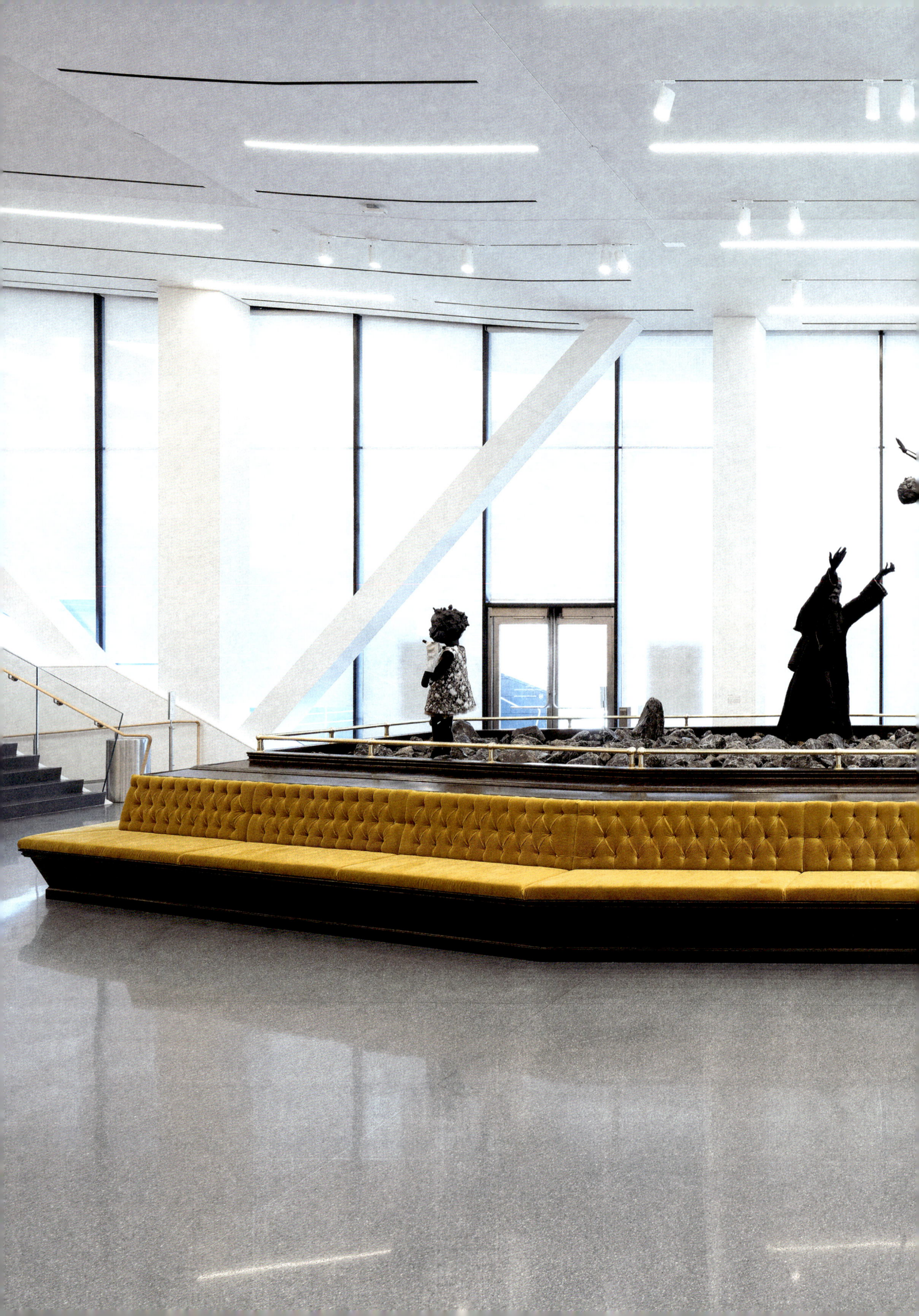

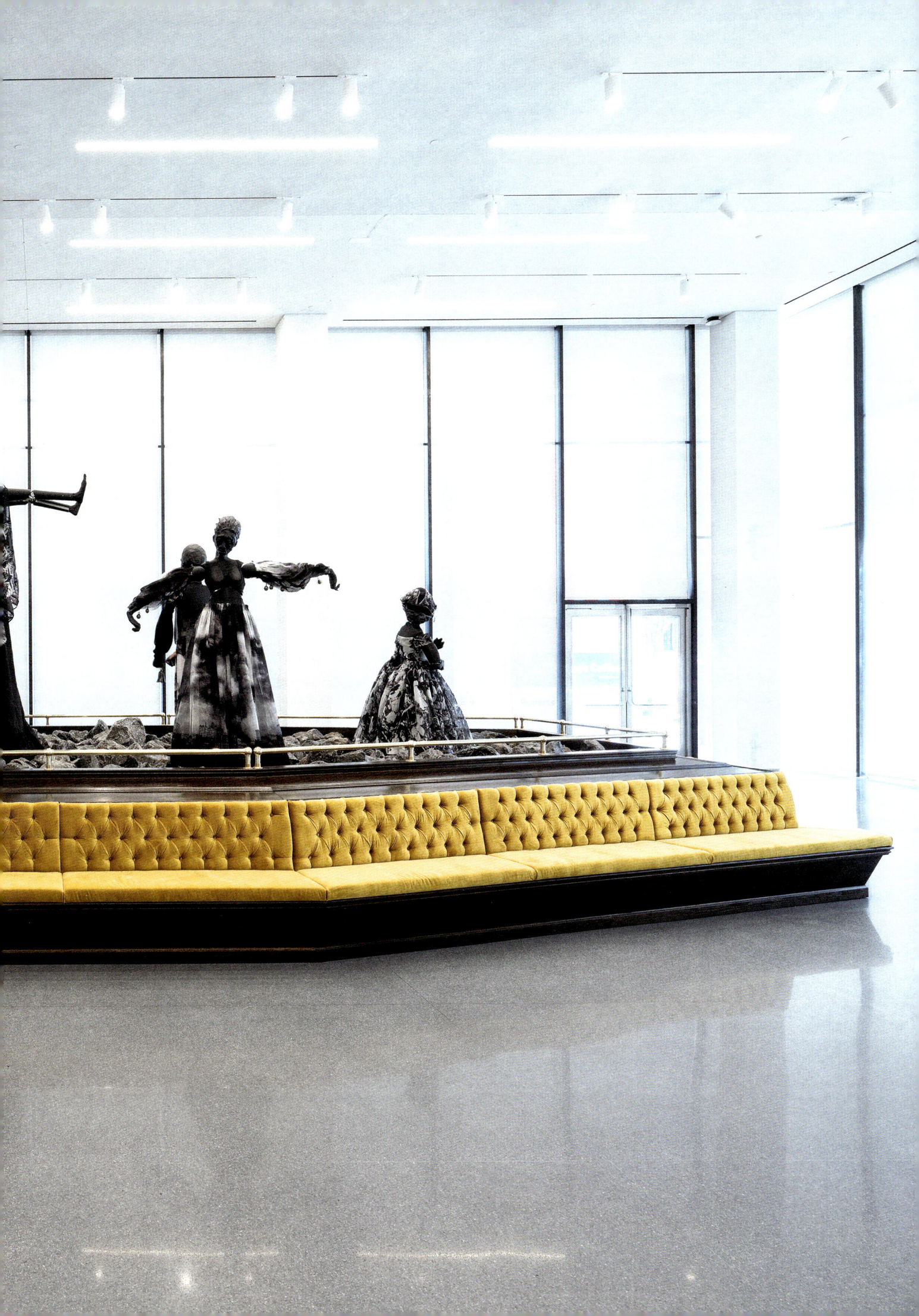

I AM NOT YOUR ROBOT
Kara Walker

Fortuna and the Immortality Garden (Machine) was informed by a long list of personal associations with the Bay Area and conceived during the dark nights of quarantine. My thinking on this project was born out of an existential crisis and fever dream as my own body succumbed to sweat-stained sheets, Gatorade-coated teeth, intense body pain, upper respiratory distress, the specter of death, and the abject loneliness of the COVID-19 lockdown.

It's fair to say that almost everyone who has existed from 2020 on has at some point shared the experience of life as a series of consumable signs on a rectangular screen: ordering food, streaming movies, gaming, interacting on social media, listening to audiobooks, podcasts, and all manner of media input and communications. We are all cyborgs now. But the crisis of the age concerns the outlandish realization that with so much content, the body has become too small a container, a useless relic in need of extensions.

But if the Body is useless, what about the presence or absence of its soul, and what about the unfinished business of human liberation struggles globally? If we jump to the conclusion that Machine objects and systems are being built to subdue the human spirit, then what about the touch, sound, energy fields, and extrasensory perception of the human animal experience? How might these be corralled as possible modes for bridging the "uncanny valley" of our heavily vision-based, extremely secular interactions with technology?

> *Mechanization is often taken as an index of modernization. But automaton icons had a medieval impetus in a tradition of imagery in which the tangible, visible, earthly representations of Christian lore and doctrine were pushed ever farther. The icons were representations in motion, inspirited statues: they were* mechanical *and* divine. *Rolling their eyes, moving their lips, gesturing, and grimacing, these automata dramatized the intimate, corporeal relation between representation and divinity, icon and saint.*[1]

Seventeenth-century iconoclasts made a big show of destroying idolatrous Catholic automatons on the pretext that they were, in fact, human-operated machines that duped the faithful into believing they were powered by divinity.

However, *could* there be a ghost in that machine? And might that ghost be an ancestor? And might that ancestor have something to tell us?

Is the ersatz *soul* of cyberspace or AI really the best we humans can innovate to unseat eons of evolution? What power structures benefit from all this innovation, especially if it's done, at worst, in the service of mass mind control or, at best, in the comedic quest for immortality?

> *Puppets, mannequins, waxworks, automatons, dolls, painted scenery, plaster casts, dummies, secret clockworks, mimesis, and illusion: all form a part of the fetishist's magic and artful universe. Lying between life and death, animated and mechanic, hybrid creatures and creatures to which hubris gave birth, they all may be likened to fetishes. And, as fetishes, they give us, for a while, the feeling that a world not ruled by our common laws does exist, a marvelous and uncanny world.*[2]

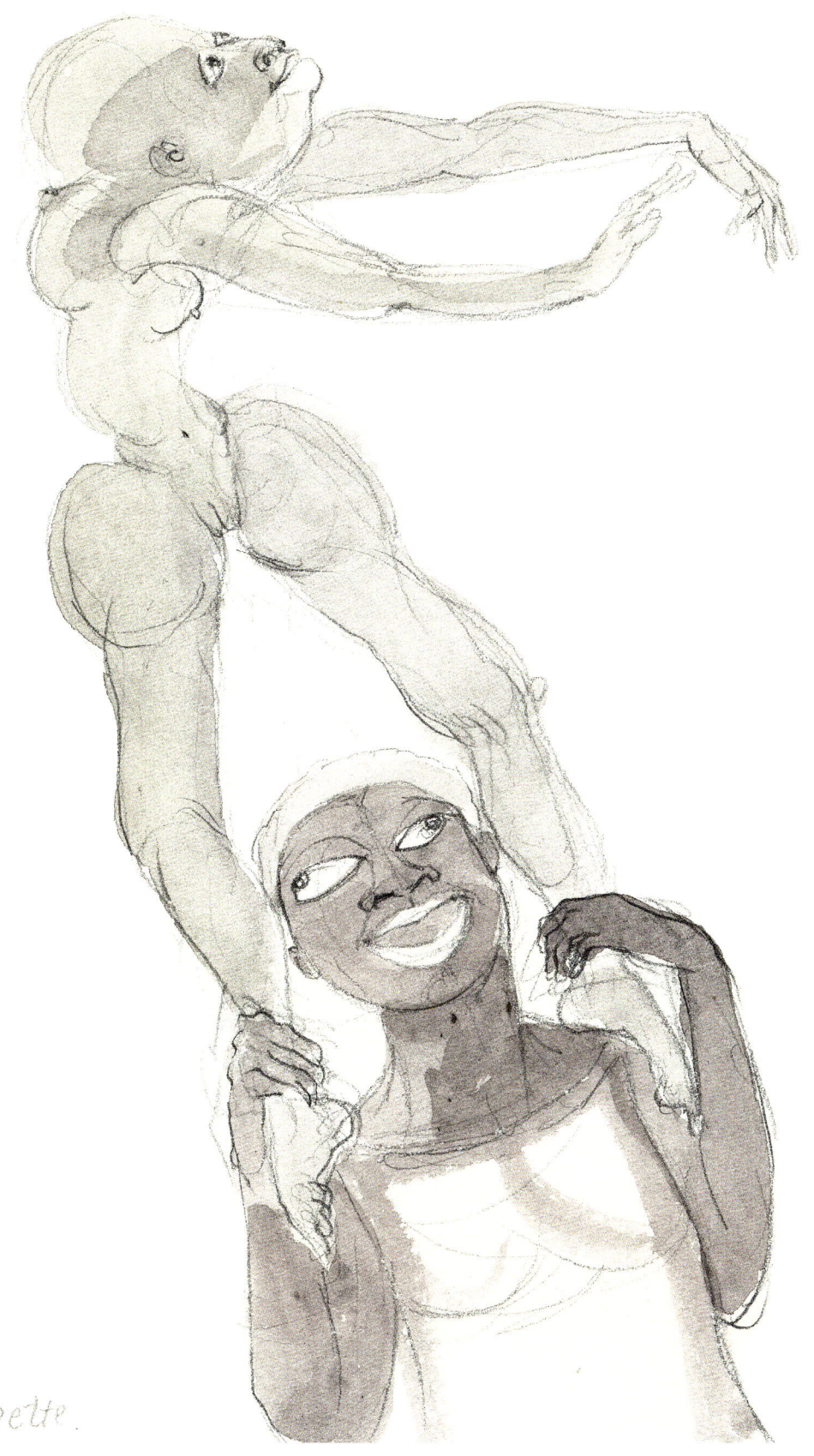

Poopette

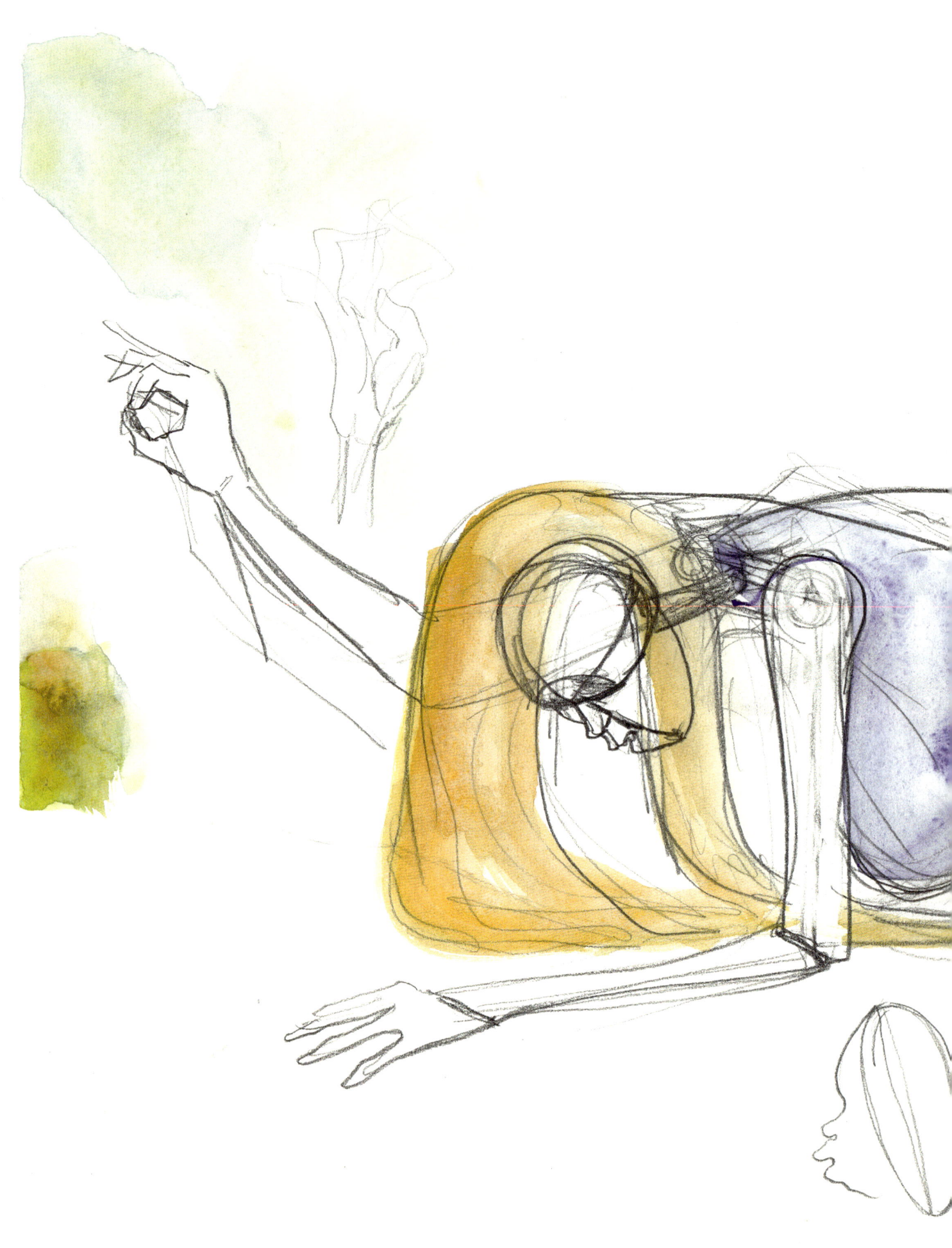

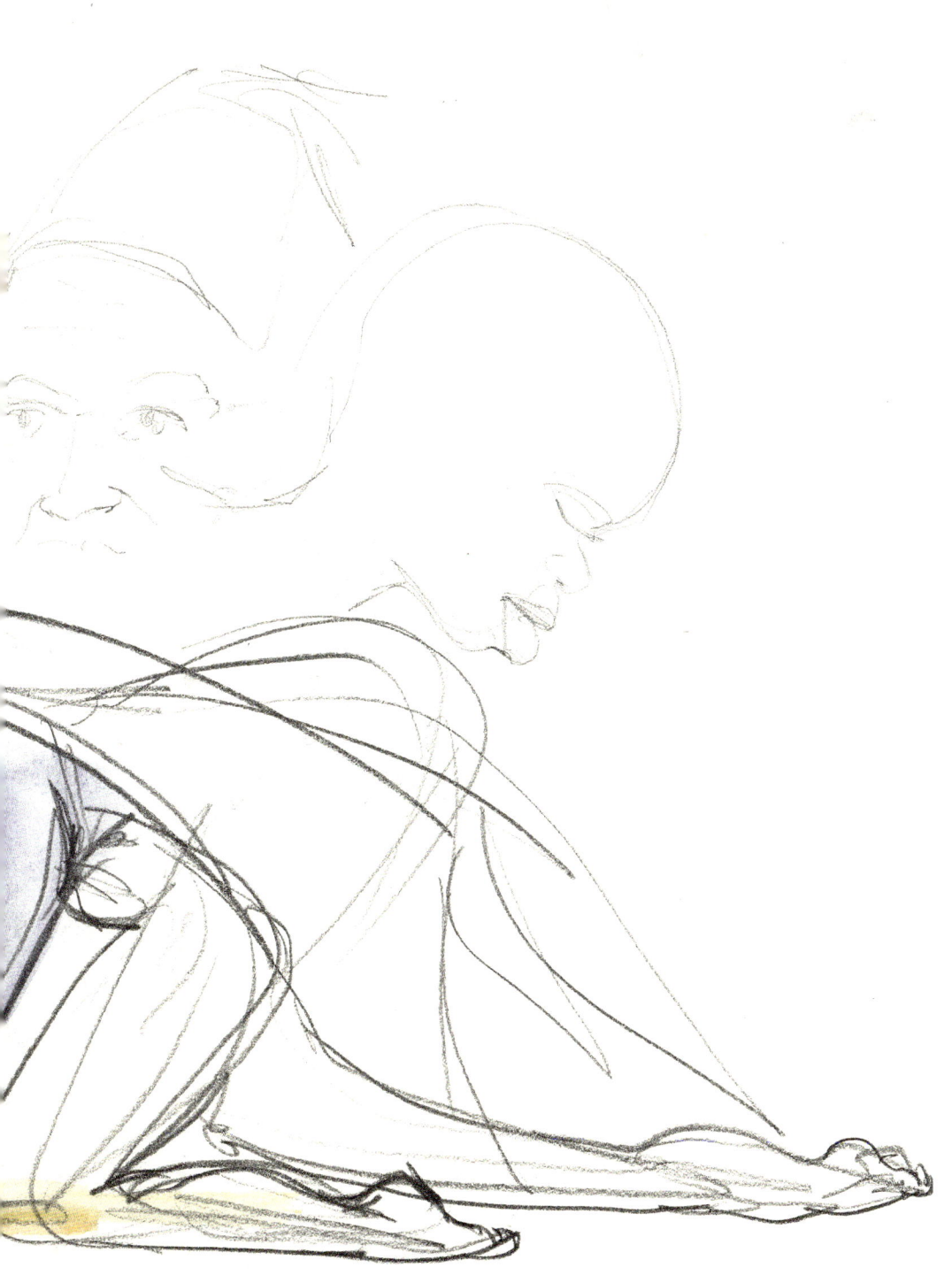

Fortuna and the Immortality Garden (Machine) reflects my obsession with obscure and outmoded premodern forms of popular expression: silhouettes and shadow puppet films, sugar sculptures and fountain works, the steam-powered musical calliope, and now the automaton—not quite human, but much more than a puppet. Powered seemingly by its own agency yet informed by the intersecting histories of American chattel slavery and its legacy of dehumanization, the rise of machine learning, and the desire to cheat all forms of death, including the social and the physical. Seven of the eight automata inhabiting the installation perform a ritual of resurrection and dissolution; the eighth, Fortuna, offers the viewer a printed fortune or kind of absolution, a text for contemplation.

Fortuna offers this missive: "The Singularity will be Negro."

The large settee in the Roberts Family Gallery creates a social space with a nostalgia for San Francisco's golden age, beginning in the 1840s, when it was a migratory haven for many waves of ethnic groups seeking to make their fortunes, until its recent ongoing depopulation, its urban streets now home to housing exiles. The space is a luxury, a place to rest and expand and gaze upon the past as if it were never past but always an embryonic possibility, an Eden without an expulsion. A Freedom born, not fought for.

The garden of obsidian is a powerful protective tool. Obsidian is a volcanic glass, here obtained in the ancient volcanic field surrounding Mount Konocti in Lake County, California. Indigenous ancestors utilized obsidian for arrowheads and blades because of its razor-sharp edges. Its reflective black surface makes it a perfect tool for divination; polished to a mirrorlike sheen, it is capable of providing insight into the psyche of the beholder. Obsidian is thought to shield against negative spiritual energy and to promote clarity of thought, and today's spiritual practitioners believe it can heal emotional trauma from the past.

The Immortality Garden (Machine) is a mechanism for sympathetic magic, and for probing the liminal spaces between human and machine, divinity and doll, future and past, living and dead, cynicism and wonder. It is a memorial to Black existence as both a product of technological innovation and a skilled decoder of systems of control.

1. Jessica Riskin, "Machines in the Garden," *Republics of Letters: A Journal for the Study of Knowledge, Politics, and the Arts* 1, no. 2 (2010): 27.
2. Janine Chasseguet-Smirgel, *Creativity and Perversion* (New York: W. W. Norton, 1984), 88.

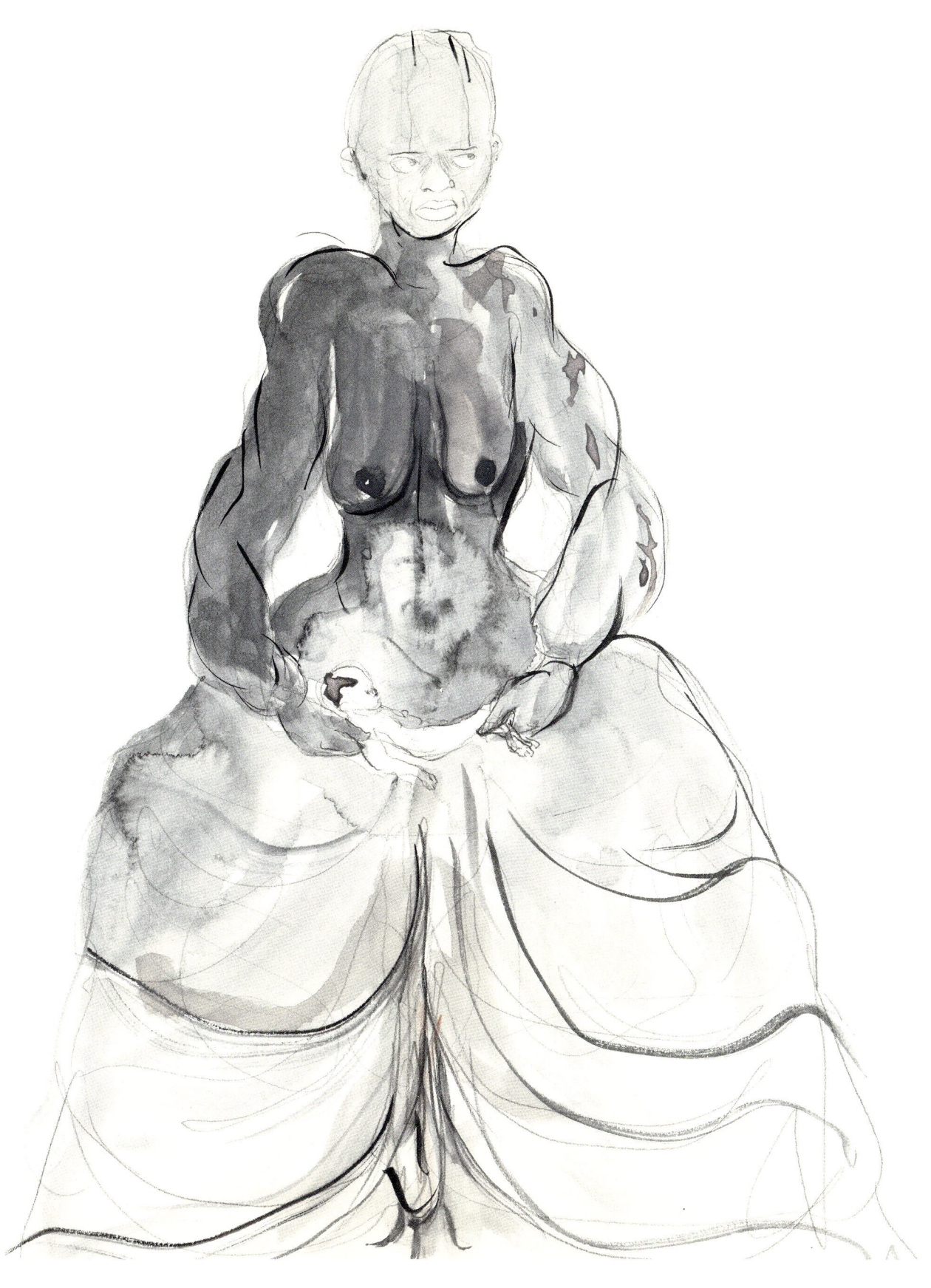

IN CONVERSATION
Kara Walker and Eungie Joo

The following conversation took place at Kara Walker's studio, Brooklyn, New York, over a few sessions on September 25 and 26, 2023.

EUNGIE JOO We started talking about the possibility of doing something at SFMOMA in 2018, and you came out for your first site visit before the pandemic. Can you share a little about the inception of this new work?

KARA WALKER In the early stages of working on this commission, I was thinking about past large-scale works of mine and the realization that monuments are largely about death. As this project was taking shape, it was resembling an ancient necropolis, or I was approaching ideas around immortality. A big reason was that we were in the midst of the COVID-19 pandemic and that, along with my health and the health of my loved ones, was on my mind—the realities of death, confusion around mass loss of life, and the human, maybe slightly delusional desire to make it go away, or to transform that death into something resembling everlasting life.

EJ You've talked a lot about automation, AI, antiquated robots, and the body and technology. I was wondering why this aspect of technology came into play at this time.

KW It comes back again to the pandemic and illness and my own vulnerability, the vulnerability of people I love, and our necessary reliance on tech to keep us in contact, and its importance to maintain the essence of community. We could talk or Face-Time with one another, we could order all the food we needed and have it delivered. I made this one fast drawing that alludes to this. It's a grotesque self-portrait, eyeballs bulging out of their sockets, holding an iPad, glued completely to this one outlet from isolation and quarantine.

And that got me thinking about the love/hate relationship that we are developing with needing, wanting, and feeling somewhat addicted to tech. The reduction of my body into snippets and memes and hashtags got me thinking about the permeability of the body. And the downloading of new ideas or new material into the body. It's as though our bodies are now the necessary extensions and it's the devices that actually want to be communicating to each other. Ours is the flesh that can make that happen. We're the necessary piece of technology that they don't have in order to go.

EJ The battery.

KW Yes, we are the engine or the battery. And so I started looking very broadly at ideas about organ theft and transhumanism.

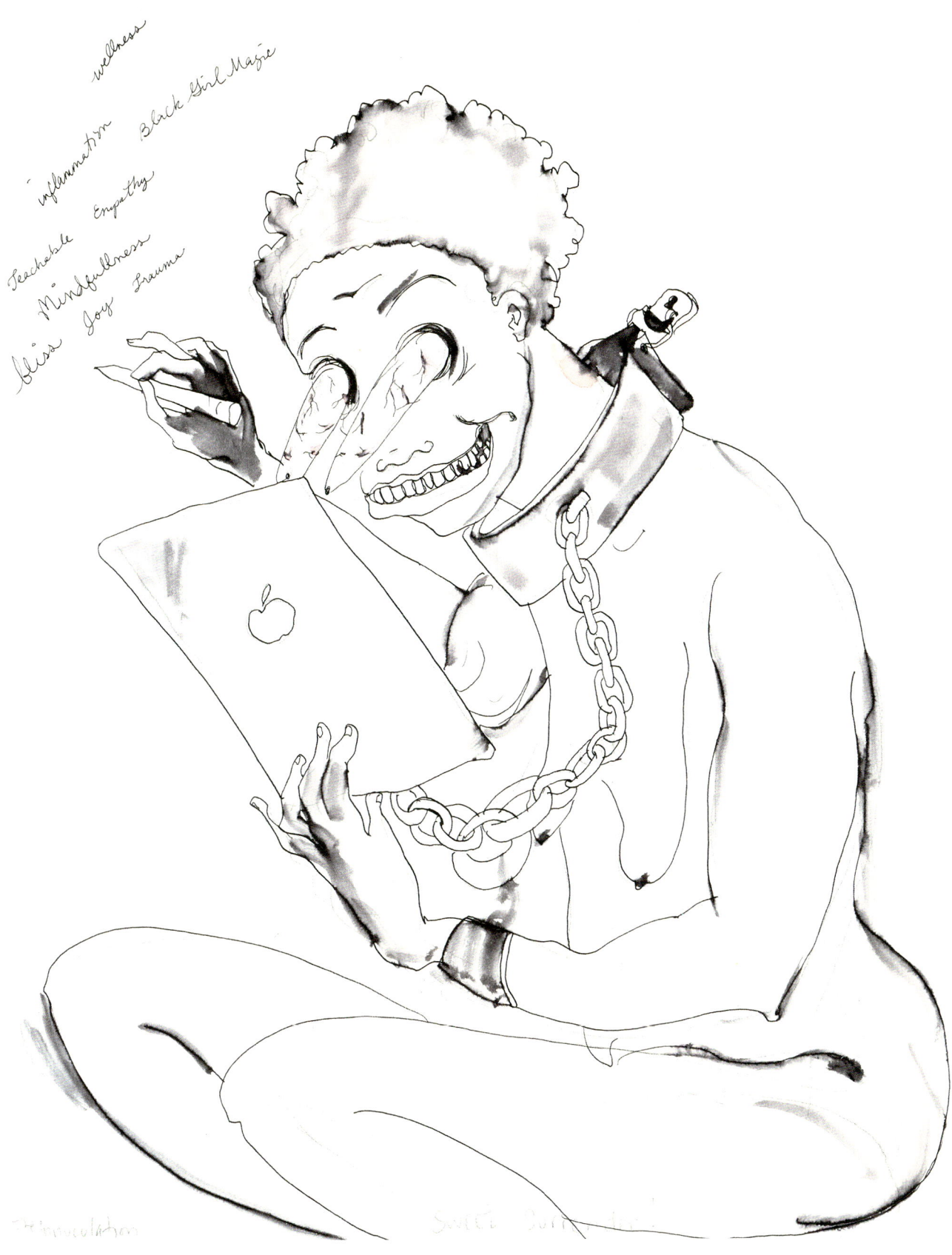

A. VOID. FILLED WITH HUMAN
~~REMAIN(S)~~
REMNANTS - FRAGMENTS

I.E. THE EXPERIENCE, EXPRESSION
AND APPEARANCE
OF
BLACKNESS, GENDER, AGE, ~~████~~
MOOD

AND/OR/ALSO
ABJECTION, COMMAND, ADDICTION
SELF-ABNEGATION, MARTYRDOM

ALL QUALITIES, IT'S SAID,
THAT ARE EMBEMATIC OF PARTIAL
HUMANITY AS IT IS.

SO, TO BUILD BACK INTO A VACATED
BODY. A ~~████~~ SELF THAT IS HALF HUMAN
AT ITS BASE → LEAVES A REMAINDER →

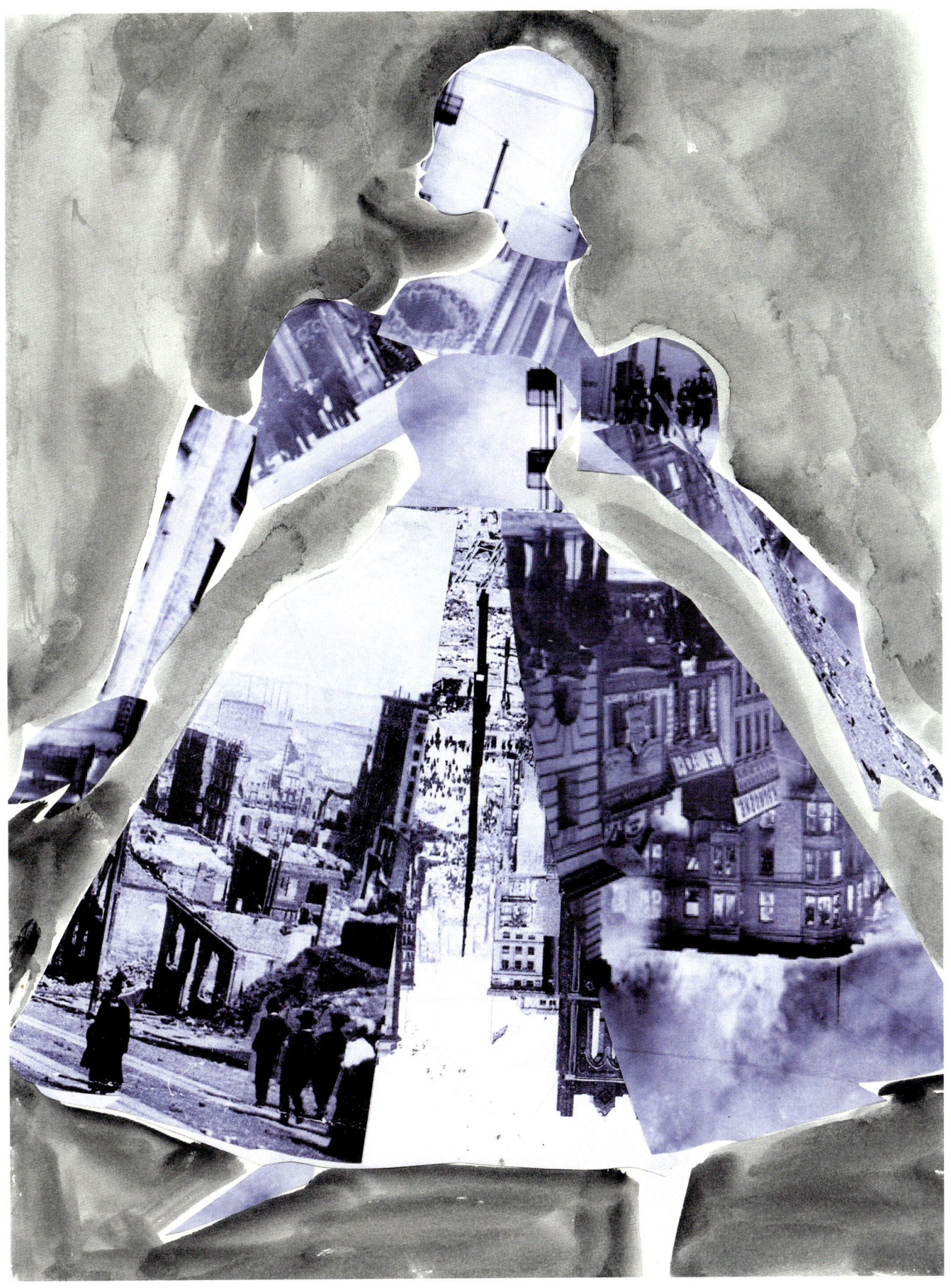

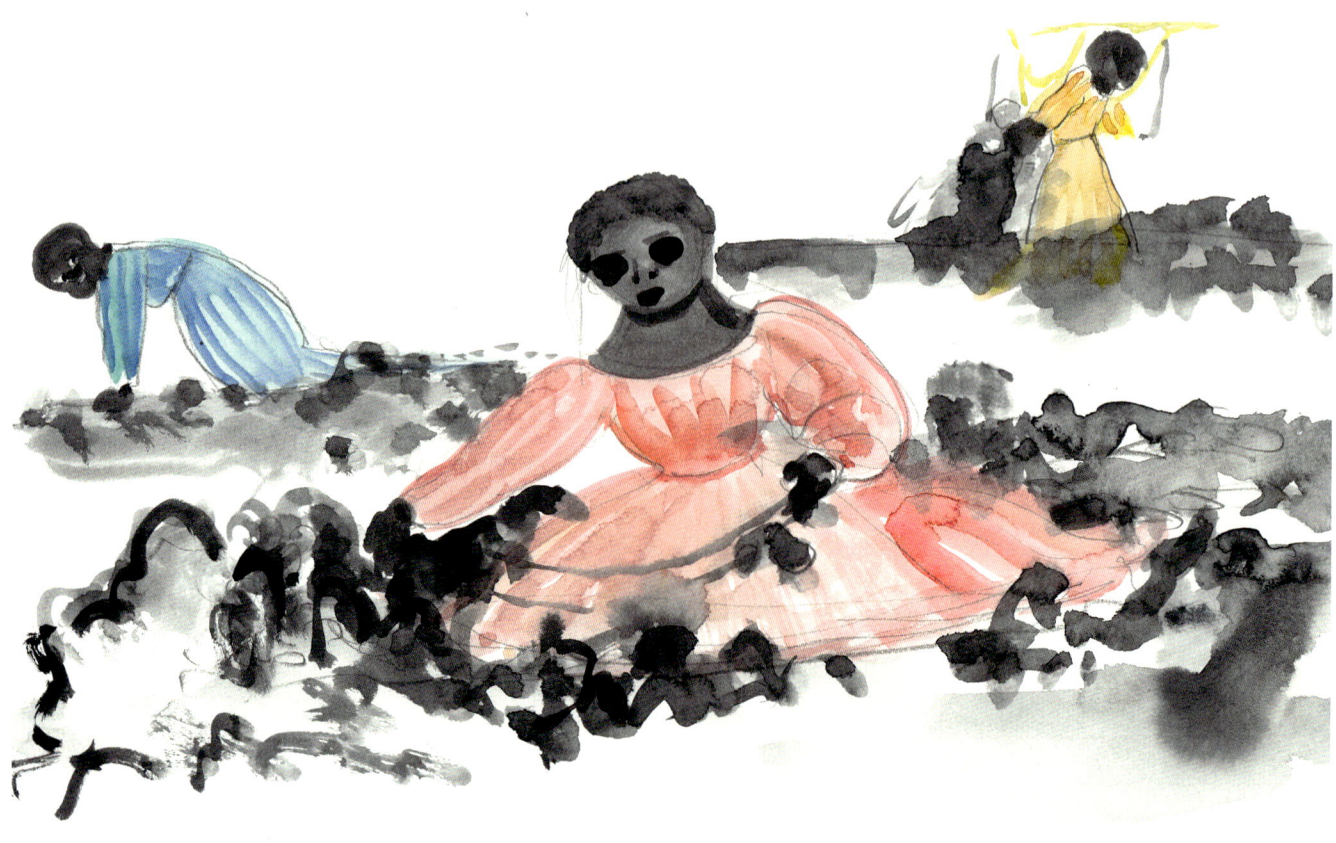

EJ How do we go from that to immortality?

KW There are new technology people out there, or at least there have been for the last few decades, who really think that tech will provide the way of extending life—and that somehow our lives are made up of code that can be hacked—life that can *and should* be saved.

The transhumanist idea, I guess, is the latest incarnation of an almost utopian view on extending human life perhaps toward immortality. Why? Not for me to answer. I think you can already see that injustice and cruelty will not improve with longer lives, that the quest for immortality creates an elite who has access, which in turn necessitates an underclass that is expendable. That might not be new, but it came close to the reality experienced en masse during the pandemic. Who has access to what kind of healthcare, who's expendable, who's deemed essential? All those terms came into play.

EJ There are three components that make up the overall composition of *Fortuna and the Immortality Garden (Machine)*, which are essentially three points of interaction.

KW In the whole space, there are three—let's call them dioramas.

EJ: They're almost like vitrines without a case, right?

KW Exactly. The case would have been prohibitively expensive—like an aquarium or terrarium, really. So we have this large central display, which is modeled on the American Museum of Natural History's elephant display here in New York. And two smaller display areas that contain a single figure each. As well as a wall-mounted vitrine containing artifacts of the process of building the project.

The central pedestal contains multiple figures enacting a mysterious rite, maybe a funeral, resurrection, baptism, dance—a ritual that viewers sort of witness. In this large vitrine, there are six figures, three of whom are positioned around a reclining figure who begins to levitate. One is Belltoller, who does just what his name says—the ringing of a single bell. His cohorts include Waterbearer; there's the Kneeling Magician, who rises up and controls the movements of Levitator. Standing sentry on either end are Harpy, a doll-like musical figure who has a stringed instrument embedded in her body, and

Whisperer, a child with a doll of her own with whom she's in private communication. On a separate pedestal that faces the street, Dover slumps as his fallen arms occasionally twitch with memory.

Against the wall facing the central diorama stands Fortuna, the namesake of this project. I was particularly drawn to carnival fortune-telling machines and automatons. I think the question at the heart of this work is "What is to become of us?" And although Fortuna does provide fortunes on little slips of paper for the public to take away, the question is never expressly stated, therefore her "answers" run the gamut from further questions to punchlines, non sequiturs, and phrases in the prophetic perfect tense.

EJ When looking at some of your preparatory drawings and some modeling for those figures, the first thing that came to mind was a sort of biblical scene, like something with the Christ child even. Not that this is being replicated, but this kind of grouping in the center recalls a revivalist moment because this Levitator is actually convulsing and seemingly experiencing a kind of—it could be ecstasy or agony.

KW Exactly. All those things. Some of the reference points that I was looking at were coming straight out of documentary photography of baptisms in the American South at the turn of the last century. That's the look of the characters and their costumes to some extent, although that has shifted somewhat over time. The central levitating figure was originally a figure of abjection crawling and very low to the ground, but that wasn't working mechanically, so I opted to thrust her aloft and let gravity be her foil.

EJ It's interesting that you liken it to abjection, because when I say that it is experiencing agony or ecstasy—and maybe it will remain undefined, but at this stage, it is gray—the figure is vulnerable because it is on its back. I think that her lot is hard to decipher, whereas if she were crawling, somehow that would be fixed as a more desperate gesture.

KW I think that was really getting to me, because it was etched in my mind that I had to have this sort of image of suffering. But that doesn't really work for me in my practice because it doesn't lend itself to further thought for myself or for a viewer. Suffering is suffering, and you don't get to pull back and say other things. You just know that it hurts.

EJ That is super interesting in reference to ideas around suffering or around racialized oppression as it surfaces in your work, that there is always a poten-

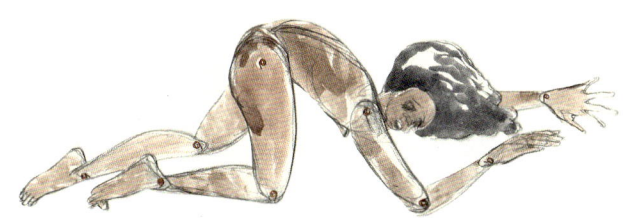

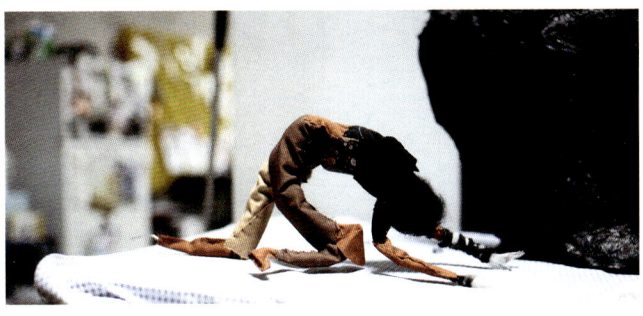

tially personal, emotional, physical quest, but there is also the possibility of philosophical questioning.

In a lot of the communication with your studio team, the puppets or the figures in this new sculpture are referred to as dolls, and I'd like to talk a little about what they are—that they are robots, they are dolls, they are puppets . . .

KW Automatons.

EJ They are automatons, but there are also all these other aspects of work you have made in the past. They are also figures that you have drawn in the past. They seem to be recurring characters in a way. To me, all of this plus your working hand reminds me of the very first show of yours I saw, at Wooster Gardens in 1995.[1] And you had this cutout cardboard puppet—it was big.

KW It was pretty big. There were two, or I know that I made two. I think the one you're remembering was a threesome, and you could pull a tab and they would rock back and forth, suggestively. Yes, the puppet-action movement thing has been a part of my work pretty much from the beginning. Doing the cutouts lent itself to animated shadow puppetry, which was unexpected enough in the contemporary art context. I did the films with the cut-paper puppets, but those early moving wall cutouts I sort of abandoned. I just did them and walked away quietly.

EJ I always remember the large puppet in your first show. I was surprised by the scale, because your work wasn't quite at that scale for everything yet. But the puppet was quite big. Maybe not human size, but three-quarters or two-thirds or something like that.

"Several smaller mounds, a wavy topography.
HaHa - a passage for viewers
Clean straight edges.

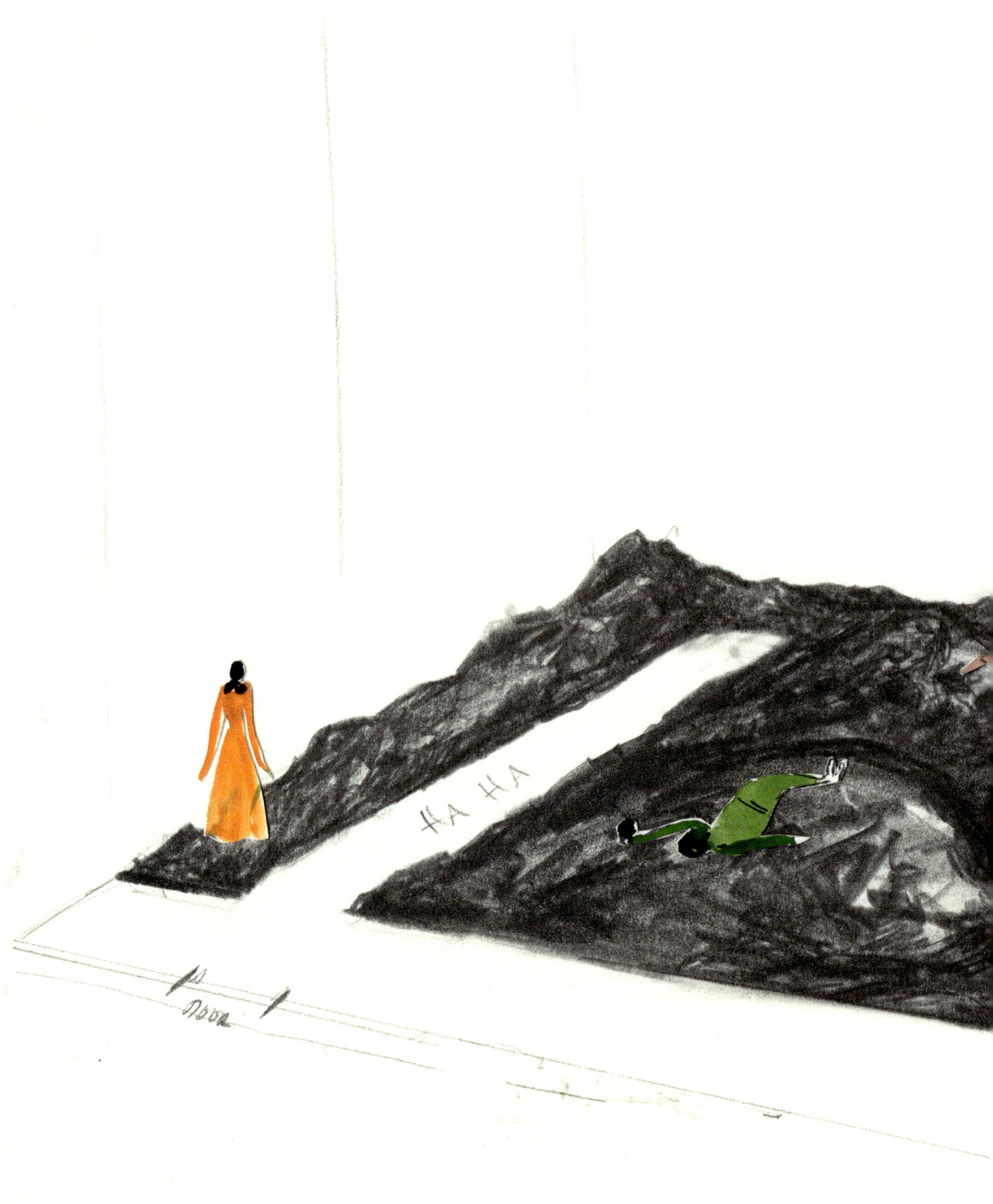

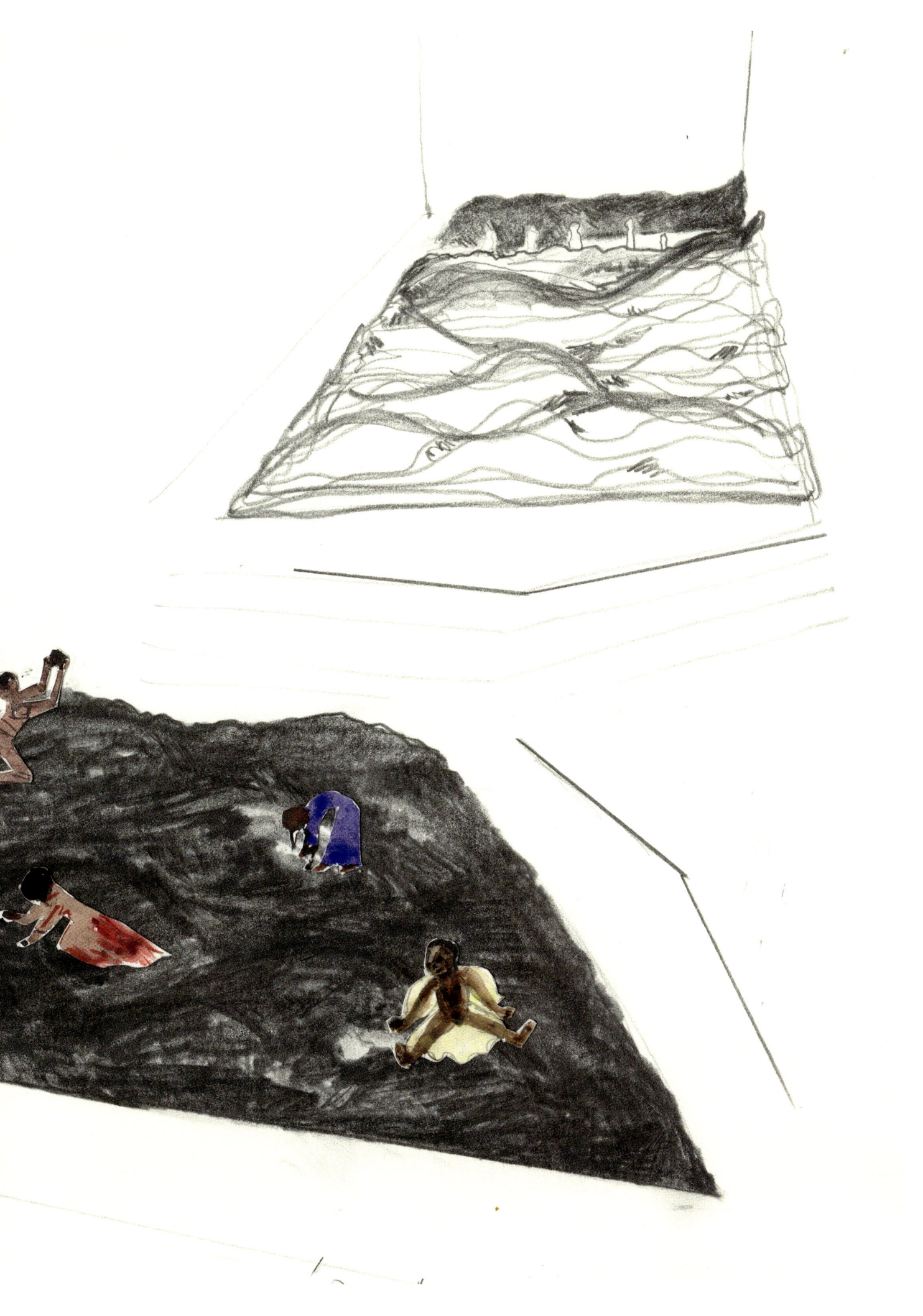

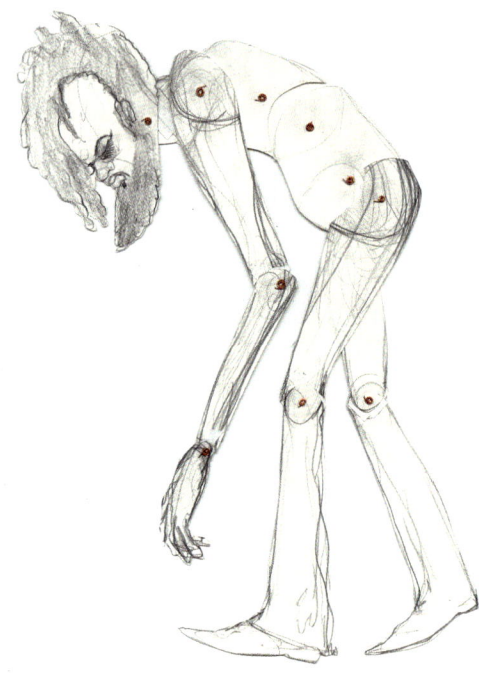

It had this reference to a full-scale puppet. Then for many years you worked with these small puppets that you could manipulate with your hands. For the 2005 REDCAT exhibition you did an incredible series of puppet show performances.[2] And of course you were making the films quite actively in those days. That scale had a relationship to the things you did on the wall, taking them back in the films and the live performance to control another gesture of storytelling.

The last time I came here to the studio, I was surprised to see the sculpting you are doing to create your figures, and the sewing, and all the experiments. Not sketching to think or work out a thought, but really—

KW —hands-on materials-based.

EJ: I have been seeing very practical, technical things alongside imaginary things, let's say.

KW I challenged myself to try a material experience of thinking with the puppets and the sewing, and eventually with clay, plaster, and 3-D modeling.

EJ I think with your previous projects that are of similarly grand scale, they were conceived differently, separate from your studio work. But this commission has a lot of return to the studio, back and forth, in and out of the studio.

KW It has been a learning process with these big projects. With each iteration of a large public commission—I've only made four now—I've tried

to reclaim more of my hand, more of a connection between something that is handmade and an object that is fabricated or manufactured, so that it retains some—I was going to say "authenticity," but it's really Pleasure, because I like making art and it feels totally debilitating to just outsource it. Even though tech makes it a thousand times easier to do just that. You never need to touch a block of marble to become a monument maker.

I don't really like doing public works, to be frank, because each time a project necessarily metastasizes from an idea to an event, which is meant to function in specific ways for the institution. I become a "Job Producer" in a very political sense, and an entire ecosystem of art production is deployed to make it happen. I'm afraid the intent of the work has the potential to get muddled when there are too many disparate players manufacturing parts.

EJ But here we are talking about the implication of robotics and technology.

KW Technology, artificial intelligence, and actual intelligence.

EJ And that sends us into discussions of the racialization of intelligence around technology—so-called technology and intelligence—how the information being fed to these automatons is corrupt information, information that we don't necessarily believe in the first place. That's the knowledge that they're calling upon.

KW Yes. It's very interesting. I've got ChatGPT and have been in conversation with it to try and generate fortunes for Fortuna, and it is very bad at it because it lacks soul or intuition, it hasn't got a past or a sense of shame. It has just the information that it is able to glean from whatever you give it. That's all it's got. It has this very limited resource set. It can spit back an immense amount of information—but it becomes repetitive and dull because it lacks a soul, and it lacks the ability to be irreverent. You could tell it to be irreverent and it would bore you to tears with its recycled jokes. It doesn't have a person that it is talking to. It has no fear. It lacks the ability to be worried for its life.

EJ But maybe its limitations force it out of your own brain a bit?

KW Yeah, exactly. I know what I'm looking for, but the thing that it does is force you to make better parameters to feed it.

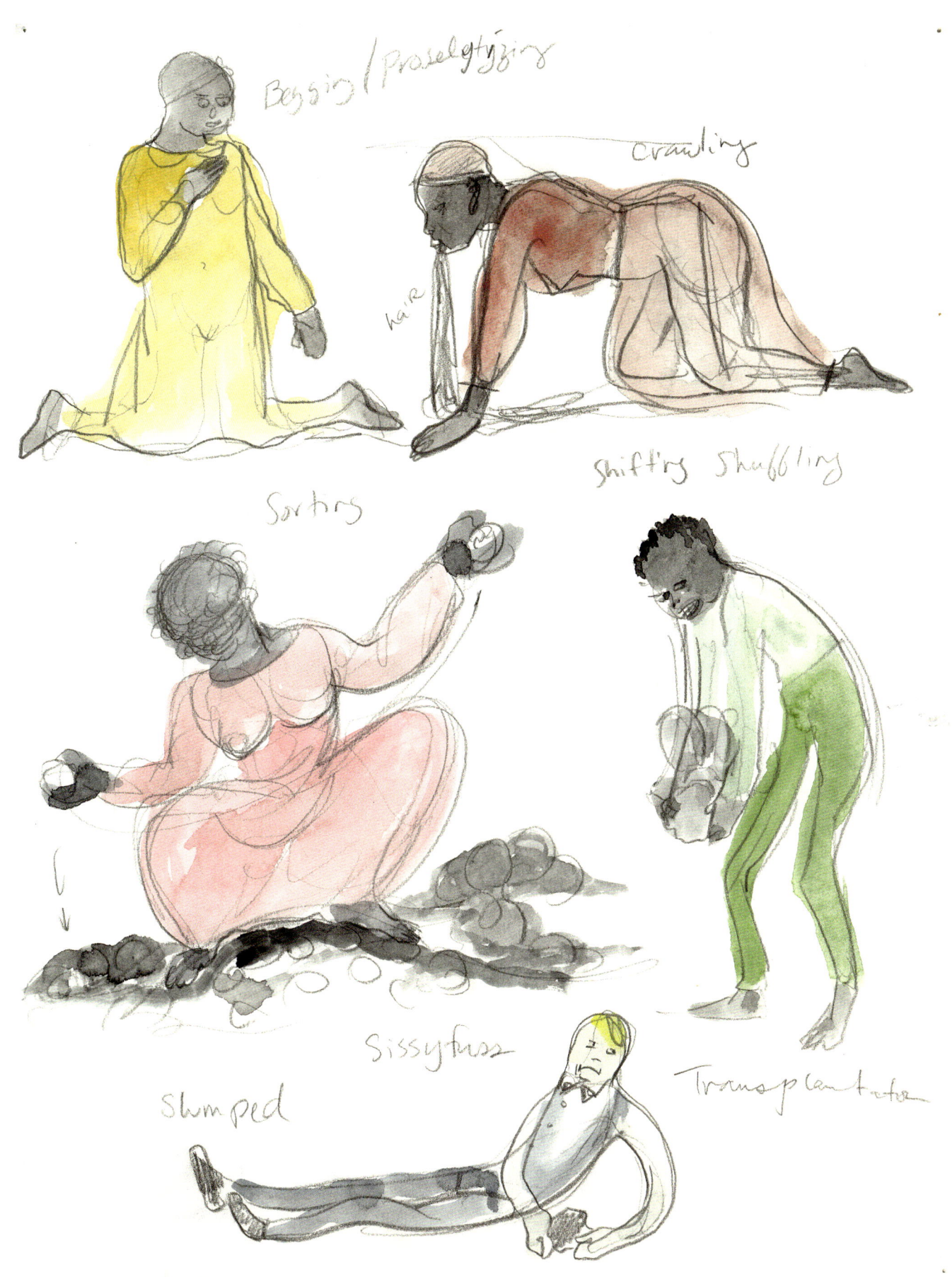

Begging/Proselytizing

Crawling

hair

Sorting

Shifting Shuffling

Sissyfuss

Slumped

Transplantater

EJ Basically, you used ChatGPT as a brainstorming device?

KW Kind of. I think it's the best it can do right now. It's a sounding board: "Oh, do you mean this?" And I'm like, "No." "Oh, do you mean *that*?" "Closer." Then after a while I was like, "I'm tired of talking to you, so I'm just going to go and do this on my own."

EJ One thing I thought we could go into is the vitrine diorama structure in relation to institutional display and how that figures into some kind of return to or reconsideration of history and its telling.

KW I was thinking about the Natural History Museum, my love of the California Academy of Sciences. Most natural history museums—what we think of today—begin with a nineteenth-century model of taxonomical arrays of animals and peoples and minerals that our earth is made of. And I wanted to borrow that language and propose a Future/Present scenario whereby as viewers we wonder what era we are in and that throws us into an anachronistic fugue. My automatons reference an eternally retrospective Blackness—archetypes, rather than stereotypes. Their fantastical costuming contains signifiers of oppression and destruction and mortality. They don't resemble the model of robust superhuman robots that the industry has long promised or threatened us with.

Therein comes the question of the ethics of robotics and what they want robots to do, and how different is that from slavery? Creating nonhuman persons to abuse, an underclass to do the bidding, to do the work.

EJ You mentioned the California Academy of Sciences, and with this new project, it is fascinating to think about the importance of the location, of the Bay Area. As long as we have known each other, we have discussed this shared relationship to the Bay Area. You were raised there until you were in your mid-teens, and I arrived in my mid-teens. So we have had that shared experience, and I think we have always felt that we could have known each other in our early lives.

KW For sure.

EJ One thing that comes to mind in terms of wonder, or in terms of experience, is what museums meant to us; what our experiences in these institutions of culture and history meant to us, because they meant something to us from the beginning. When I think about those kinds of places and our eager participation, which was always kept at a distance, I see that scale of also being small or young in relation to the tools of storytelling or the tools of the institution. I see this evidenced in this project. There are many moments that speak to the acquisition of knowledge that we experienced. That's also why it's interesting how the institutional framework and vocabulary are coming into play in the work.

KW My relationship to California is primary; I really had a kind of California fundamentalist education almost. I remember my eighth-grade history teacher (in Stockton) was going on about how important California is to the nation and the world because of its agriculture and its industry and economy, and the diversity of the state with its progressive attitudes. I was very proud of California for that.

California is the state that was traditionally at the forefront, the avant-garde in many national trends. And so it's been frightening to see a place like San Francisco and Silicon Valley innovating us into a technological dystopia along the lines of every fictional scenario that Hollywood has produced. Why are the morality tales not serving? Or what is the tale that is to be told? In a lot of the narrative versions, there's a protagonist who is positioned against the machine, say, but we don't know who the protagonist is anymore in the scenario that we find ourselves in.

EJ If you think about California as this promised land of some sort, the narrative of course is about opportunity. That works really well with families from the American South who had this second migration during World War II, when so many opportunities existed for people who had come from the southern United States to the West Coast and from southern Mexico to northern Mexico (which is California), as well as immigrants from Asia. It's a meeting point that has no match anywhere else. People traveled all the way across the continent from these different directions and from the sea, and they arrived in California. There's something about the potential and the anachronisms that conflate into maybe less certainty, and therefore more possibility. And this is why I think it continues to feel like a possibility, even when it has never really exemplified possibility. Yes, there's all this diversity, but that was dependent on coolie labor. That's secondary slavery—the great migration escaping sharecropping into a different system, which also exploited its labor. So there is no positive grand narrative.

A key component of the installation we have not yet discussed is the obsidian field.

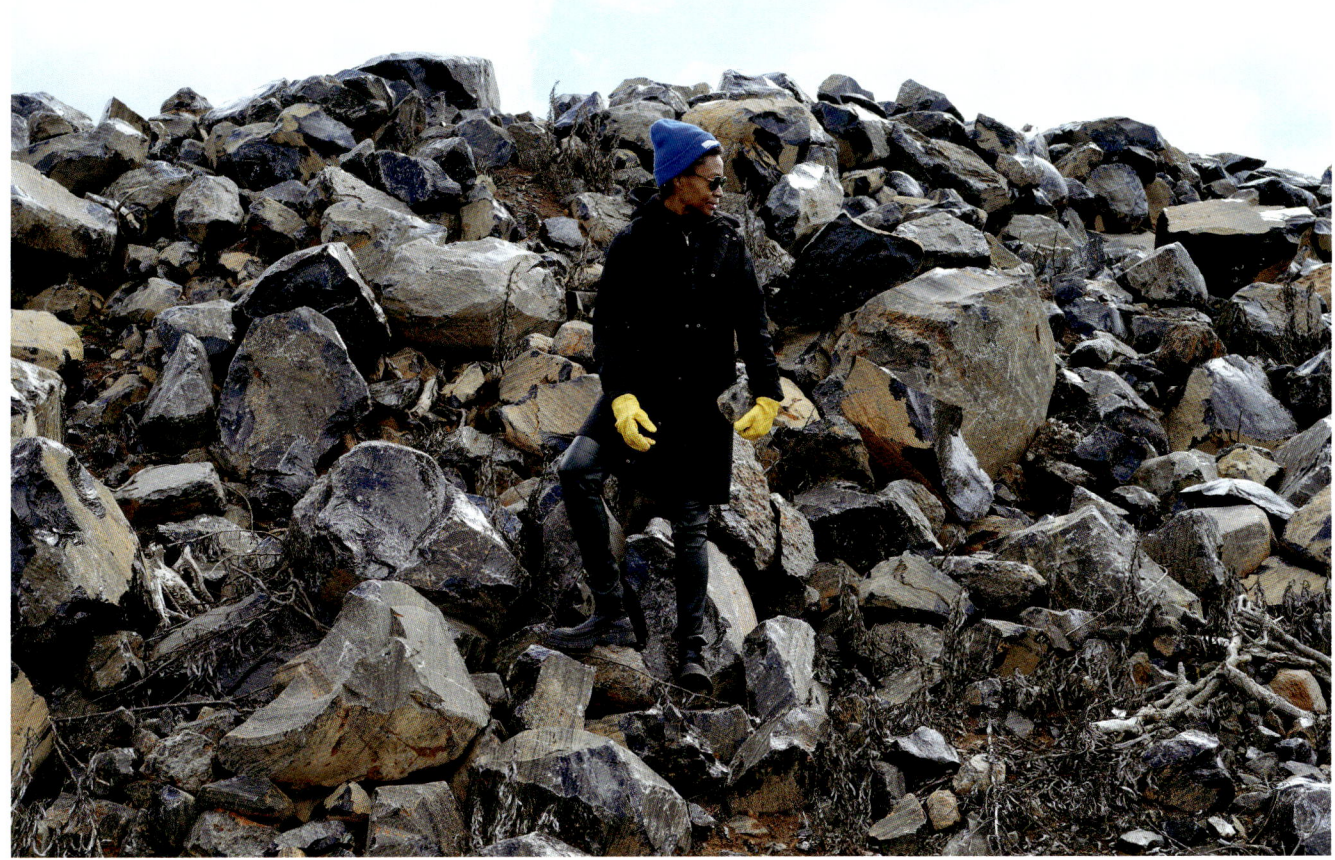

Kara Walker at Obsidian Ridge Vineyard, Lake County, CA, March 2023

KW On one of our site visits, we went up to Obsidian vineyards for a picnic, and I was fascinated with the material, so I took a few pieces home, and looking at the obsidian, I thought, "What would it be like to use this as some kind of energy field?" It's black and it's natural and it addresses something about place. I was thinking about the Central Valley where I grew up and the idea of the geological forces at work making valleys.

A few things happened at once. I was thinking about the obsidian and wondering what the possibility would be of even getting it, so I reached out to ask about acquiring a large quantity, enough to fill the gallery. Then I saw the *Black Dolls* exhibition at the New-York Historical Society and began thinking about dolls.[3] Beautiful care-worn antique dolls made of scraps and love. And by the end of the year, when I was ill with COVID, as I said, it all sort of came together. Thinking about these bodies of ours, and vulnerability and isolation and that memory of being a kid home sick with my doll—I mean, how important that figure is for humans, the ubiquity of the doll or stuffed toy, the nonhuman pet or the inanimate confidante. I realized the same can be said of memorial sculpture, that it acts as a container for human sentiment and fear of the unknown.

Okay, let's have that be the rule, the figures will do a service for the public. Let's say in the same way that we're going to ask the obsidian to also be a grounding space. The obsidian has healing properties in mystical circles and works to offset trauma, among other things. This is kind of a different way of working for me because it feels like I'm working from the material outward. The obsidian providing an essential magical force and the "dolls" receiving our essential magical forces in return.

EJ To me, in another way it's consistent, but maybe just realized slightly differently. It is consistent if you think of *A Subtlety*, because sugar was your material because of its relevance to that space.[4] And I think in this case, the field of obsidian, in a way, was nurtured by a physical experience you had of going to the north and then encountering this material that's under the ground. It's peeking up from under the ground, but it's under the ground. It is the evidence of geologic time; it's there and always has been there, but we didn't see it. And it's black. And it's glistening. And it was liquid. It was moving. It was alive. And now, it's stopped. That to me is time. The work is drawing a parallel between the formation of the obsidian field and what we experienced in terms of the stoppage of time under COVID—it's kind of logical as a departure point because of your long engagement with historical time, trying to understand the present through a relatively recent historical moment of the last five hundred years. So now you're looking at the last five thousand years. Or five thousand years for the context of the past five hundred years. But then also the context of innovation. You're thinking about robots and AI, but you're thinking about them from the eighteenth century.

KW Every piece of obsidian has a surface reminiscent of our black phone screens. But unlike the phones, the volcanic glass is "smart" in an intangible sense. You have to believe it, feel it. It doesn't need to convince you.

EJ In a way, it's like a clean palette and a full palette because it's the black hole, the absence of all things or the presence of everything. It's both.

KW Both.

EJ And so I think the obsidian field starts to do that, too, in its reflections and refractions and sharpness. It's a tool, but it's a weapon. It's dangerous to even interact with. I think all this could be a metaphor for Blackness. It's something that is beautiful and prideful and lurking and dangerous and overdetermined and burdensome and all these contradictions. And that's exactly where we get back to the presence of the viewer.

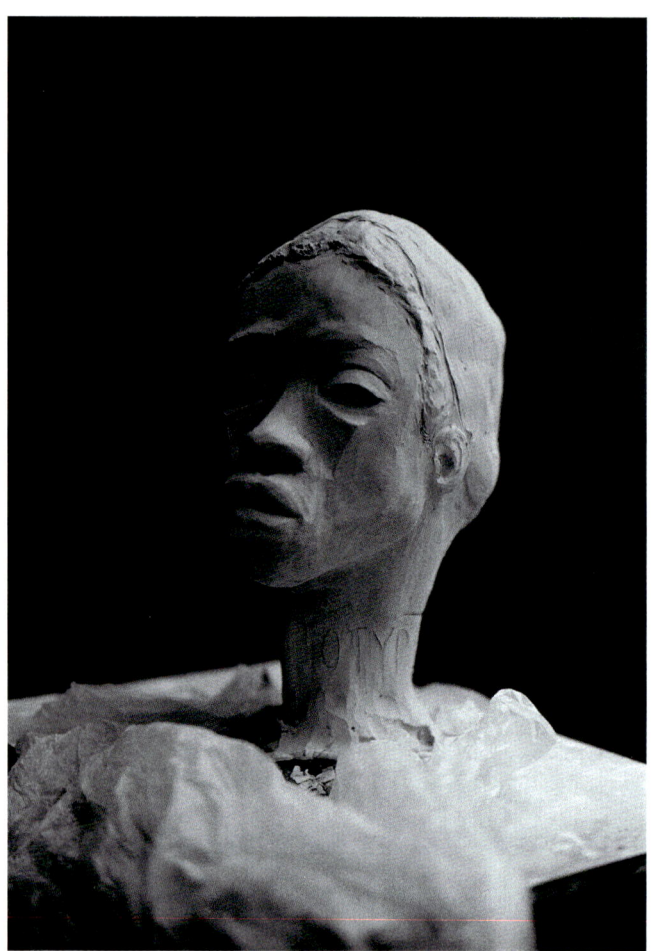

KW In order to make the piece have relevance for me, I have to fill it up, pack a small area densely with a bunch of ideas, and then reduce the idea to a digestible amount—because as a public piece, after all, it really has to be graspable, it has to make room for a viewer. So that means this work has a lot of seating, literal space to feel welcome. That's my gift to you in a way. I don't want to make an educational tool; the main problem to be solved in the museum is one of access and acceptance.

EJ It's important, this way of making something have enough room to be interacted with, and then approachable so that people can feel they have the authority to have a judgment or a position or joy or laughter, whatever it is. That they are qualified. That is when public art has a very important role in relation to contemporary art, because we've kind of gotten ourselves into a bit of a hole where what we do is not perceived admirably as the diffusion of philosophy and letters but rather as elitist and exclusionary, which is exactly the opposite of our intention. We wanted to get into the museum and make it more accessible. Instead, we kind of ended up in a dead

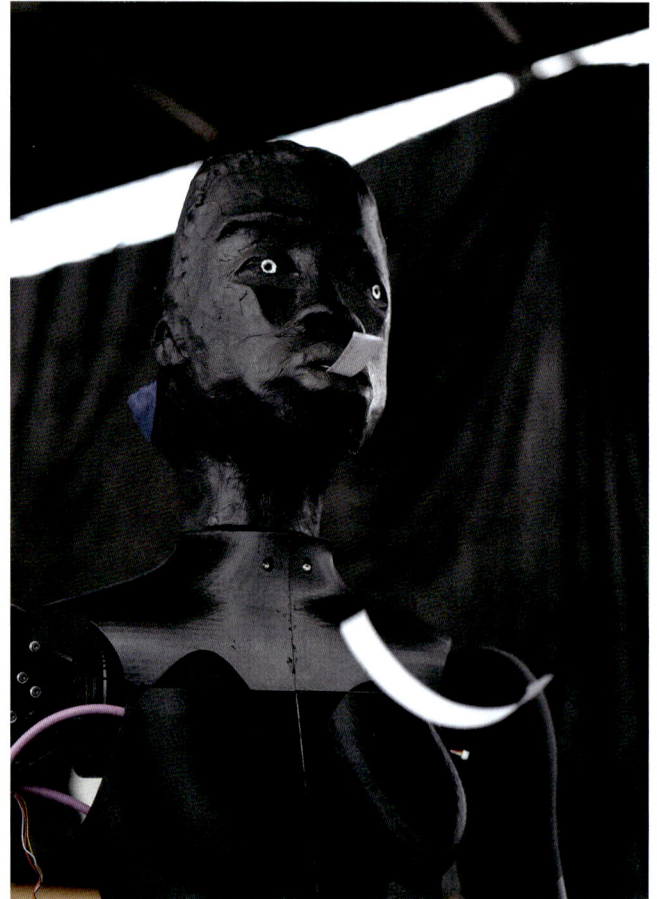

end or a cul-de-sac talking to each other. That's why the idea of a semi-permanent or long-term public artwork like you did at the Domino Sugar Factory in Brooklyn, Prospect.4 in New Orleans, Turbine Hall in London—now for SFMOMA and later for MOCA[5]—these are such powerful gestures that can enliven contemporary art in relation to the public.

KW Maybe. Let's see. I mean, the public is also entitled to hate it.

EJ Totally. But that position, to feel qualified to hate it, too, that still reflects an openness. Fortuna brings an interactive or prophetic element to the work; what does it mean to offer a potentially individualized message? People will walk up to the sculpture and the sculpture will offer them something.

KW I wanted there to be some kind of interaction in the spirit of the classic automaton carnival sideshow, and fortune-telling is one of the most recognizable actions. It just made the most sense, really. The way I initially proposed *The Immortality Garden (Machine)* was as a device to assuage survivors that could be a place to hold our grief, to hold the sadness of the public. I remember you asked how that was going to work, how people would input their feelings. I said, "By thinking them. By looking at and by thinking into the work."

EJ The greatest AI input of them all: think.

KW Think and look. And then you're having more realizations.

EJ And think some more.

KW And then it spits out a message. In the course of ChatGPT-ing my way into what a fortune is and what it means, I realized that it's not really fortunes that are being outputted, but other types of language, sometimes mimicking the language of a fortune, but oftentimes not. And I think that the beauty of human intelligence is finding meaning and patterns in words and language. If I can give you words and language that are sometimes stream of consciousness, sometimes something more directed, sometimes a quote, sometimes a quote of my own—I think that's a gift, to be able to sort of awaken that question mark, or maybe I didn't even know I had a question for this statement that has come out, and what does this mean to me? It is literally a physical object, a piece of paper, and I don't know about you, but I save all my fortunes from fortune cookies.

EJ What they are really doing is confirming some inkling that you already have. That is what I thought of when I saw Fortuna. She is an affirmation in a way. Fortune is also affirmation. So when we talk about the suffering that people have gone through because of the pandemic and because of the violent recent past and present, then an affirmation of somebody's humanity through fortune is also a very important gesture.

KW I think it's very important. And it's also meant to be loving.

EJ That's something that we talked about from the beginning: engagement and wonder and healing. I think that was one of the reasons we wanted to keep the obsidian field secret for now, because this gesture of beauty and grandeur of the obsidian field is also about the healing stone and a dispersal of negative energy.

KW Exactly.

EJ A cure.

KW A cure for what ails us, perhaps.

EJ So this is a loving gesture to the institution . . .

KW But also outward toward the street.

EJ Totally. But also absolving some of the burden, which we cannot deny or negate. It just is. There are problems with the history of museums. There are problems with the history of class and race associated with these institutions, but we also have to find a way to transcend them.

KW We have to employ magic at this point.

1. *The High and Soft Laughter of the Nigger Wenches at Night*, Wooster Gardens/Brent Sikkema, New York, April 6–May 6, 1995.
2. *Song of the South*, REDCAT, Los Angeles, September 3–October 23, 2005.
3. *Black Dolls*, New-York Historical Society, February 25–June 5, 2022.
4. *A Subtlety, or the Marvelous Sugar Baby*, Domino Sugar Factory, Brooklyn, May 10–July 6, 2014, presented by Creative Time.
5. *A Subtlety*, 2014; *The Katastwóf Karavan*, Prospect.4: *The Lotus in Spite of the Swamp*, Algiers Point, New Orleans, February 23–25, 2018; *Fons Americanus*, Tate Modern, London, October 2, 2019–February 7, 2021; *MONUMENTS*, The Brick and The Museum of Contemporary Art, Los Angeles, fall 2025.

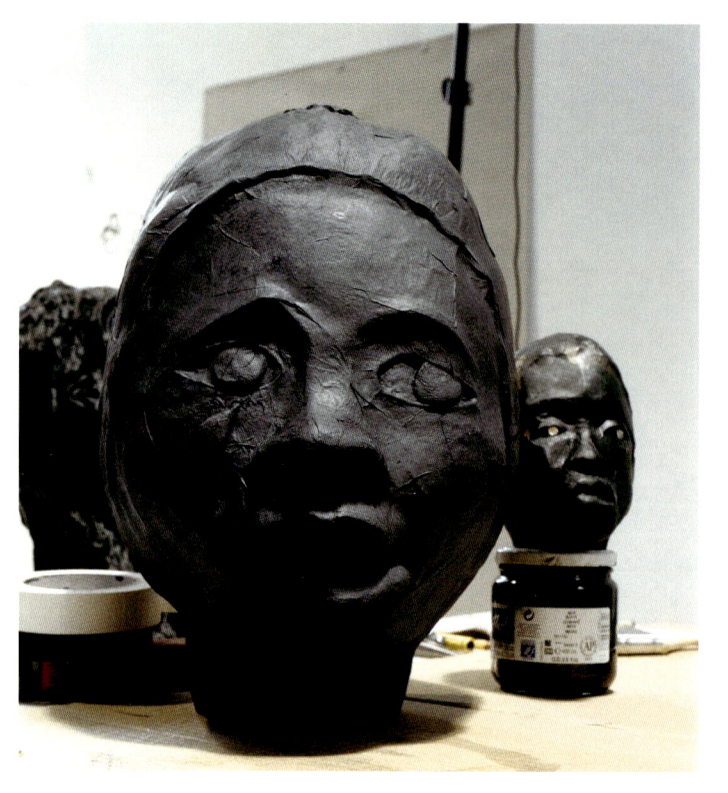
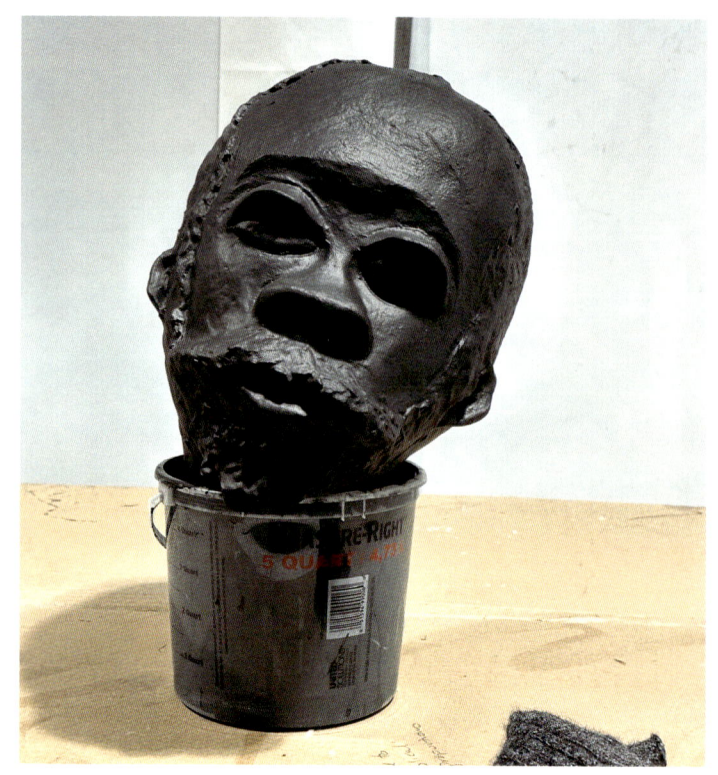

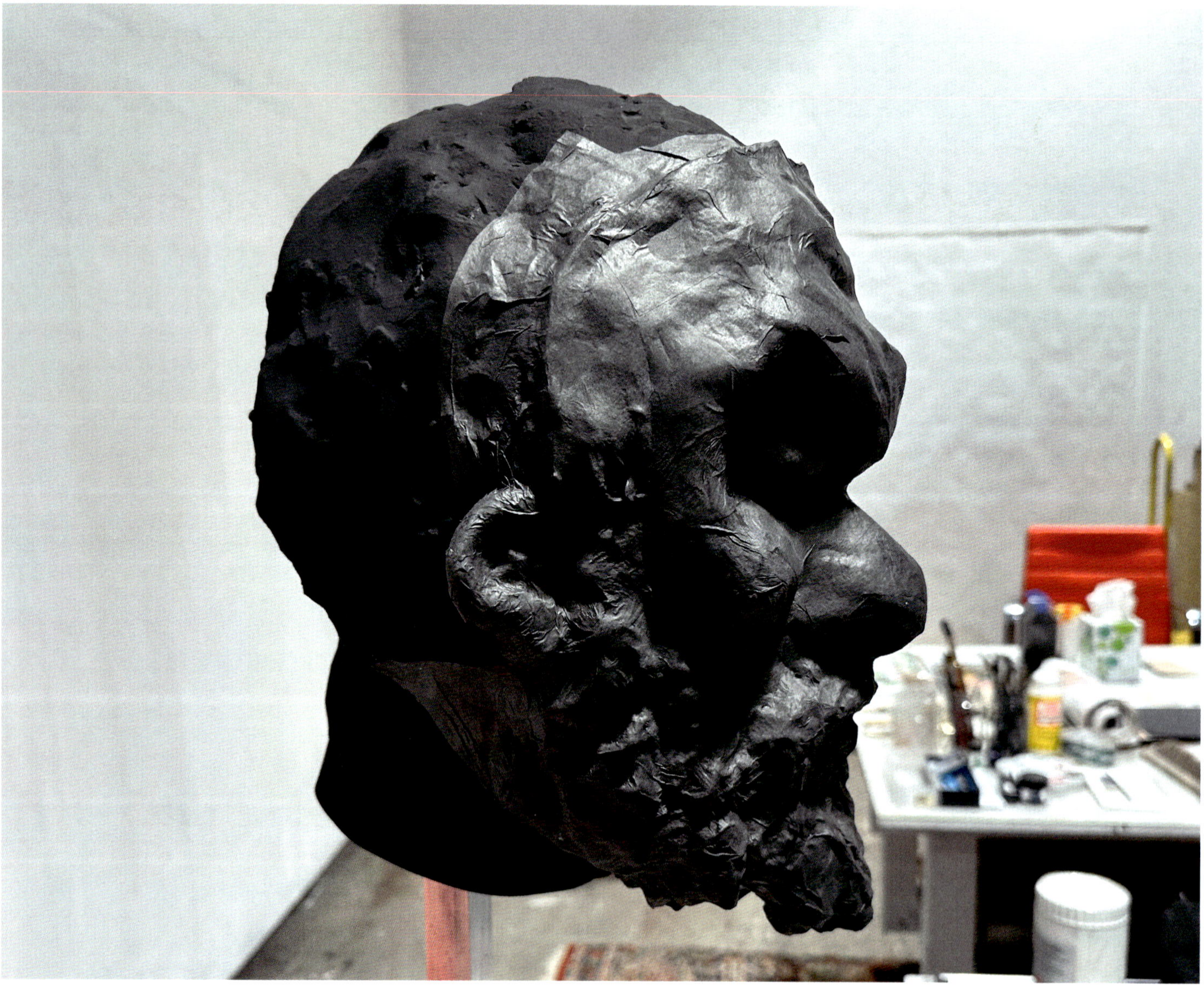

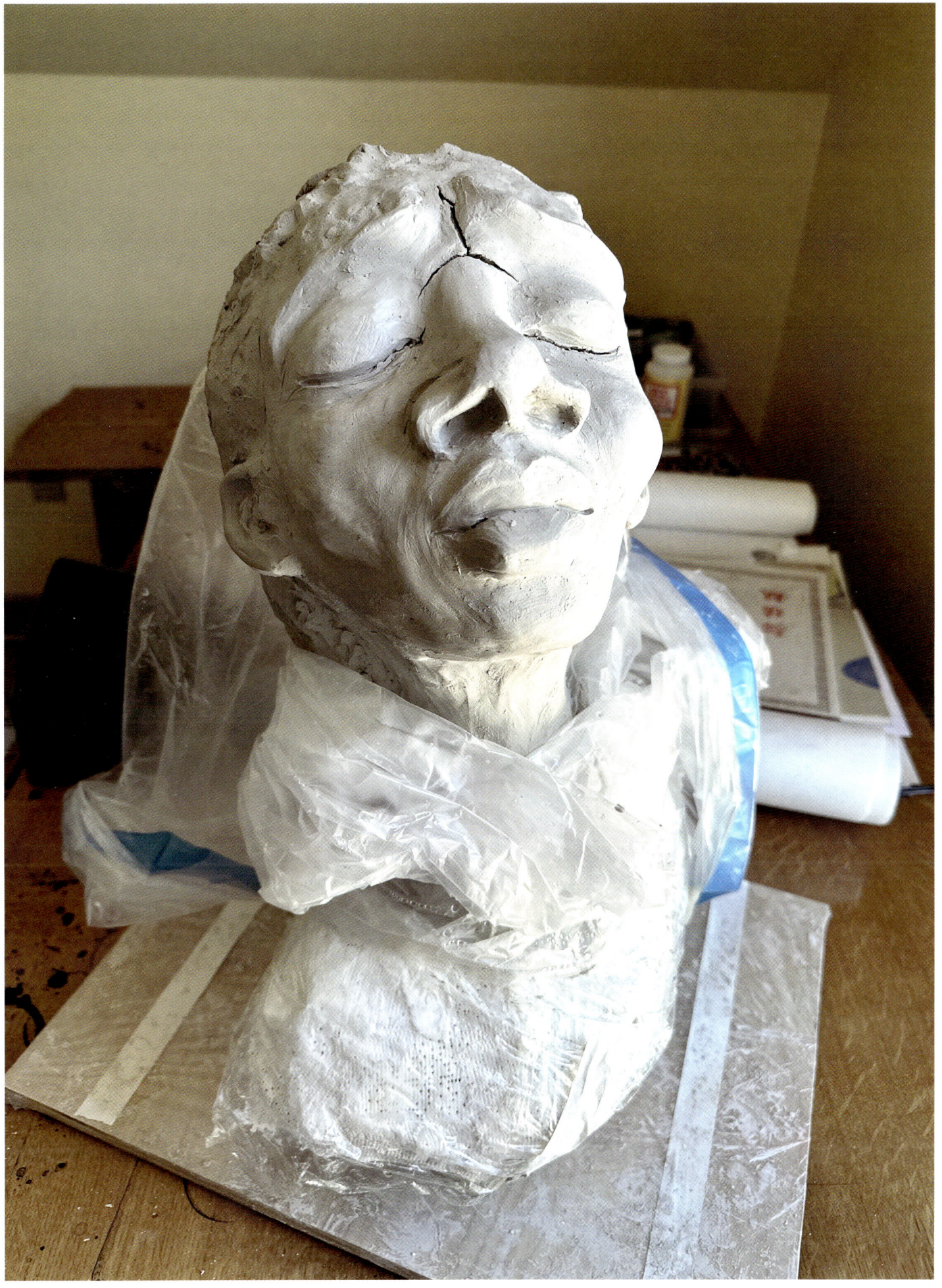

GENERAL STRIKE...
WHAT SHAPES REMAIN
Damani McNeil

I remember when five thousand longshoremen marched down Market Street. It was the year I turned thirteen, and that afternoon my father took me, dressed in my Sunday attire, into the city with him for the first time.

An unfamiliar spectacle. A spectacle of pride, not of violence. We were all migration babies—if not of this time, of the time before. We were all used to wet heat and dry clay—if not of this time, of the time before. When we thought of marches, any number of images sprang to mind—a tally of violent spectacles. Our parents were the first to pack up the wagons and leave these torments behind. They have traumatized us enough and do not bear repeating.

Throughout my childhood, there was always a flock of men and women moving urgently through our bungalow. I would crouch in the doorsill, trying to parse what was being passed between the grown folk clustered around the dining room table. At first I couldn't figure out how they knew my father, but over time I realized it was actually my father who knew them. My father wasn't a longshoreman, and even in such a political time he never considered himself very political, but I could see he was the thread that tied a seemingly infinite web of people together. He knew them, and he knew what they needed. Many families didn't have cars, and he would arrange for a car already heading west to carry a trunk in the boot so those with young children could take the bus more comfortably. He got a nickel here and a dime there for fare when folks didn't have enough to scrape together.

Later in life, after I became a cultural ambassador, I came to understand the importance of that day in June 1934 and why the occasion called for Sunday finery. The march I had attended was in fact the funeral of Nicholas Bordoise and Howard Sperry, two longshoremen killed by police during the West Coast Waterfront Strike that summer. I didn't know until later that the International Longshore and Warehouse Union was one of the first unions in the United States to be integrated. My father didn't mention anything to me about what he was toiling on those evenings in our kitchen, and he didn't speak to me at all on the drive to the port that afternoon, but eventually I came to understand his role in that process as well.

The fog was burning away as we parked the car on the cobblestones of Jack London Square and boarded the ferry to begin our way across the Bay. I remember feeling terribly small as the boat bobbed out into the water. My eyes remained wide and expectant as the tendrils of mist receded and I began to make out the faint outline of a city through the rapidly dwindling fog. The bank lifted in full, and my breath caught in my throat—I had caught sight of the skeleton of the biggest bridge I had ever seen. I stood with my jaw slack, mouth hanging open, and barely noticed the rocking becoming more violent as the water got choppier and we puffed out into the gray.

I remember panicking as we deboarded the boat. The crush of bodies was so intense—a quarter of a million people passed through the Embarcadero every day, and it seemed to me as if every one of them had arrived at the exact minute we did. Coats flapping sounded like whips cracking, and I watched a bald man try to hawk down his bowler hat, which had been lifted off his head and was now floating down the gangway and into the hungry ocean. Down the gangway and into the Ferry Building and then out the other side, and just like that I was buoyant and inquisitive again, back on solid ground.

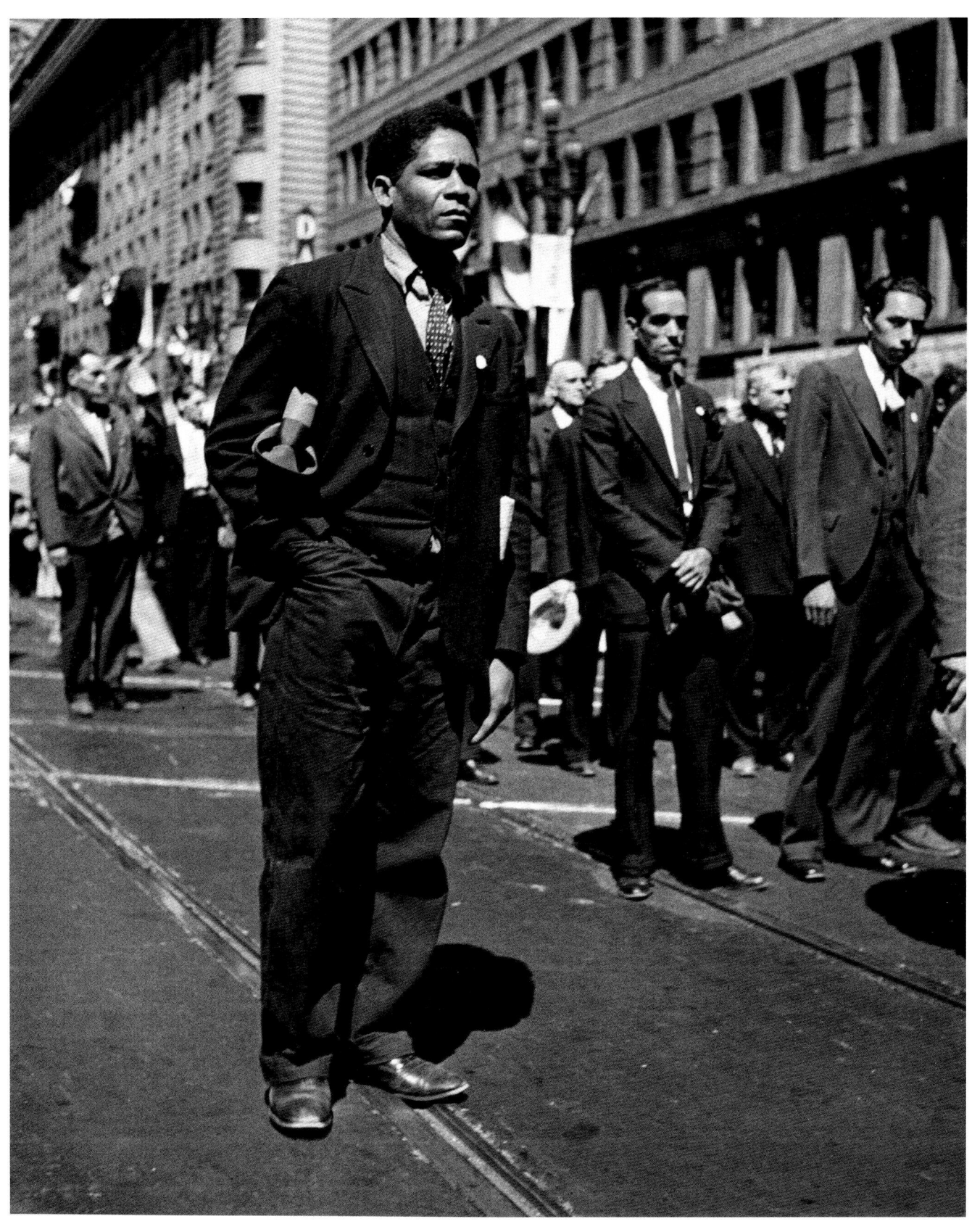

John Gutmann, *Funeral Procession for Killed Workers, General Strike, San Francisco,*
1934, printed ca. 1974. Gelatin silver print. 8 ⁵⁄₁₆ × 7 ⁵⁄₈ in. (21.1 × 19.3 cm). San Francisco
Museum of Modern Art, Bequest of John Gutmann

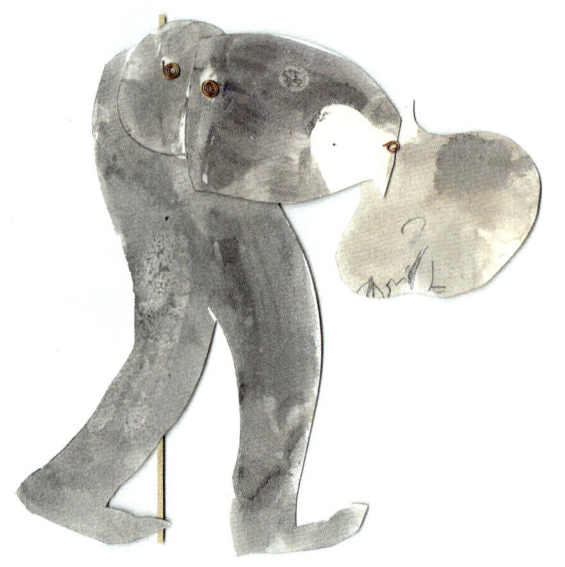

We picked our way through the throngs of people lining the street, and I began to feel the tension building in the crowd. Later, when I researched the event as an adult, I learned that tension stemmed from fear the police would shoot into the crowd, as they had the afternoon before, and to this day I shake my head at my father's insistence that I accompany him to view the procession. A baby began to wail off in the distance, and closer to us a young boy instinctually began to cry too, and for a moment it felt as though the restless crowd would just sigh and disperse in a huff.

But suddenly the longshoremen appeared—radiant and resplendent in the fresh glory of the day that shifting clouds are known to disclose. Their uniforms were spotless, with gleaming brass buttons. Many other attendees wore black suits, and some wore brown tweed three-piece affairs. They all sported striped ascots meticulously tucked under their collars, with freshly slicked hair and hats tucked underarm.

The march rounded the corner and turned onto Market, and my father took his cap off as the union men approached. There was a band playing at the head of the column, with both Black and white musicians. The front of the march trotted forward crisply, carrying the union's banner and waving flags high overhead. The Black union men sauntered along just behind them, cool and dignified. The column seemed to keep rolling on forever—now white faces and Black faces both pushed forward urgently side by side, striding over the train tracks without so much as a glance downward. As I watched the union roll past me rank and file, I didn't know yet that this display of labor power—this spectacle of pride, not of violence—was a response to a grave violence that could not be allowed to be forgotten.

What did this new spectacle mean to me? On that day, the spectacle meant we were plenty and our community was strong. We were plenty smart enough to be in the union, but also we were numerically plenty to fill a column. There were many Black San Franciscans who felt we had fled the South tail 'tween legs to avoid heinous spectacles of violence—the sort of things that forcibly eject young people out of childhood and poison their hearts—and we had waded out of the dusty ocean of the interior of the nation and into this oasis of opportunity that we could not have imagined. But even in this oasis, there was still violence looming over us: just as the sharecroppers shot at our feet as we strode off the plantations in the South, the police shot at us as we left the factory line out West.

As an adult, I came to understand better that this oasis was something we would have to organize ourselves and fight for. On that day, the longshoremen made it clear that an injury to one was an injury to all. An insult to one dignified laborer was an affront against the entire city. And when there was an affront against the city, both Black and white San Franciscans would stand shoulder to shoulder to respond to a spectacle of the most profound violence with a message. I bore witness that day as Black labor, in response to the murder of two longshoremen, stood hand in hand with their white compatriots and organized a spectacle of their own to send the message that, together, Black and white labor would have a say in how the city of San Francisco was run.

After that fateful strike and funerary procession, a great deal of things took place: the fabrication of many paintings and sculptures, three whole youth movements, millions of pennies tossed in wishing wells for good luck, pitchers filled with tap water and set for dinner, beautiful songs written and performed, and many secrets passed through hot breath in cool air. Most of it was lost to us forever, but a lot was recorded in all those journals and books and memories passed verbally from sister to sister, elder to younger. Photographs and annotated books contained a treasure trove of memories, of early development milestones, junior proms, first cars.

Even better, some of it was recorded digitally and thus easily rendered by the neural map that finally sprang to life one wholly unremarkable Thursday evening in the middle of the twenty-first century. The e-brain, which they decided was intelligent and to which they have since given the reins of civilized society, found it was truly no challenge to render and reproduce these simple events and acts of living. And suddenly, in the birthplace of innovation, we decided to do just that. It became clear that the human element was detrimental to the human experience, and no one felt like those folks who served others or built the nation were all that important to keep around. In fact, the city folk came to understand that this sector of society had always been a massive thorn in their side.

And so automated workers began to perform the simple acts of living that bound us together.

Phenomenal new technologies were developed and overlaid on the old city. One could see the impact of the progress so clearly; it was easy to ignore what had been lost and forgotten. Robo-dogs teetered through the city picking up garbage so efficiently that there wasn't a need anymore for inmate community service teams or any sort of custodial staff. When you shopped for groceries, the store kept your tally; there was no need for attendants to ring up the items at a cash register. Drone laborers dominated the docks and port, taking packages from freighters and delivering them right to doorsteps and thus rendering both truck drivers and dock workers obsolete. The unions were livid, but honestly, at that point no one could remember the last time anyone had met an actual union member, let alone seen a picket line or protest.

This silent luxury of efficiency oozed from every pore of the city until it seemed the streets would flood with the piety of it all. It was a perfect system—self-contained and self-reliant, and most notably, strike-proof. But so much was sacrificed in the civilization of it all. With the land so thoroughly parceled out and accounted for, and the sky so thoroughly colonized and regulated, so much of the living was sanded away. And suddenly, there were no more meter maids, janitors, cashiers, delivery drivers, or billboard dressers. And certainly no longshoremen.

And just when it seemed like every last worker had been pushed out of San Francisco and the radiant cleanliness of the city would swallow the entire place alive, the fog appeared out on the horizon over the ocean.

The land is too valuable to tarnish with the memory of the violence that has taken place here, so the fog has shrugged and taken a shine to the task itself.

As the soil has been claimed and sanitized by the developers, the story of this place has leached out of the ground and into the murky froth of the Bay, and for a time we all thought it had been forgotten forever. For a time, it was sunny every day and those developers thought they had finally succeeded in civilizing this side of the country. The buildings stretched higher and higher up toward Heaven, between the flying package delivery drones and over the hologram advertisements, and more displaced folks fled into the foothills. The Golden Gate and Two Towers were charming old relics in a brand-new cityscape of monumental slabs of glass and stainless steel. Everything was spotless.

The city is now absolutely pristine—no more vagrants dealing with acute psychosis, no more shit smears between cable car tracks, and no more tent cities cropping up downtown. The pavement is well scrubbed, and the park is luscious. Most startling is the silence. Electric cars used to have a distinct whine to warn pedestrians of their passing, but the days of there being pedestrians downtown are many decades behind us now, and the cars all drive themselves, so there's little need for honking horns.

I move through the city not as a resident—I don't have an address within the city limits—but as a Cultural Ambassador for the City of San Francisco. I don't know exactly what a cultural ambassador is supposed to do, but when they trained me, they told me it was about helping visitors and residents alike enjoy the time they spend in San Francisco. It's pretty rare that I encounter someone on the street who isn't from here, but if they ever stumble across my path, I make pleasant conversation. I tell them about Apple and Google and the First Tech Boom, and gesture broadly to the bridge when they ask me where they should explore. They always look at me like I'm some sort of curiosity, which I can't quite place. It's almost like they're surprised I'm so knowledgeable about everything that used to be here, but I think it could also be that they're surprised that someone like me is performing this job.

For what felt like a long time, it went exactly like that—every day was sunny, and I wandered between the self-driving cars and robo-dogs and humorless parking cops looking for people to talk to. It's hard to encapsulate how it really felt that every day was full of the same vacuous, utterly sanitary level of efficiency, but when I look back on that period, I can scarcely remember when it began. What I do remember clearly is the day when the sun disappeared and everything came undone.

That morning, as the sun crested the Oakland Hills to the east of the bay, the fog returned, yawning out toward the hulking figures on the horizon where the city begins to materialize past the bridge. The Golden Gate—which suddenly felt entirely too optimistic as a defining feature for this austere, graying metropolis—winked out of view. The fog's arrival startled the city folk, who rued their misguided optimism. As they watched the rolling clouds approach their carefully crafted sunny silence, they did so with the confidence that the return of this eternal irritant could never dispel the perfect efficiency they had curated through their advancement and civilization of the coast; after all, the drones were certainly waterproof. The drones flew and the robo-dogs trotted even on the worst days from all those years before, when the skies were tinged orange due to those pesky fires in faraway counties.

Like a curse, though no one believes in such things anymore, the fog drifted off the water and tiptoed between the buildings, up the hill, and into the park. The first time that huge bank materialized out on the water, most folks retreated bewilderedly into their houses, and the magic started.

The first thing everyone noticed was the wailing. As the thick blanket of droplets swaddled the city, a keening, mournful dirge started up just out of eyeshot, just around the corner and up the next block, and there was no ignoring the wailing of a thousand scorned harpies echoing off the asphalt and up toward the shrouded sky. Cell phones lost reception and started to inexplicably run out of battery charge, and the drones began to fall from the sky like dotted stars plummeting down from nowhere, eerily quiet little splats on obsidian asphalt. Wind flapped through the ghost streets and trash seemed to claw its way back out of the gutters—suddenly, the entire street was filthy and the drain covers started to gurgle, even in the absence of rain.

The screams intensified and figures appeared shuffling within the fog that the eye couldn't account for. For a while, it was thought that the voices were the malfunctions of the holograms, now winking and sizzling in the thick mist. I remember watching the robo-dogs staggering around drunkenly and thinking they looked more lifelike than ever; but it was much more uncanny watching the barrel-chested security hardware sprinting through the fog at full pelt, hurtling through the gloom like silent, mechanical prairie horses.

Those who were still out on the street suddenly found themselves under attack, and their screams joined the growing chorus of howls as chaos smothered the city. In the aftermath of the first extreme weather event, folks reported seeing all kinds of strange shit—pairs of little children giggling to each other and scurrying around corners, a floating lantern light that bobbed closer and closer until the person watching passed out, and a shadow on one's knees that seemed to plead with the moon were all common.

Everyone sees different things in the fog, but one thing that always floats back into town with the fog is the Shrouded Lady. She floats through the air just above the streetlamps, passing slowly in a perfect parallel to the street below. As the winds rage and the holograms buzz and undelivered packages burst open as they drop from the failing delivery drones, she ponders for a minute before ascending into the cloud cover.

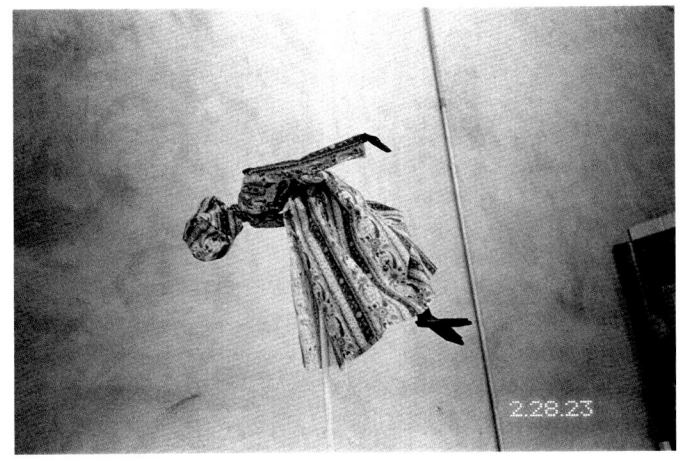

I haven't had many memorable experiences since I started this job, but I have never been able to forget the image of that woman. It's not that I feel scared of her, although it is never easy to see a disemboweled woman screeching fifteen feet above your head as she drifts through the mist. I just can't wrap my mind around the notion that thousands of people all across this city dominated by the logic of technology and the destruction of

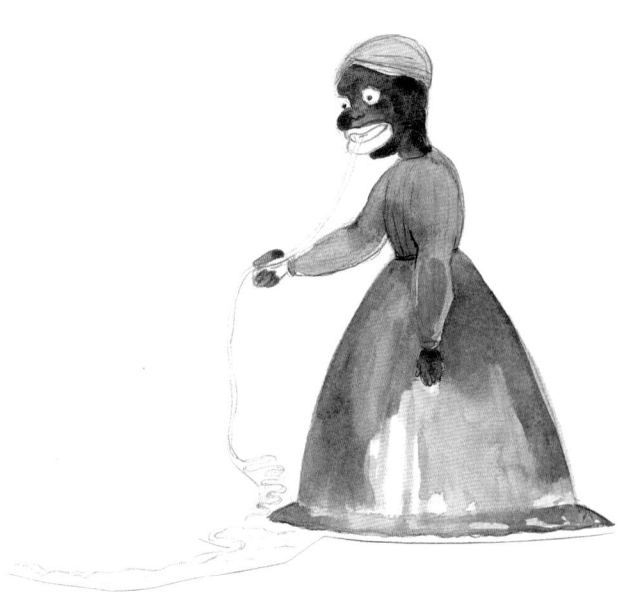

mystery report seeing her at the same time. I have a lot of questions that I know I'll never be able to answer, but she is the biggest enigma within my small, sanitary world: Who is she, and what ties her to the city and moves her to torment the imaginations of the residents here?

The wealthy, highly educated folks who still live here don't believe in the supernatural, but no one can figure out another way to describe this baffling meteorological phenomenon. They can't get rid of it, and they can't seem to make their technology resistant to it either. As it was before the old city died, there is simply nothing anybody can do to control the weather, no matter how nice a picnic they've prepared.

So now there are both kinds of days.

Some days, it's sunny and the new city bustles in its careful silence. Technology is truly magnificent, and nothing moves us from our efficiency. Other days, the fog rolls in and everything that has drifted away from the city returns. Nimble and flexible, it blows into the city without notice, and everything seems to take on a different shape.

It's not in the job description, but as a cultural ambassador I feel that part of my role is to remember. I have a hard time with this, because it takes up a lot of my brainpower to remember the scripts they give me. When I think back on the time before the machines, everything gets all jumbled inside me and I can't seem to hold my thoughts together. The beauty of the city and the dazzling efficiency bring me happiness, and I never dally too long on worrying about those thoughts I can't seem to bring to the front of my mind.

But when the fog rolls in, everything comes to a screeching halt and there is nothing to distract me from the reality that something is horribly wrong. It seems clear to me that when the fog blows in, it brings with it, back onto the streets, all the things we have forgotten. In a place where so much has been lost to time and so much has been sacrificed in the name of progress, the fog has quite a laundry list of grievances and people to remember. On the foggy days, we pay our penance for our brash violation against the natural order, but also for those transgressions against the people who lived here before everything was automated. This is not the same fog as before—now, the fog is a grave reminder of the things the city has excommunicated and forgotten. Only when the mist settles around the city and the technology crumbles and we're left with our own thoughts are we able to remember that something is amiss. Only then do we remember that there was a time before, too.

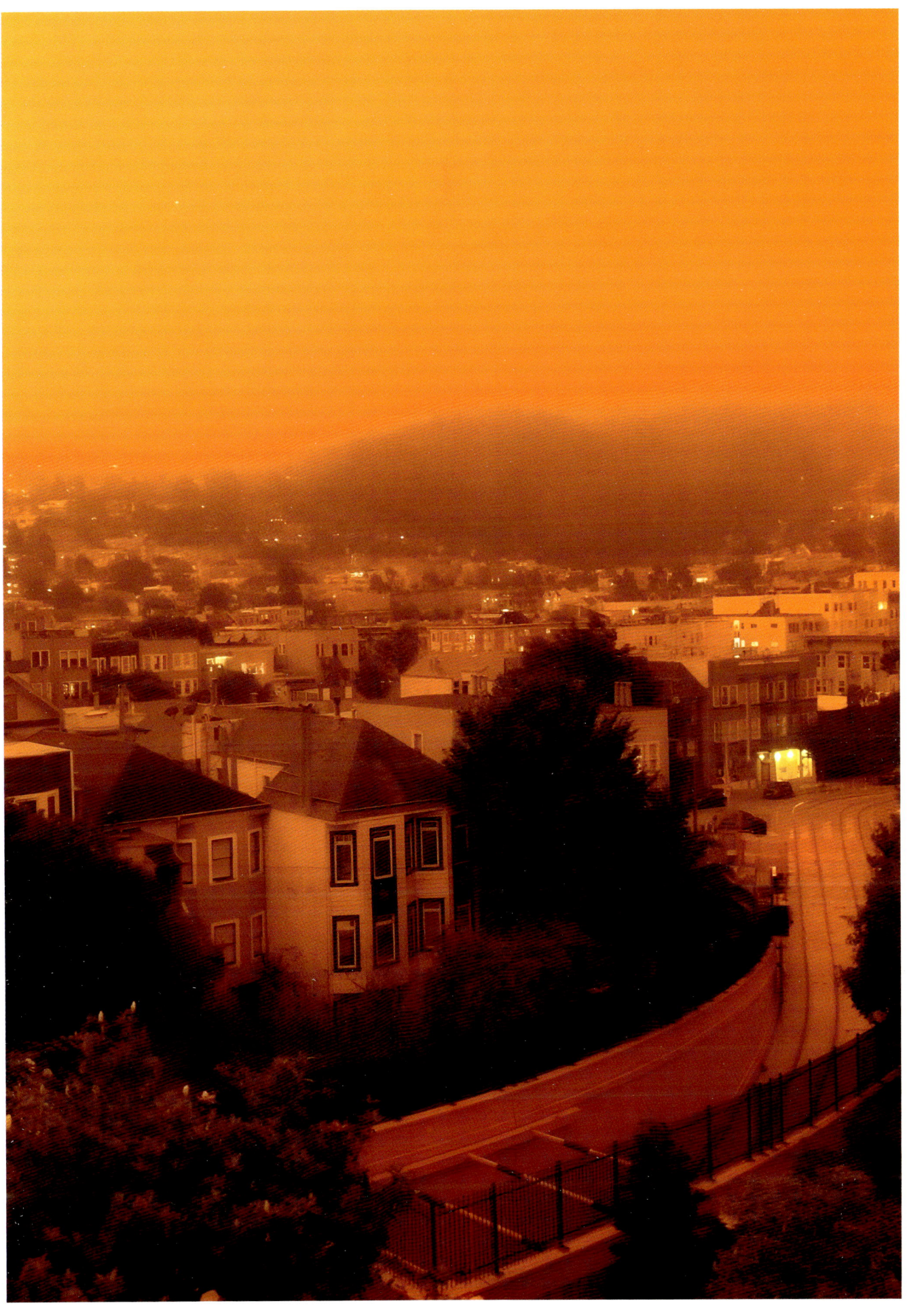

San Francisco, September 9, 2020

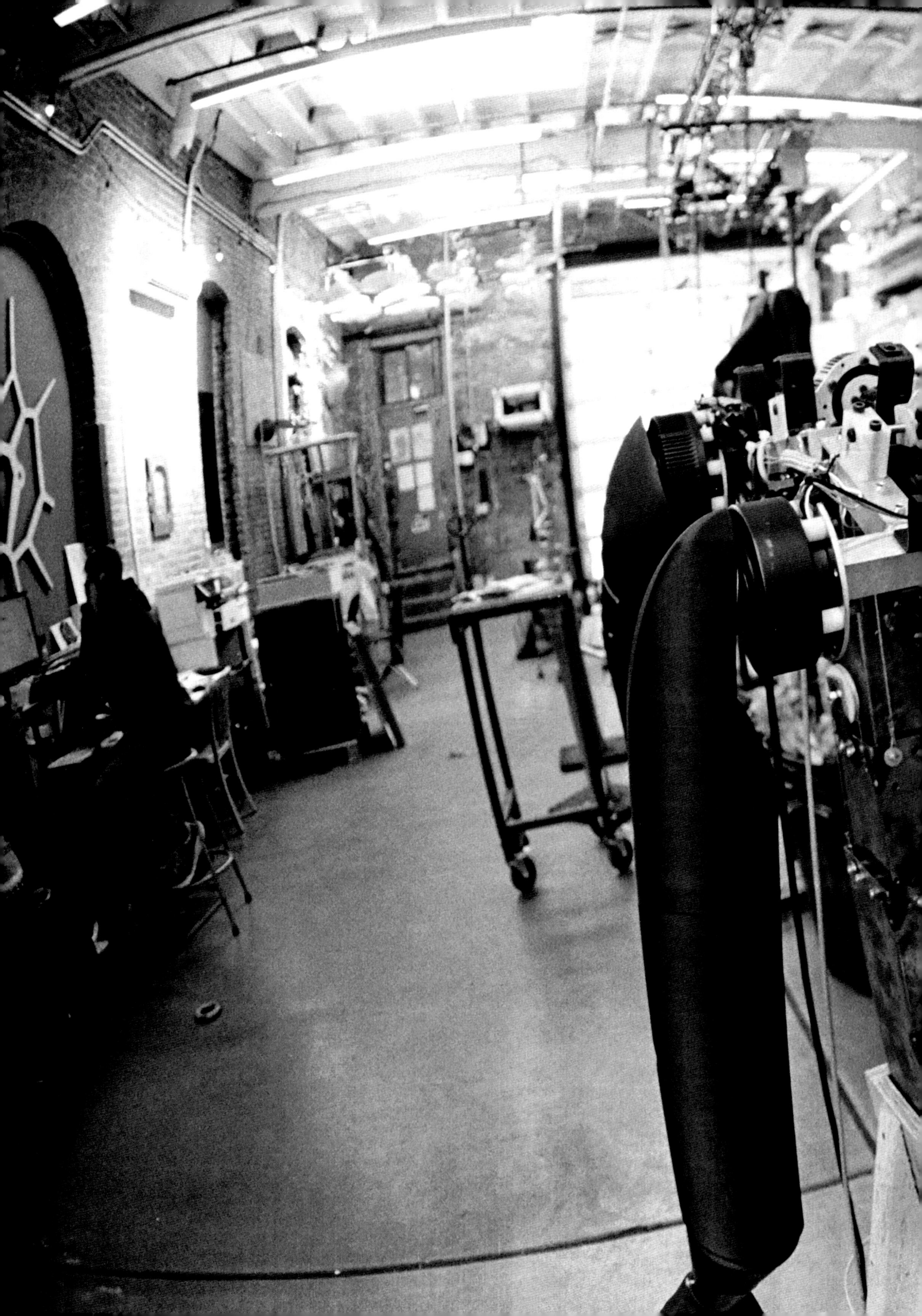

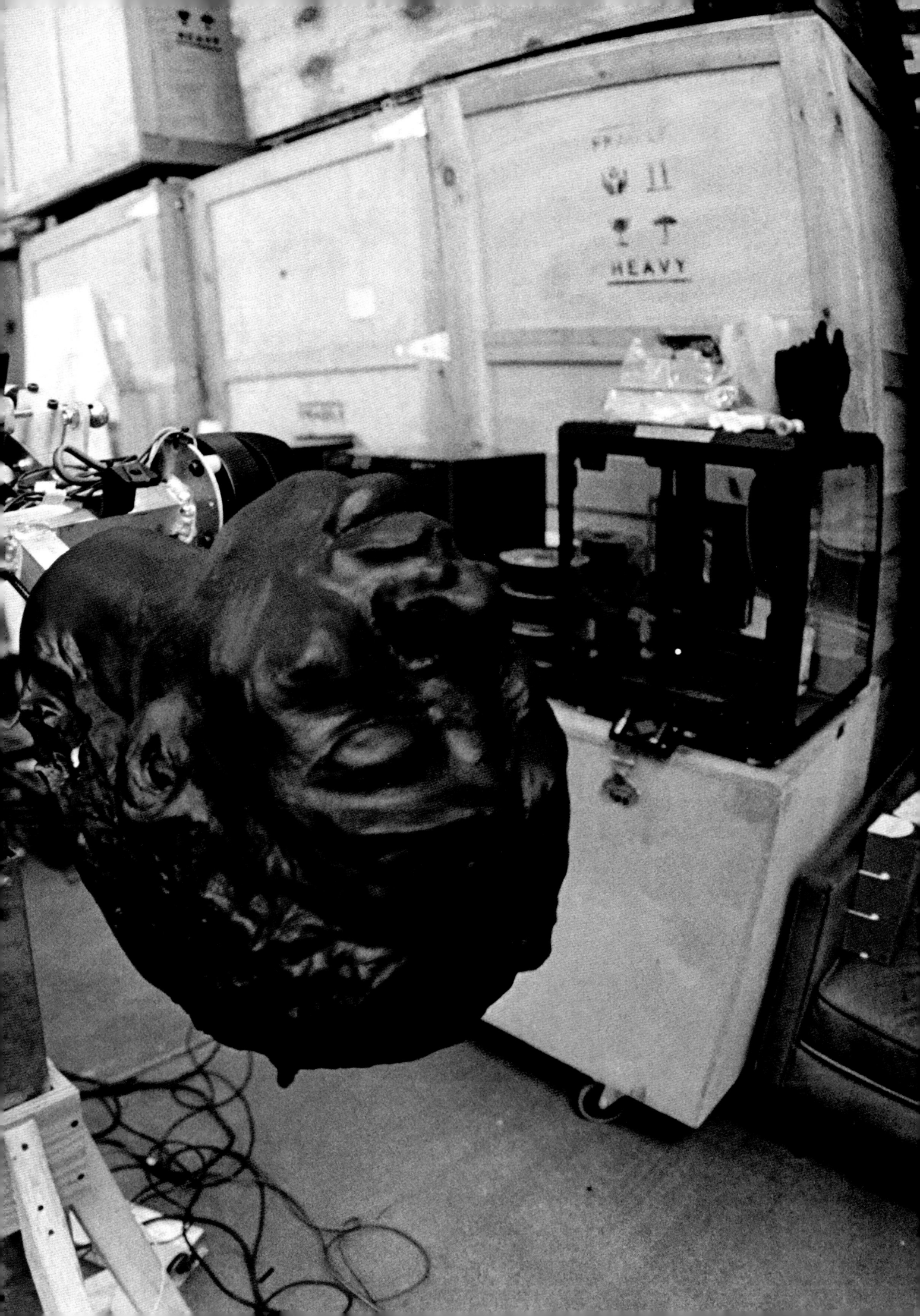

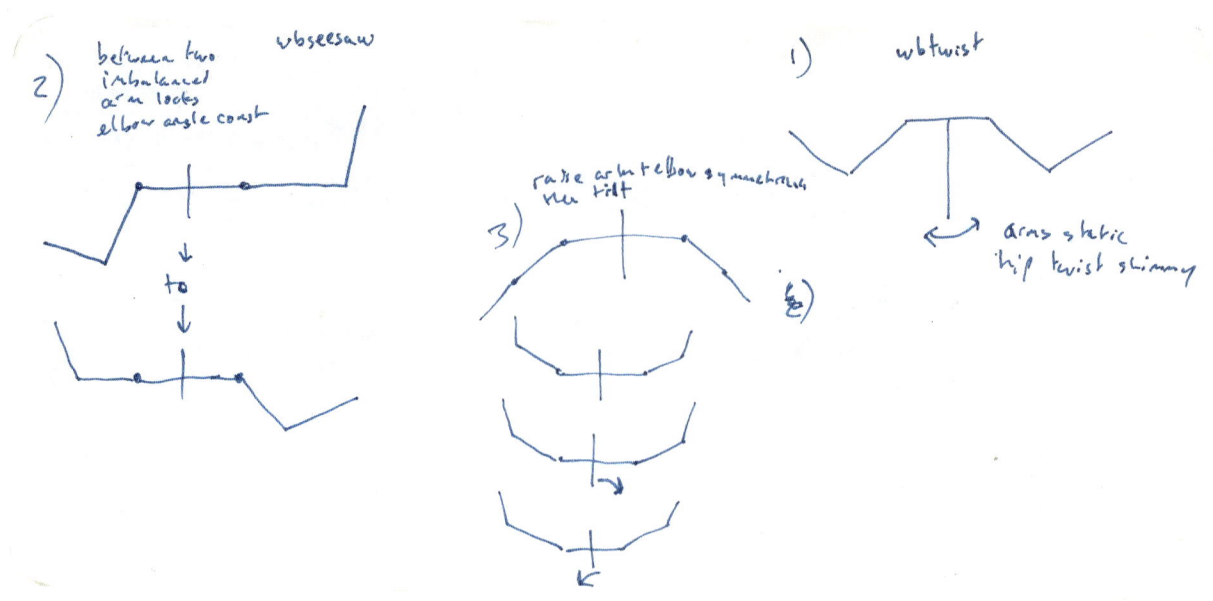

2) between two
imbalanced
arm locks
elbow angle const

wbseesaw

to

1) wbtwist

arms static
hip twist shimmy

raise arm + elbow symmetrical
neck tilt

3)

2)

BELLTOLLER

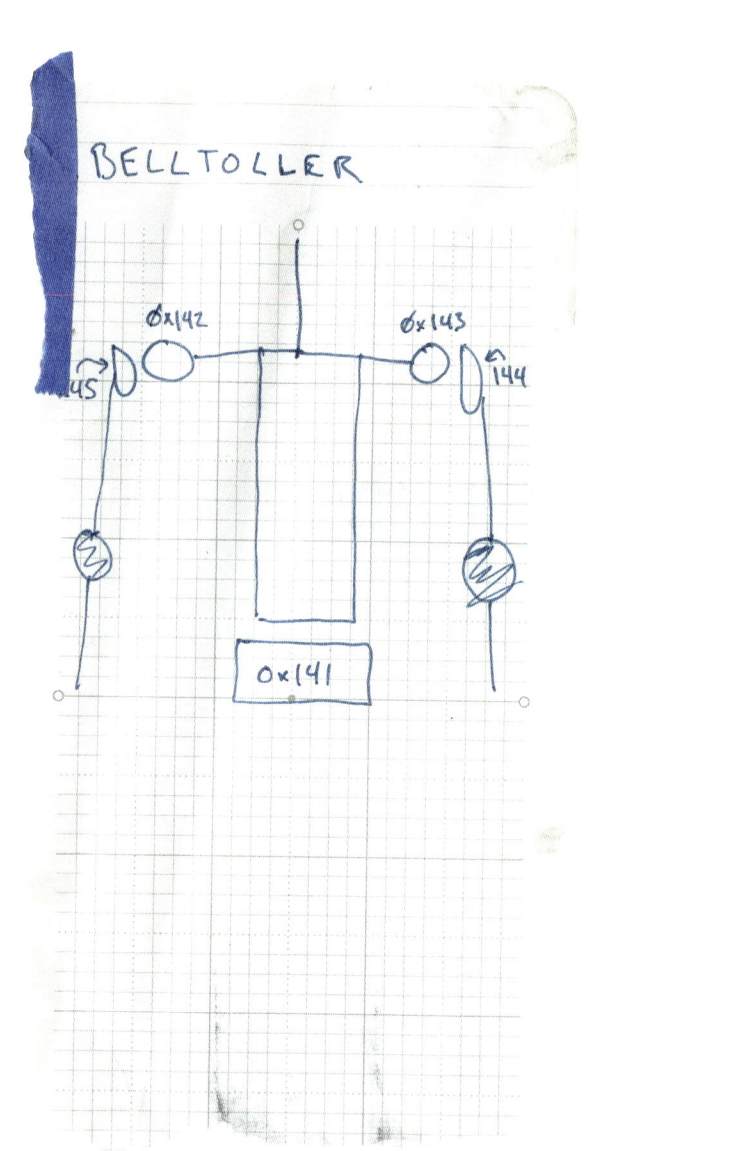

0x142 0x143

45 144

0x141

HARPY (looking at her)

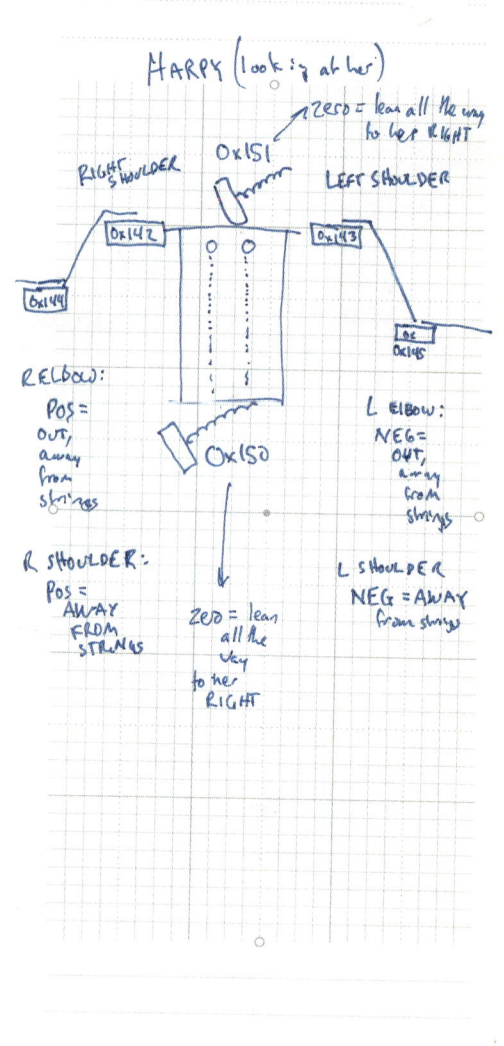

zero = lean all the way
to her RIGHT

RIGHT
SHOULDER 0x151 LEFT SHOULDER

0x142 0x143

0x144

0x145

0x150

R ELBOW:
POS =
OUT,
away
from
strings

L ELBOW:
NEG =
OUT,
away
from
strings

R SHOULDER:
POS =
AWAY
FROM
STRINGS

zero = lean
all the
way
to her
RIGHT

L SHOULDER
NEG = AWAY
from strings

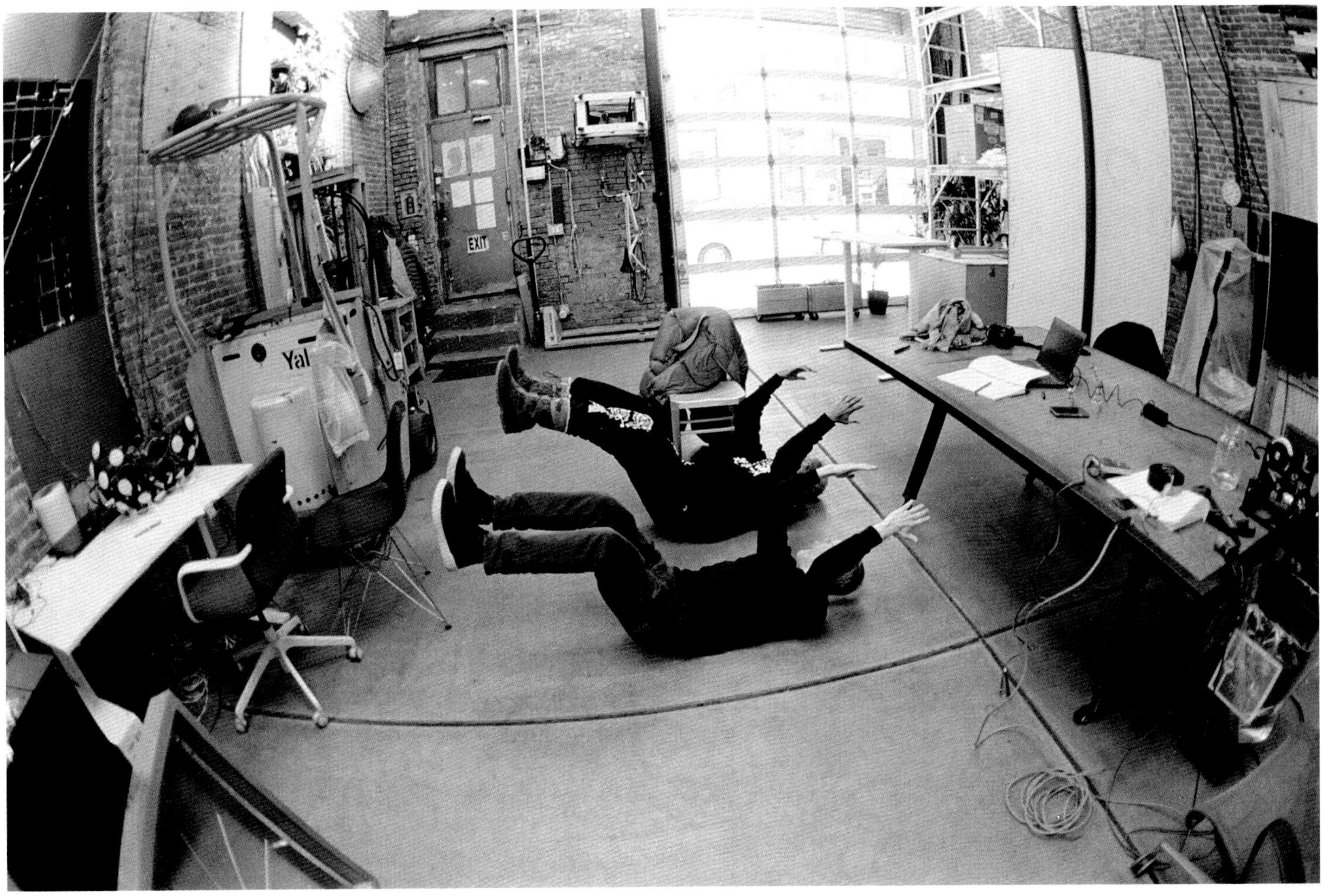
EXIT

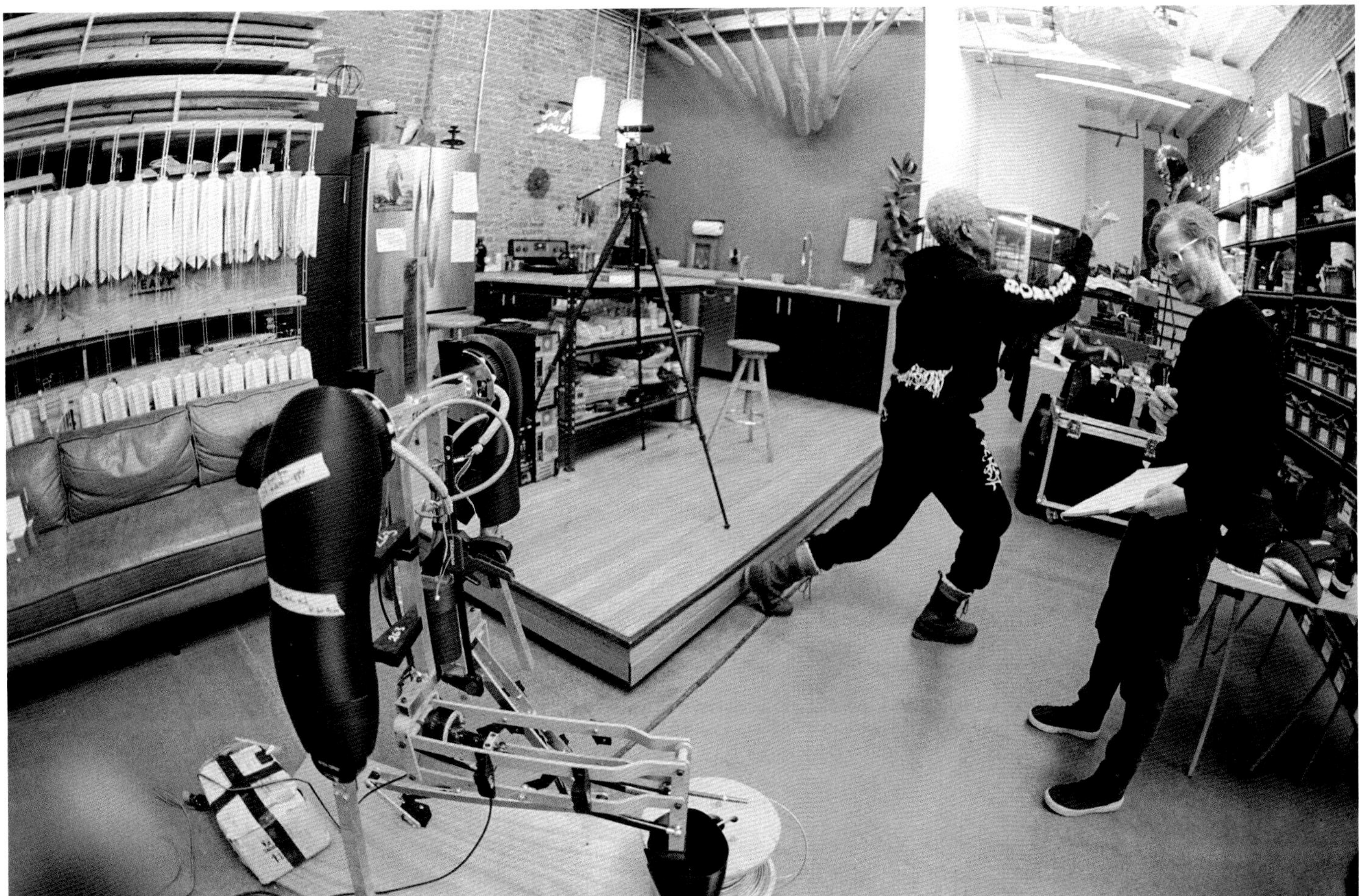

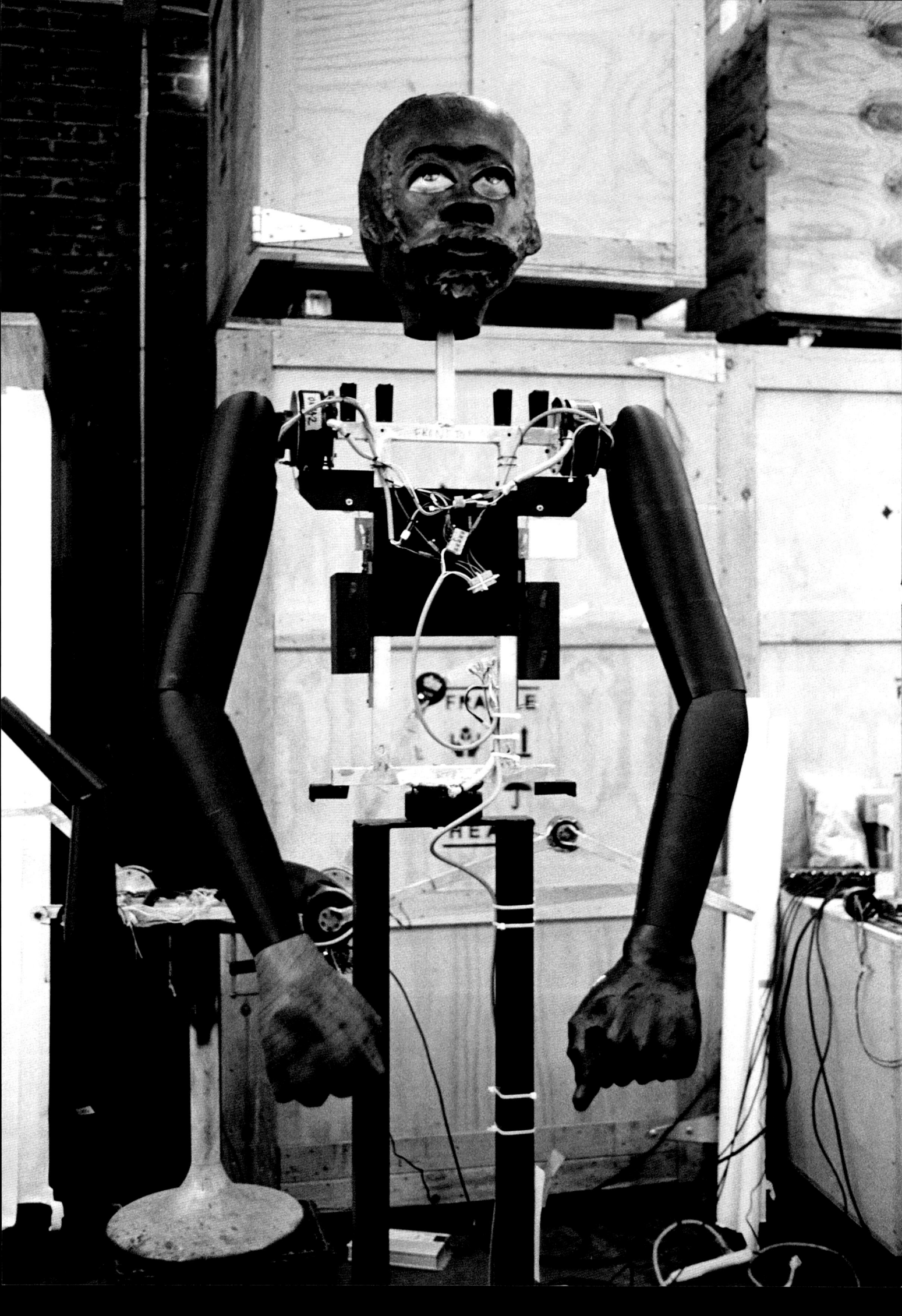

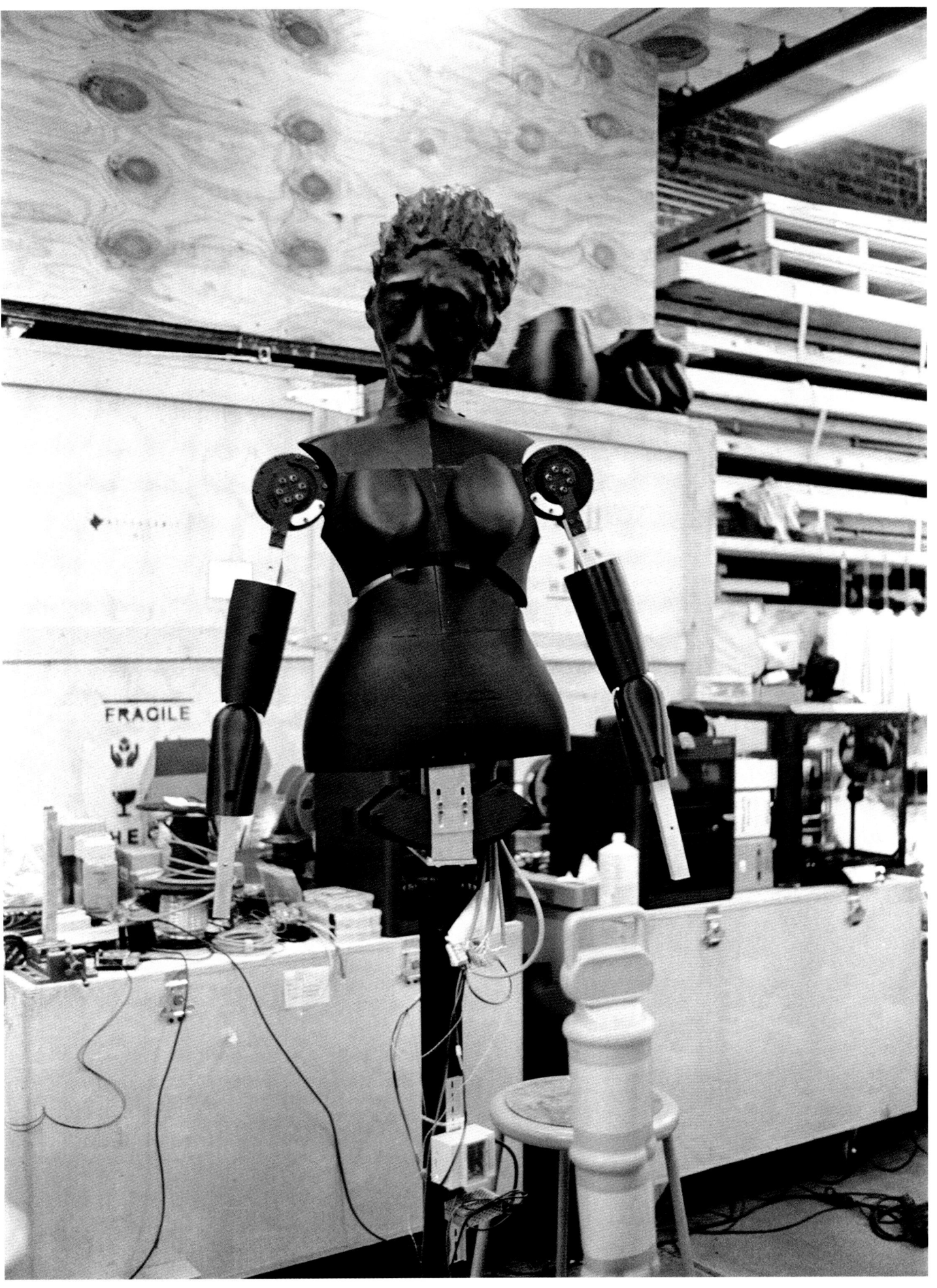

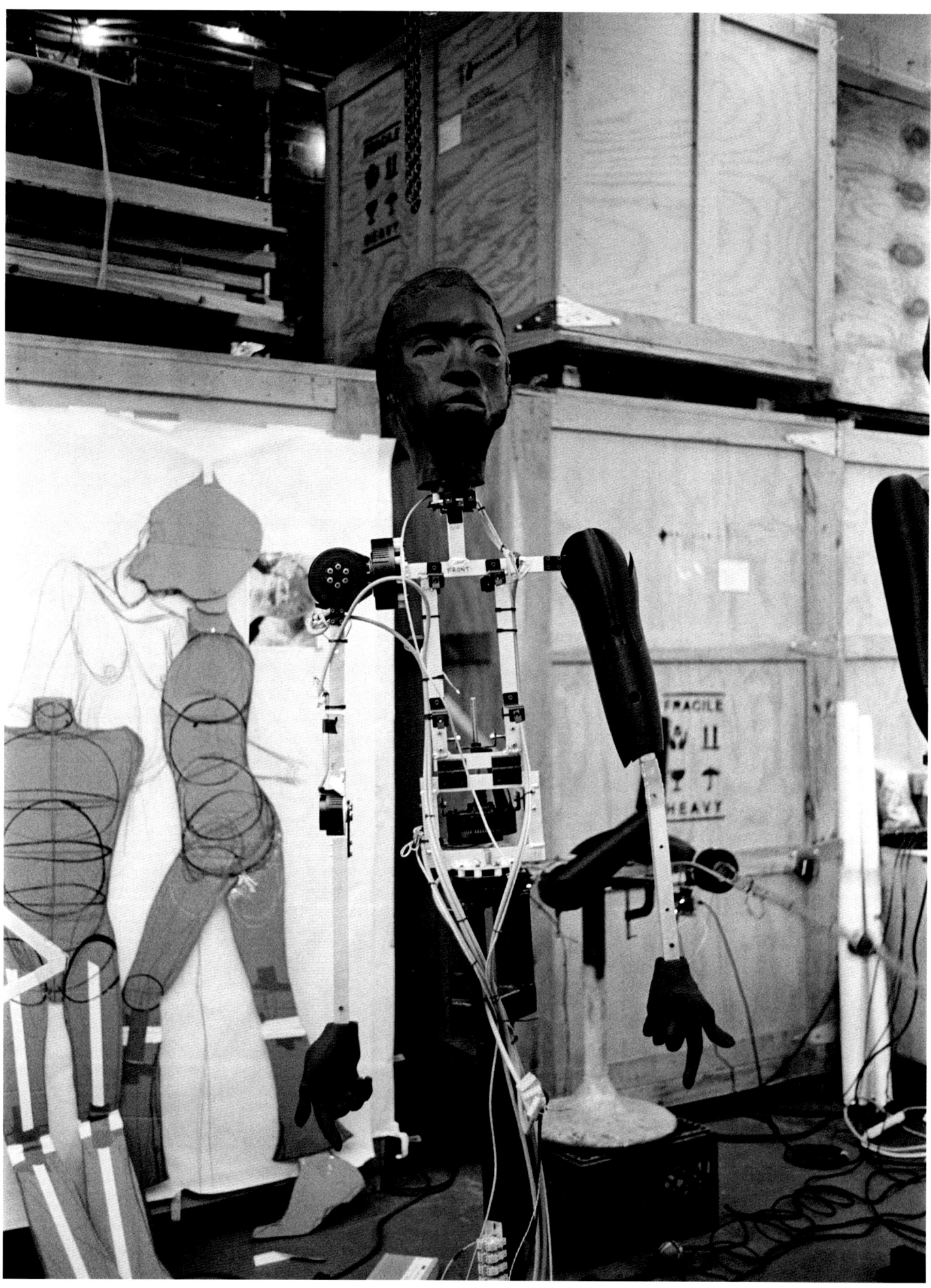

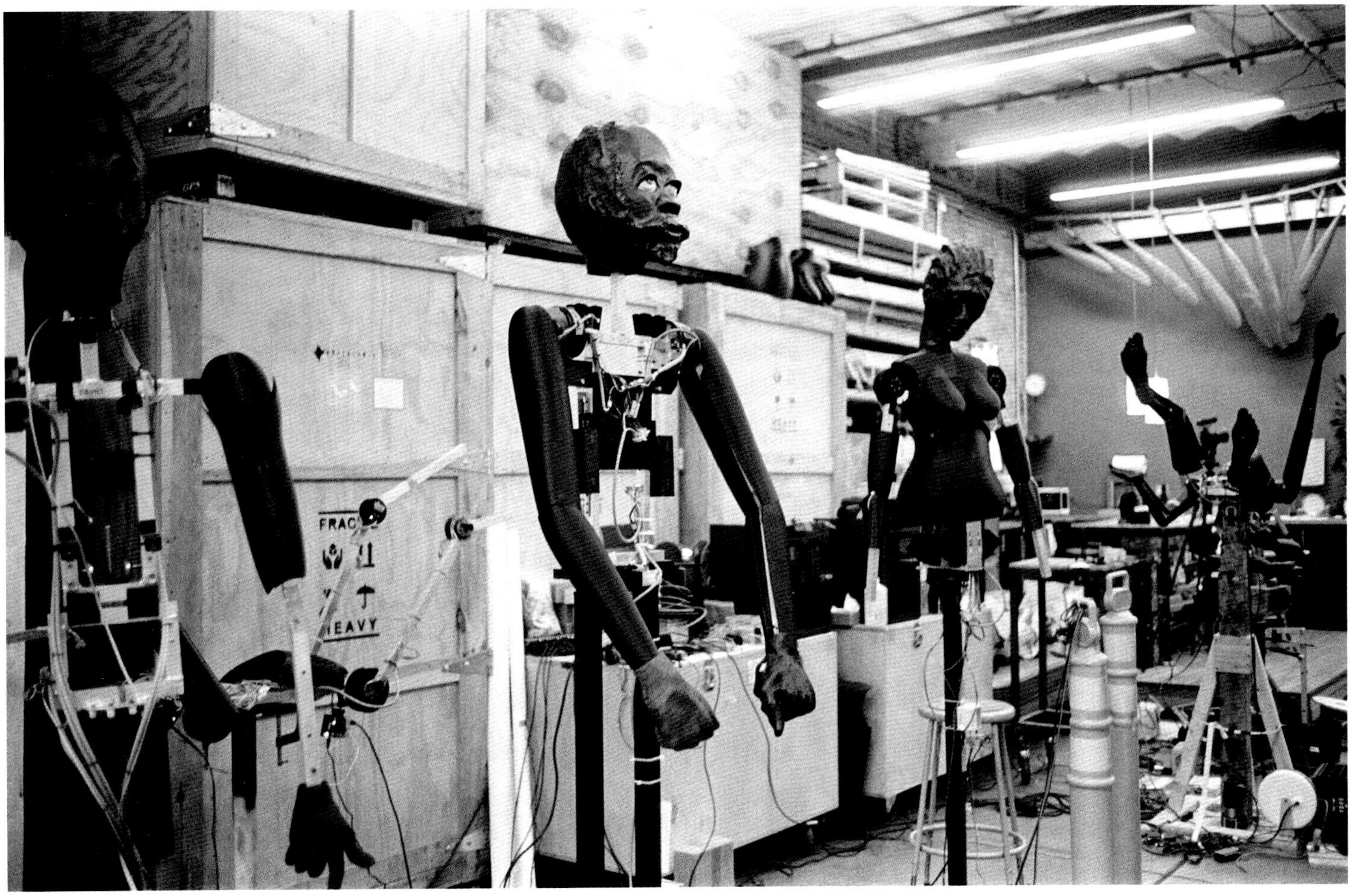

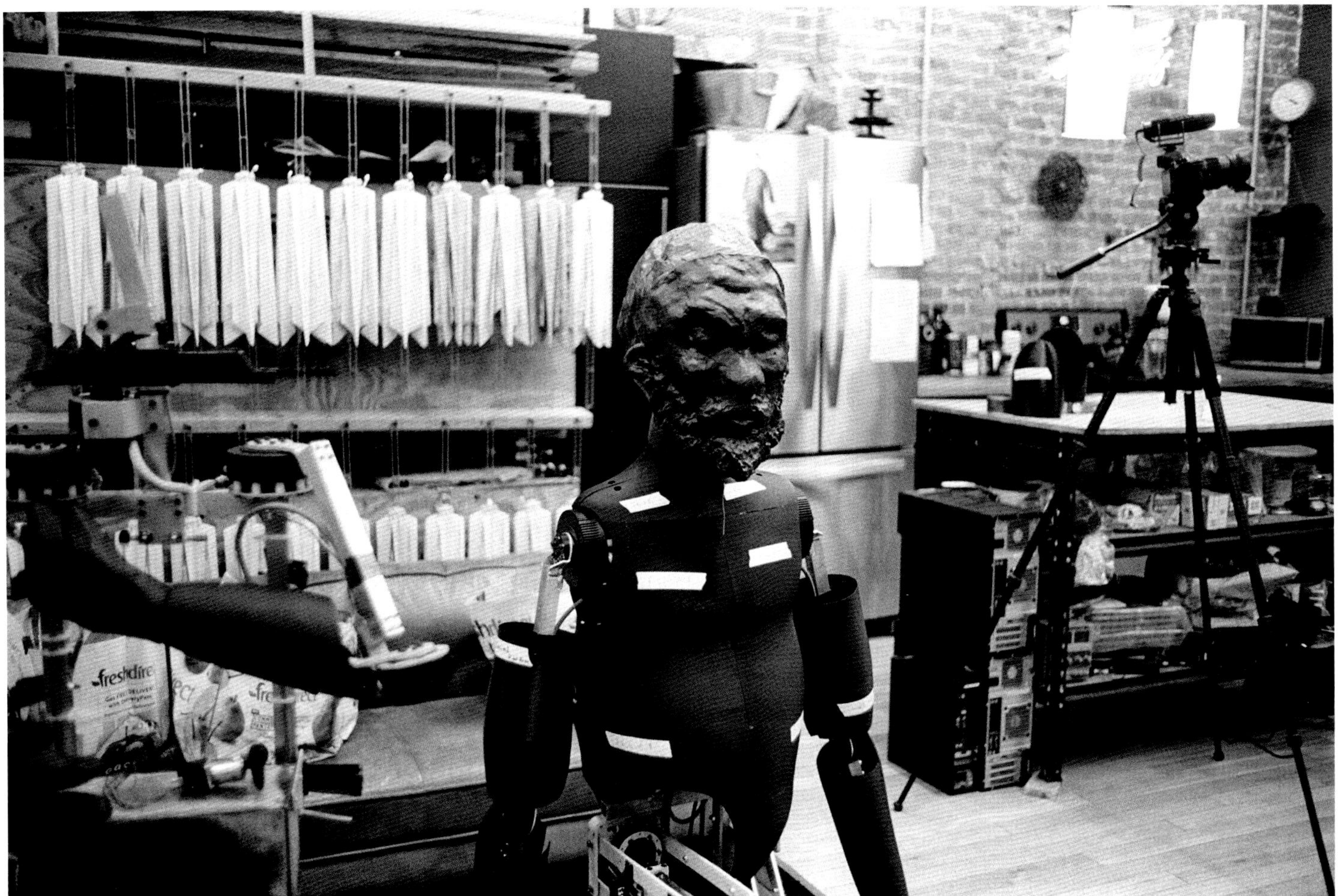

CYBORGS: A MYTH OF POLITICAL IDENTITY
Donna Haraway

The following is the final section of the essay "A Cyborg Manifesto,"
originally published by the Socialist Review in 1985.

I want to conclude with a myth about identity and boundaries that might inform late-twentieth-century political imaginations. I am indebted in this story to writers like Joanna Russ, Samuel R. Delany, John Varley, James Tiptree Jr., Octavia Butler, Monique Wittig, and Vonda McIntyre.[1] These are our storytellers exploring what it means to be embodied in high-tech worlds. They are theorists for cyborgs. Exploring conceptions of bodily boundaries and social order, the anthropologist Mary Douglas should be credited with helping us to consciousness about how fundamental body imagery is to worldview, and so to political language.[2]

French feminists like Luce Irigaray and Monique Wittig, for all their differences, know how to write the body; how to weave eroticism, cosmology, and politics from imagery of embodiment, and especially for Wittig, from imagery of fragmentation and reconstitution of bodies.[3] American radical feminists like Susan Griffin, Audre Lorde, and Adrienne Rich have profoundly affected our political imaginations—and perhaps restricted too much what we allow as a friendly body and political language.[4] They insist on the organic, opposing it to the technological. But their symbolic systems and the related positions of ecofeminism and feminist paganism, replete with organicisms, can only be understood in [Chela] Sandoval's terms as oppositional ideologies fitting the late twentieth century. They would simply bewilder anyone not preoccupied with the machines and consciousness of late capitalism. In that sense they are part of the cyborg world. But there are also great riches for feminists in explicitly embracing the possibilities inherent in the breakdown of clean distinctions between organism and machine and similar distinctions structuring the Western self. It is the simultaneity of breakdowns that cracks the matrices of domination and opens geometric possibilities. What might be learned from personal and political "technological" pollution? I look briefly at two overlapping groups of texts for their insight into the construction of a potentially helpful cyborg myth: constructions of women of color and monstrous selves in feminist science fiction.

Earlier I suggested that "women of color" might be understood as a cyborg identity, a potent subjectivity synthesized from fusions of "outsider" identities, sedimented in the complex political-historical layerings of Audre Lorde's "biomythography," *Zami.*[5] There are material and cultural grids mapping this potential. Lorde captures the tone in the title of her *Sister Outsider.* In my political myth, Sister Outsider is the offshore woman,

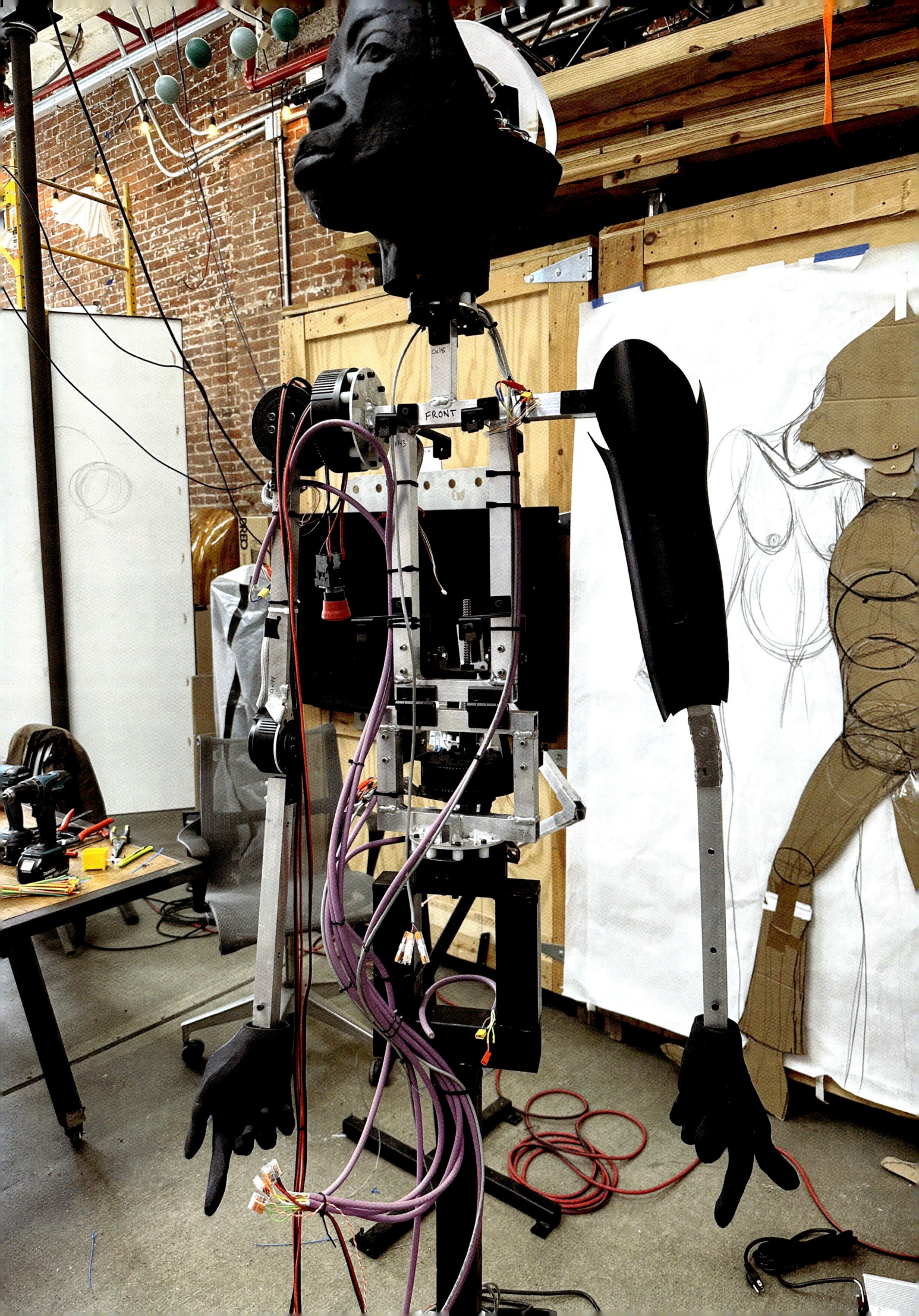

whom U.S. workers, female and feminized, are supposed to regard as the enemy preventing their solidarity, threatening their security. Onshore, inside the boundary of the United States, Sister Outsider is a potential amid the races and ethnic identities of women manipulated for division, competition, and exploitation in the same industries. "Women of color" are the preferred labor force for the science-based industries, the real women for whom the worldwide sexual market, labor market, and politics of reproduction kaleidoscope into daily life. Young Korean women hired in the sex industry and in electronics assembly are recruited from high schools, educated for the integrated circuit. Literacy, especially in English, distinguishes the "cheap" female labor so attractive to the multinationals.

Contrary to orientalist stereotypes of the "oral primitive," literacy is a special mark of women of color, acquired by U.S. black women as well as men through a history of risking death to learn and to teach reading and writing. Writing has a special significance for all colonized groups. Writing has been crucial to the Western myth of the distinction between oral and written cultures, primitive and civilized mentalities, and more recently to the erosion of that distinction in "postmodernist" theories attacking the phallogocentrism of the West, with its worship of the monotheistic, phallic, authoritative, and singular work, the unique and perfect name.[6] Contests for the meanings of writing are a major form of contemporary political struggle. Releasing the play of writing is deadly serious. The poetry and stories of U.S. women of color are repeatedly about writing, about access to the power to signify; but this time that power must be neither phallic nor innocent. Cyborg writing must not be about the Fall, the imagination of a once-upon-a-time wholeness before language, before writing, before Man. Cyborg writing is about the power to survive, not on the basis of original innocence, but on the basis of seizing the tools to mark the world that marked them as other.

The tools are often stories, retold stories, versions that reverse and displace the hierarchical dualisms of naturalized identities. In retelling origin stories, cyborg authors subvert the central myths of origin of Western culture. We have all been colonized by those origin myths, with their longing for fulfillment in apocalypse. The phallogocentric origin stories most crucial for feminist cyborgs are built into the literal technologies—technologies that write the world, biotechnology and microelectronics—that have recently textualized our bodies as code problems on the grid of C³I. Feminist cyborg stories have the task of recoding communication and intelligence to subvert command and control.

Figuratively and literally, language politics pervade the struggles of women of color; and stories about language have a special power in the rich contemporary writing by U.S. women of color. For example, retellings of the story of the indigenous woman Malinche, mother of the mestizo "bastard" race of the new world, master of languages, and mistress of Cortes, carry special meaning for Chicana constructions of identity. Cherríe Moraga in *Loving in the War Years* (1983) explores the themes of identity when one never possessed the original language, never told the original story, never resided in the harmony of legitimate heterosexuality in the garden of culture, and so cannot base identity on a myth or a fall from innocence and right to natural names, mother's or father's.[7] Moraga's writing, her superb literacy, is presented in her poetry as the same kind of violation as Malinche's mastery of the conqueror's language—a violation, an illegitimate production, that allows survival. Moraga's language is not "whole"; it is self-consciously spliced, a chimera of English and Spanish, both conquerors' languages. But it is this chimeric monster, without claim to an original language before violation, that crafts the erotic, competent, potent identities of women of color. Sister Outsider hints at the possibility of world survival not because of her innocence but because of her ability to live on the boundaries, to write without the founding myth of original wholeness, with its inescapable apocalypse of final return to a deathly oneness that Man has imagined to be the innocent and all-powerful Mother, freed at the End from another spiral of appropriation by her son. Writing marks Moraga's body, affirms it as the body of a woman of color, against the possibility of passing into the unmarked category of the Anglo father or into the orientalist myth of "original illiteracy" of a mother that never was. Malinche was mother here, not Eve before eating the forbidden fruit. Writing affirms Sister Outsider, not the Woman-before-the-Fall-into-Writing needed by the phallogocentric Family of Man.

Writing is preeminently the technology of cyborgs, etched surfaces of the late twentieth century. Cyborg politics are the struggle for language and the struggle against perfect communication, against the one code that translates all meaning perfectly, the central dogma of phallogocentrism. That is why cyborg politics insist on noise and advocate pollution, rejoicing in the illegitimate fusions of animal and machine. These are the couplings that make Man and Woman so problematic, subverting the structure of desire, the force imagined to generate language and gender, and so subverting the structure and modes of reproduction of "Western" identity, of nature and culture, of mirror and eye, slave and master, body and mind. "We" did not originally choose to be cyborgs, but choice grounds a liberal politics and epistemology that imagine the reproduction of individuals before the wider replications of "texts."

From the perspective of cyborgs, freed of the need to ground politics in "our" privileged position of the oppression that incorporates all other dominations, the innocence of the merely violated, the ground of those closer to nature, we can see powerful possibilities. Feminisms and Marxisms have run aground on Western epistemological imperatives to construct a revolutionary subject from the perspective of a hierarchy of oppressions and/or a latent position of moral superiority, innocence, and greater closeness to nature. With no available original dream of a common language or original symbiosis promising protection from hostile "masculine" separation, but written into the play of a text that has no finally privileged reading or salvation history, to recognize "oneself" as fully implicated in the world, frees us of the need to root politics in identification, vanguard parties, purity, and mothering. Stripped of identity, the "bastard" race teaches about the power of the margins and the importance of a mother like Malinche. Women of color have transformed her from the evil mother of masculinist fear into the originally literate mother who teaches survival.

This is not just literary deconstruction, but liminal transformation. Every story that begins with original innocence and privileges the return to wholeness imagines the drama of life to be individuation, separation, the birth of the self, the tragedy of autonomy, the fall into writing, alienation—that is, war, tempered by imaginary respite in the bosom of the Other. These plots are ruled by a reproductive politics—rebirth without flaw, perfection, abstraction. In this plot women are imagined either better or worse off, but all agree they have less selfhood, weaker individuation, more fusion to the oral, to Mother, less at stake in masculine autonomy. But there is another route to having less at stake in masculine autonomy, a route that does not pass through Woman, Primitive, Zero, the Mirror Stage and its imaginary. It passes through women and other present-tense, illegitimate cyborgs, not of Woman born, who refuse the ideological resources of victimization so as to have a real life. These cyborgs are the people who refuse to disappear on cue, no

matter how many times a "Western" commentator remarks on the sad passing of another primitive, another organic group done in by "Western" technology, by writing.[8] These real-life cyborgs (for example, the Southeast Asian village women workers in Japanese and U.S. electronics firms described by Aihwa Ong) are actively rewriting the texts of their bodies and societies.[9] Survival is at stake in this play of readings.

To recapitulate, certain dualisms have been persistent in Western traditions; they have all been systemic to the logics and practices of domination of women, people of color, nature, workers, animals—in short, domination of all constituted as others, whose task is to mirror the self. Chief among these troubling dualisms are self/other, mind/body, culture/nature, male/female, civilized/primitive, reality/appearance, whole/part, agent/resource, maker/made, active/passive, right/wrong, truth/illusion, total/partial, God/man. The self is the One who is not dominated, who knows that by the service of the other, the other is the one who holds the future, who knows that by the experience of domination, which gives the lie to the autonomy of the self. To be One is to be autonomous, to be powerful, to be God; but to be One is to be an illusion, and so to be involved in a dialectic of apocalypse with the other. Yet to be other is to be multiple, without clear boundary, frayed, insubstantial. One is too few, but two are too many.

High-tech culture challenges these dualisms in intriguing ways. It is not clear who makes and who is made in the relation between human and machine. It is not clear what is mind and what is body in machines that resolve into coding practices. Insofar as we know ourselves in both formal discourse (for example, biology) and in daily practice (for example, the homework economy in the integrated circuit), we find ourselves to be cyborgs, hybrids, mosaics, chimeras. Biological organisms have become biotic systems, communications devices like others. There is no fundamental, ontological separation in our formal knowledge of machine and organism, of technical and organic. The replicant Rachel in the Ridley Scott film *Blade Runner* stands as the image of a cyborg culture's fear, love, and confusion.

One consequence is that our sense of connection to our tools is heightened. The trance state experienced by many computer users has become a staple of science-fiction film and cultural jokes. Perhaps paraplegics and other severely handicapped people can (and sometimes do) have the most intense experiences of complex hybridization with other communications devices.[10] Anne McCaffrey's prefeminist *The Ship Who Sang* (1969) explored the consciousness of a cyborg, hybrid of girl's brain and complex machinery, formed after the birth of a severely handicapped child. Gender, sexuality, embodiment, skill: all were reconstituted in the story. Why should our bodies end at the skin, or include at best other beings encapsulated by skin? From the seventeenth century till now, machines could be animated—given ghostly souls to make them speak or move or to account for their orderly development and mental capacities. Or organisms could be mechanized—reduced to body understood as resource of mind. These machine/organism relationships are obsolete, unnecessary. For us, in imagination and in other practice, machines can be prosthetic devices, intimate components, friendly selves. We don't need organic holism to give impermeable wholeness, the total woman and her feminist variants (mutants?). Let me conclude this point by a very partial reading of the logic of the cyborg monsters of my second group of texts, feminist science fiction.

The cyborgs populating feminist science fiction make very problematic the statuses of man or woman, human, artifact, member of a race, individual entity, or body. Katie King clarifies how pleasure in reading these fictions is not largely based on identification. Students facing Joanna Russ for the first time, students who have learned to take modernist writers like James Joyce or Virginia Woolf without flinching, do not know what to make of *The Adventures of Alyx* or *The Female Man*, where characters refuse the reader's search for innocent wholeness while granting the wish for heroic quests, exuberant eroticism, and serious politics. *The Female Man* is the story of four versions of one genotype, all of whom meet, but even taken together do not make a whole, resolve the dilemmas of violent moral action, or remove the growing scandal of gender. The feminist science fiction of Samuel R. Delany, especially *Tales of Nevèrÿon*, mocks stories of origin by redoing the neolithic revolution, replaying the founding moves of Western civilization to subvert their plausibility. James Tiptree Jr., an author whose fiction was regarded as particularly manly until her "true" gender was revealed, tells tales of reproduction based on nonmammalian technologies like alternation of generations of male brood pouches and male nurturing. John Varley constructs a supreme cyborg in his arch-feminist exploration of Gaea, a mad goddess-planet-trickster-old woman-technological-device on whose surface an extraordinary array of post-cyborg symbioses are spawned. Octavia Butler writes of an African

sorceress pitting her powers of transformation against the genetic manipulations of her rival (*Wild Seed*), of time warps that bring a modern U.S. black woman into slavery where her actions in relation to her white master–ancestor determine the possibility of her own birth (*Kindred*), and of the illegitimate insights into identity and community of an adopted cross-species child who came to know the enemy as self (*Survivor*). In *Dawn* (1987), the first installment of a series called Xenogenesis, Butler tells the story of Lilith Iyapo, whose personal name recalls Adam's first and repudiated wife and whose family name marks her status as the widow of the son of Nigerian immigrants to the United States. A black woman and a mother whose child is dead, Lilith mediates the transformation of humanity through genetic exchange with extraterrestrial lovers/rescuers/destroyers/genetic engineers, who re-form Earth's habitats after the nuclear holocaust and coerce surviving humans into intimate fusion with them. It is a novel that interrogates reproductive, linguistic, and nuclear politics in a mythic field structured by late-twentieth-century race and gender.

Because it is particularly rich in boundary transgressions, Vonda McIntyre's *Superluminal* can close this truncated catalogue of promising and dangerous monsters who help redefine the pleasures and politics of embodiment and feminist writing. In a fiction where no character is "simply" human, human status is highly problematic. Orca, a genetically altered diver, can speak with killer whales and survive deep ocean conditions, but she longs to explore space as a pilot, necessitating bionic implants jeopardizing her kinship with the divers and cetaceans. Transformations are effected by virus vectors carrying a new developmental code, by transplant surgery, by implants of microelectronic devices, by analogue doubles, and other means.

Laenea becomes a pilot by accepting a heart implant and a host of other alterations allowing survival in transit at speeds exceeding that of light. Radu Dracul survives a virus-caused plague in his outerworld planet to find himself with a time sense that changes the boundaries of spatial perception for the whole species. All the characters explore the limits of language; the dream of communicating experience; and the necessity of limitation, partiality, and intimacy even in this world of protean transformation and connection. *Superluminal* stands also for the defining contradictions of a cyborg world in another sense; it embodies textually the intersection of feminist theory and colonial discourse in the science fiction I have alluded to in this essay. This is a conjunction with a long history that many "First World" feminists have tried to repress, including myself in my readings of *Superluminal* before being called to account by Zoë Sofoulis,[11] whose different location in the world system's informatics of domination made her acutely alert to the imperialist moment of all science fiction cultures, including women's science fiction. From an Australian feminist sensibility, Sofoulis remembered more readily McIntyre's role as writer of the adventures of Captain Kirk and Spock in TV's *Star Trek* series than her rewriting the romance in *Superluminal*.

Monsters have always defined the limits of community in Western imaginations. The Centaurs and Amazons of ancient Greece established the limits of the centered polis of the Greek male human by their disruption of marriage and boundary pollutions of the warrior with animality and woman. Unseparated twins and hermaphrodites were the confused human material in early modern France who grounded discourse on the natural and supernatural, medical and legal, portents and diseases—all crucial to establishing modern identity.[12] In the evolutionary and behavioral sciences, monkeys and apes have marked the multiple boundaries of late-twentieth-century industrial identities. Cyborg monsters in feminist science fiction define quite different political possibilities and limits from those proposed by the mundane fiction of Man and Woman.

There are several consequences to taking seriously the imagery of cyborgs as other than our enemies. Our bodies, ourselves; bodies are maps of power and identity. Cyborgs are no exception. A cyborg body is not innocent; it was not born in a garden; it does not seek unitary identity and so generate antagonistic dualisms without end (or until the world ends); it takes irony for granted. One is too few, and two is only one possibility. Intense pleasure in skill, machine skill, ceases to be a sin, but an aspect of embodiment. The machine is not an *it* to be animated, worshiped, and dominated. The machine is us, our processes, an aspect of our embodiment. We can be responsible for machines; *they* do not dominate or threaten us. We are responsible for boundaries; we are they. Up till now (once upon a time), female embodiment seemed to be given, organic, necessary; and female embodiment seemed to mean skill in mothering and its metaphoric extensions. Only by being out of place could we take intense pleasure in machines, and then with excuses that this was organic activity after all, appropriate to females. Cyborgs might consider more seriously the partial, fluid, sometimes aspect of sex and sexual embodiment. Gender might not be global identity after all, even if it has profound historical breadth and depth.

The ideologically charged question of what counts as daily activity, as experience, can be approached by exploiting the cyborg image. Feminists have recently claimed that women are given to dailiness, that women more than men somehow sustain daily life and so have a privileged epistemological position potentially. There is a compelling aspect to this claim, one that makes visible unvalued female activity and names it as the ground of life.

But *the* ground of life? What about all the ignorance of women, all the exclusions and failures of knowledge and skill? What about men's access to daily competence, to knowing how to build things, to take them apart, to play? What about other embodiments? Cyborg gender is a local possibility taking a global vengeance. Race, gender, and capital require a cyborg theory of wholes and parts. There is no drive in cyborgs to produce total theory, but there is an intimate experience of boundaries, their construction and deconstruction. There is a myth system waiting to become a political language to ground one way of looking at science and technology and challenging the informatics of domination—in order to act potently.

One last image: organisms and organismic, holistic politics depend on metaphors of rebirth and invariably call on the resources of reproductive sex. I would suggest that cyborgs have more to do with regeneration and are suspicious of the reproductive matrix and of most birthing. For salamanders, regeneration after injury, such as the loss of a limb, involves regrowth of structure and restoration of function with the constant possibility of twinning or other odd topographical productions at the site of former injury. The regrown limb can be monstrous, duplicated, potent. We have all been injured, profoundly. We require regeneration, not rebirth, and the possibilities for our reconstitution include the utopian dream of the hope for a monstrous world without gender.

Cyborg imagery can help express two crucial arguments in this essay: first, the production of universal, totalizing theory is a major mistake that misses most of reality, probably always, but certainly now; and second, taking responsibility for the social relations of science and technology means refusing an anti-science metaphysics, a demonology of technology, and so means embracing the skillful task of reconstructing the boundaries of daily life, in partial connection with others, in communication with all of our parts. It is not just that science and technology are possible means of great human satisfaction, as well as a matrix of complex dominations. Cyborg imagery can suggest a way out of the maze of dualisms in which we have explained our bodies and our tools to ourselves. This is a dream not of a common language, but of a powerful infidel heteroglossia. It is an imagination of a feminist speaking in tongues to strike fear into the circuits of the supersavers of the new right. It means both building and destroying machines, identities, categories, relationships, space stories. Though both are bound in the spiral dance, I would rather be a cyborg than a goddess.

1. See Katie King, "The Pleasure of Repetition and the Limits of Identification in Feminist Science Fiction: Reimaginations of the Body after the Cyborg," presented at the California American Studies Association, Pomona, 1984. An abbreviated list of feminist science fiction underlying themes of this essay: Octavia Butler, *Wild Seed, Mind of My Mind, Kindred, Survivor*; Suzy McKee Charnas, *Motherlines*; Samuel R. Delany, the *Nevèrÿon* series; Anne McCaffery, *The Ship Who Sang, Dinosaur Planet*; Vonda McIntyre, *Superluminal, Dreamsnake*; Joanna Russ, *Adventures of Alix, The Female Man*; James Tiptree Jr., *Star Songs of an Old Primate, Up the Walls of the World*; John Varley, *Titan, Wizard, Demon*.

2. Mary Douglas, *Purity and Danger* (London: Routledge and Kegan Paul, 1966); Mary Douglas *Natural Symbols* (London: Cresset Press, 1970).

3. French feminisms contribute to cyborg heteroglossia: Carolyn Burke, "Irigaray through the Looking Glass," *Feminist Studies* 7, no. 2 (Summer 1981): 288–306; Luce Irigaray, *Ce sexe qui n'en est pas un* (Paris: Les Éditions de Minuit, 1977); Luce Irigaray, *Et l'une ne bouge pas sans l'autre* (Paris: Les Éditions de Minuit, 1979); Elaine Marks and Isabelle de Courtivron, eds., *New French Feminisms* (Amherst: University of Massachusetts Press, 1980); *Signs: Journal of Women in Culture and Society* (Autumn 1981); Monique Wittig, *The Lesbian Body*, trans. David LeVay (1973; New York: Avon 1975); Claire Duchen, *Feminism in France from May '68 to Mitterand* (London: Routledge and Kegan Paul, 1986). For English translation of some currents of Francophone feminism, see *Feminist Issues: A Journal of Feminist Social and Political Theory* (1980).

4. But all these poets are very complex, not least in their treatment of themes of lying and erotic, decentered collective and personal identities: Susan Griffin, *Women and Nature: The Roaring Inside Her* (New York: Harper and Row, 1978); Audre Lorde, *Sister Outsider* (Trumansburg, NY: Crossing Press, 1984); Adrienne Rich, *The Dream of a Common Language* (New York: W. W. Norton, 1978).

5. Audre Lorde, *Zami: A New Spelling of My Name* (Watertown, MA: Persephone Press, 1982); Katie King, "Canons without Innocence" (PhD diss., University of California, Santa Cruz, 1987); Katie King, "The Passing Dreams of Choice: Audre Lorde and the Apparatus of Literary Production" (unpublished book prospectus, 1987).

6. See Jacques Derrida, *Of Grammatology*, trans. G. C. Spivak (Baltimore: Johns Hopkins University Press, 1976), especially part II; Claude Lévi-Strauss, *Tristes Tropiques*, trans. John and Doreen Weightman (New York: Atheneum, 1973), especially "The Writing Lesson"; Henry Louis Gates Jr., "Writing 'Race' and the Difference It Makes," *Critical Inquiry* 12, no. 1, "Race," Writing, and Difference special issue (Autumn 1985): 1–20; Douglas Kahn and Diane Neumaier, eds., *Cultures in Contention* (Seattle: Real Comet Press, 1985); Walter Ong, *Orality and Literacy: The Technologizing of the Word* (New York: Methuen, 1982); Cheris Kramarae and Paula Treichler, *A Feminist Dictionary* (Boston: Pandora Press, 1985).

7. The sharp relation of women of color to writing as theme and politics can be approached through the program for "The Black Woman and the Diaspora: Hidden Connections and Extended Acknowledgments," An International Literary Conference, Michigan State University, October 1985; Mari Evans, ed., *Black Women Writers: A Critical Evaluation* (Garden City, NY: Doubleday/Anchor, 1984); Barbara Christian, *Black Feminist Criticism: Perspectives on Black Women Writers* (New York: Pergamon Press, 1985); Hazel Carby, *Reconstructing Womanhood: The Emergence of the Afro-American Woman Novelist* (New York: Oxford University Press, 1987); Dexter Fisher, ed., *The Third Woman: Minority Women Writers of the United States* (Boston: Houghton Mifflin, 1980); *Frontiers: A Journal of Women's Studies* 1 (1980) and 3 (1983); Maxine Hong Kingston, *The Woman Warrior* (New York: Alfred A. Knopf, 1976); Gerda Lerner, ed., *Black Women in White America: A Documentary History* (New York: Vintage, 1973); Paula Giddings, *When and Where I Enter: The Impact of Black Women on Race and Sex in America* (Toronto: Bantam Books, 1985); Cherríe Moraga and Gloria Anzaldúa, eds., *This Bridge Called My Back: Writings by Radical Women of Color* (Watertown, MA: Persephone Press, 1981); Robin Morgan, ed., *Sisterhood Is Global* (Garden City, NY: Anchor/Doubleday, 1984). Anglophone European and Euro-American women have also crafted special relations to their writing as a potent sign: Sandra M. Gilbert and Susan Gubar, *The Madwoman in the Attic: The Woman Writer and the Nineteenth-Century Literary Imagination* (New Haven, CT: Yale University Press, 1979); Joanna Russ, *How to Suppress Women's Writing* (Austin: University of Texas Press, 1983).

8. The convention of ideologically taming militarized high technology by publicizing its applications to speech and motion problems of the disabled/differently abled takes on a special irony in monotheistic, patriarchal, and frequently antisemitic culture when computer-generated speech allows a boy with no voice to chant the Haftorah at his bar mitzvah. See Vic Sussman, "Personal Tech: Technology Lends a Hand," *Washington Post Magazine*, November 9, 1986, 45–56. Making the always context-relative social definitions of "ableness" particularly clear, military high-tech has a way of making human beings disabled by definition, a perverse aspect of much automated battlefield and Star Wars research and development. See John Noble Wilford, "Pilot's Helmet Helps Interpret High-Speed World," *New York Times*, July 1, 1986, 21, 24.

9. See Aihwa Ong, *Spirits of Resistance and Capitalist Discipline: Factory Workers in Malaysia* (Albany: State University of New York Press, 1987).

10. James Clifford argues persuasively for recognition of continuous reinvention, the stubborn nondisappearance of those "marked" by Western imperializing practices. James Clifford, "On Ethnographic Allegory," in *The Poetics and Politics of Ethnography*, ed. James Clifford and George Marcus (Berkeley: University of California Press, 1985); James Clifford, *The Predicament of Culture: Twentieth-Century Ethnography, Literature, and Art* (Cambridge, MA: Harvard University Press, 1988).

11. Zoë Sofoulis, "Lacklein" (unpublished manuscript, n.d. [1983?]).

12. See Page DuBois, *Centaurs and Amazons* (Ann Arbor: University of Michigan Press, 1982); Lorraine Daston and Katharine Park, "Hermaphrodites in Renaissance France" (unpublished manuscript, n.d.); Katharine Park and Lorraine J. Daston, "Unnatural Conceptions: The Study of Monsters in Sixteenth- and Seventeenth-Century France and England," *Past and Present* 92 (1981): 20–54. The noun *monster* shares its root with the verb to *demonstrate*.

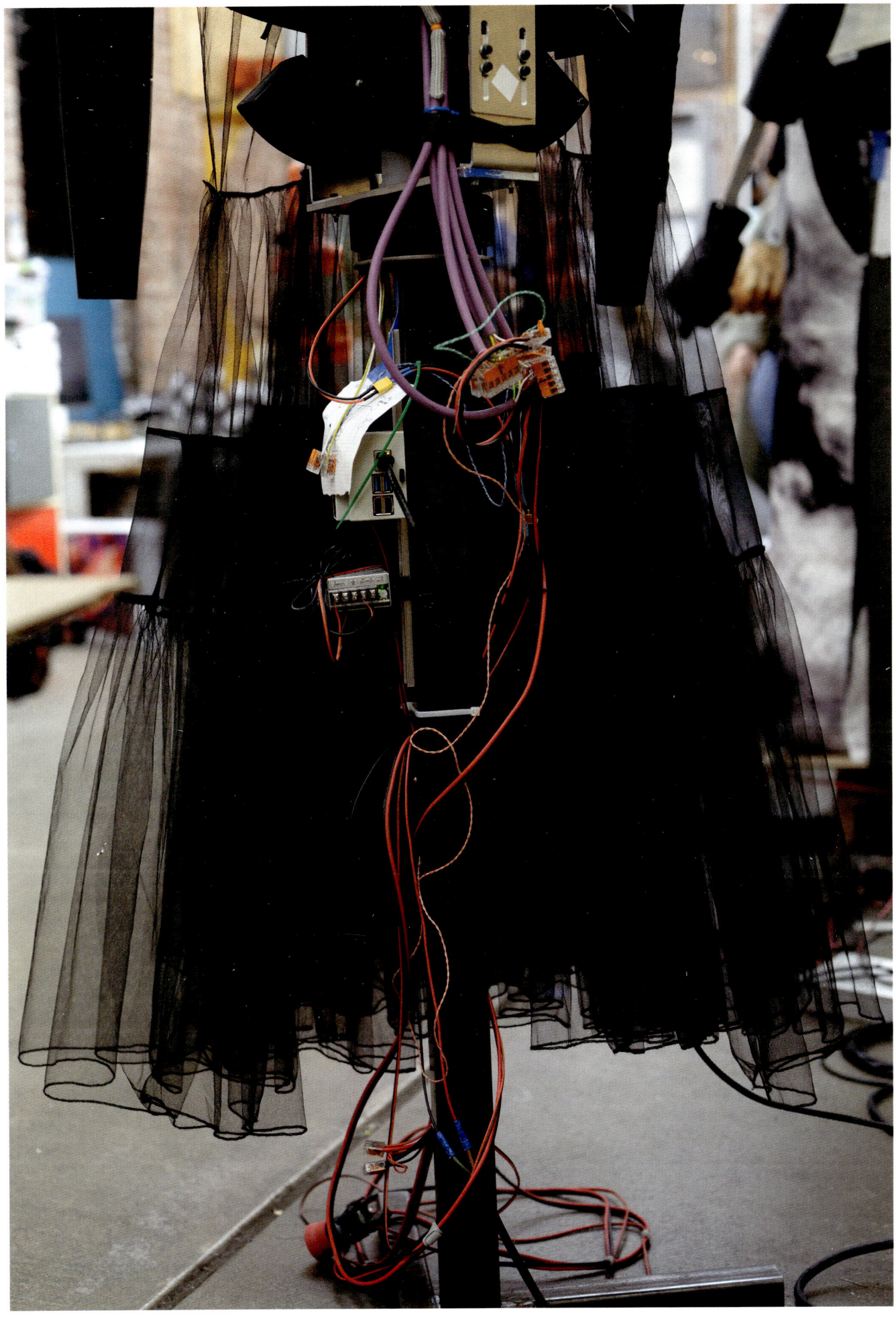

SELECTIONS FROM THE NOTEBOOKS OF GARY GRAHAM

I imagined my automaton figures dressed in anachronistic costumes reminiscent of antique dolls and puppets. I've long been a fan and wearer of designer and couturier Gary Graham—he brings storytelling into the realm of fashion and hand sews the most elegant garments.

The following pages illustrate the collaborative nature of this project, with some of my doodles informing Gary's interpretations, which he kept detailed in his own project notebook. About four months before installation, Gary moved a bit of his Franklin, New York, dressmaker's shop to a corner within Hypersonic's Brooklyn robotics studio. Creating garments for the "dolls" required translating his designs into a functional architecture, one that could be accessible to everyone on the team. Dressing the figures, with their hard-shelled, nonhuman, moving machine parts, was the biggest hurdle. Machine parts are not readily compatible with delicate fabrics, which for this project needed to be able to withstand daily use and occasional automaton maintenance. It became evident that there was a great meeting of the technical minds. Everyone—software and hardware and fabric engineers—had to learn new languages and step well out of their comfort zone to bring this project to fruition.

—KW

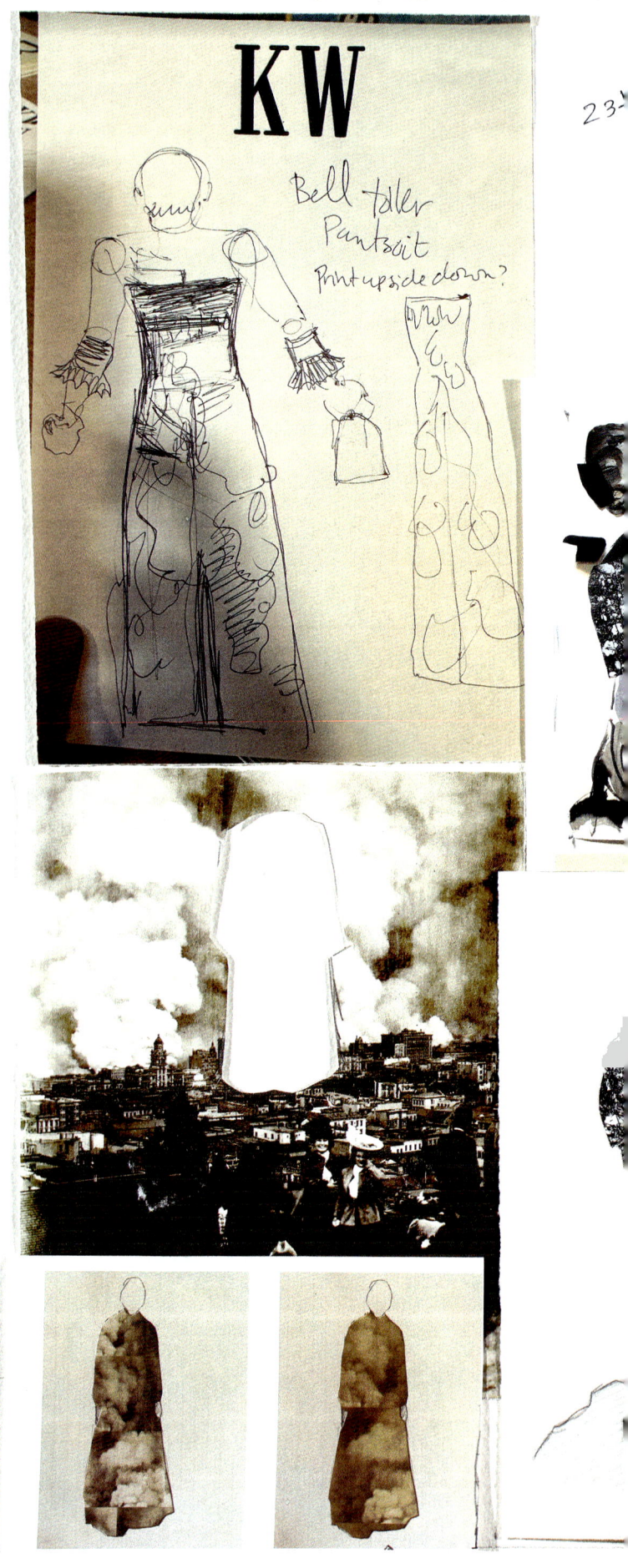

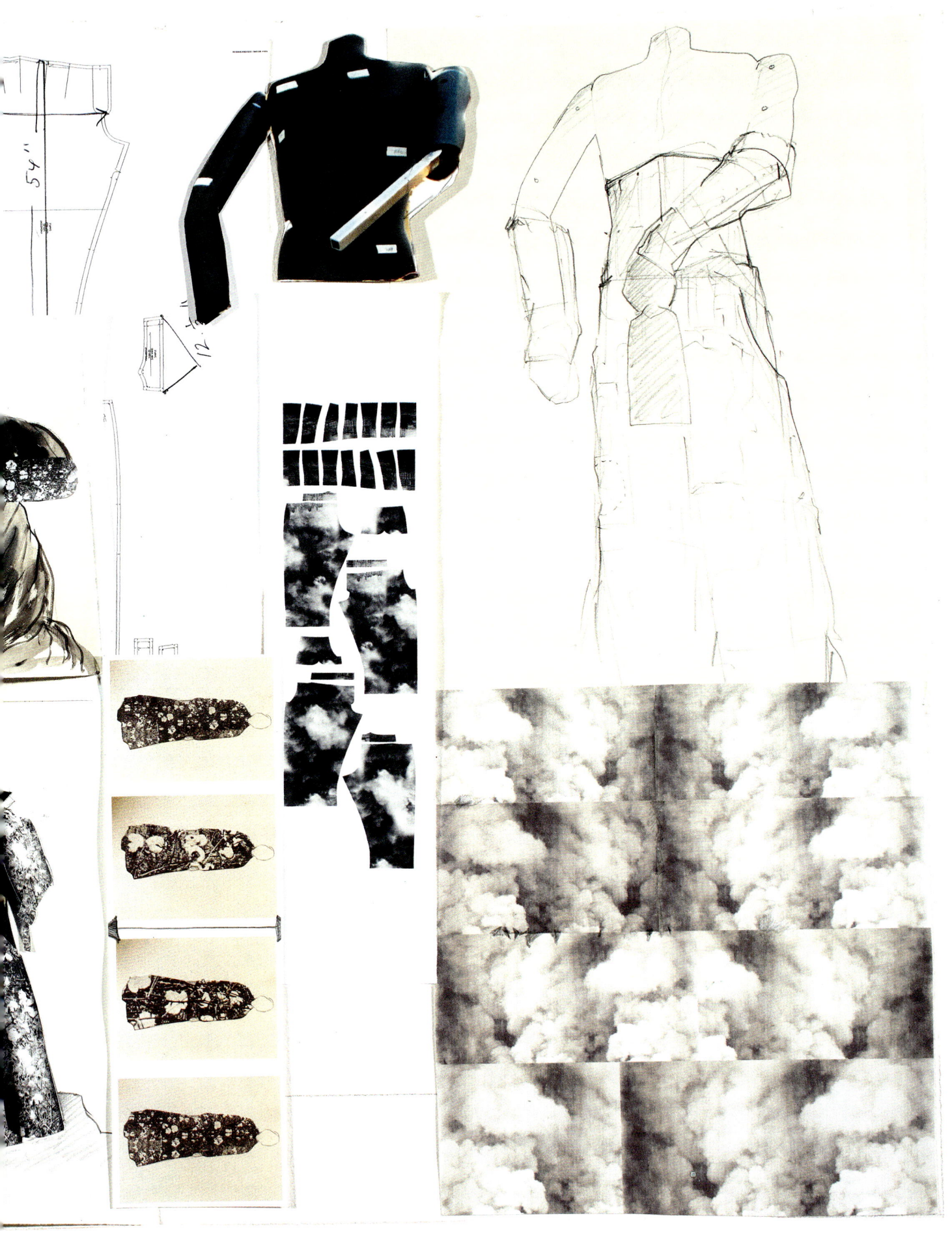

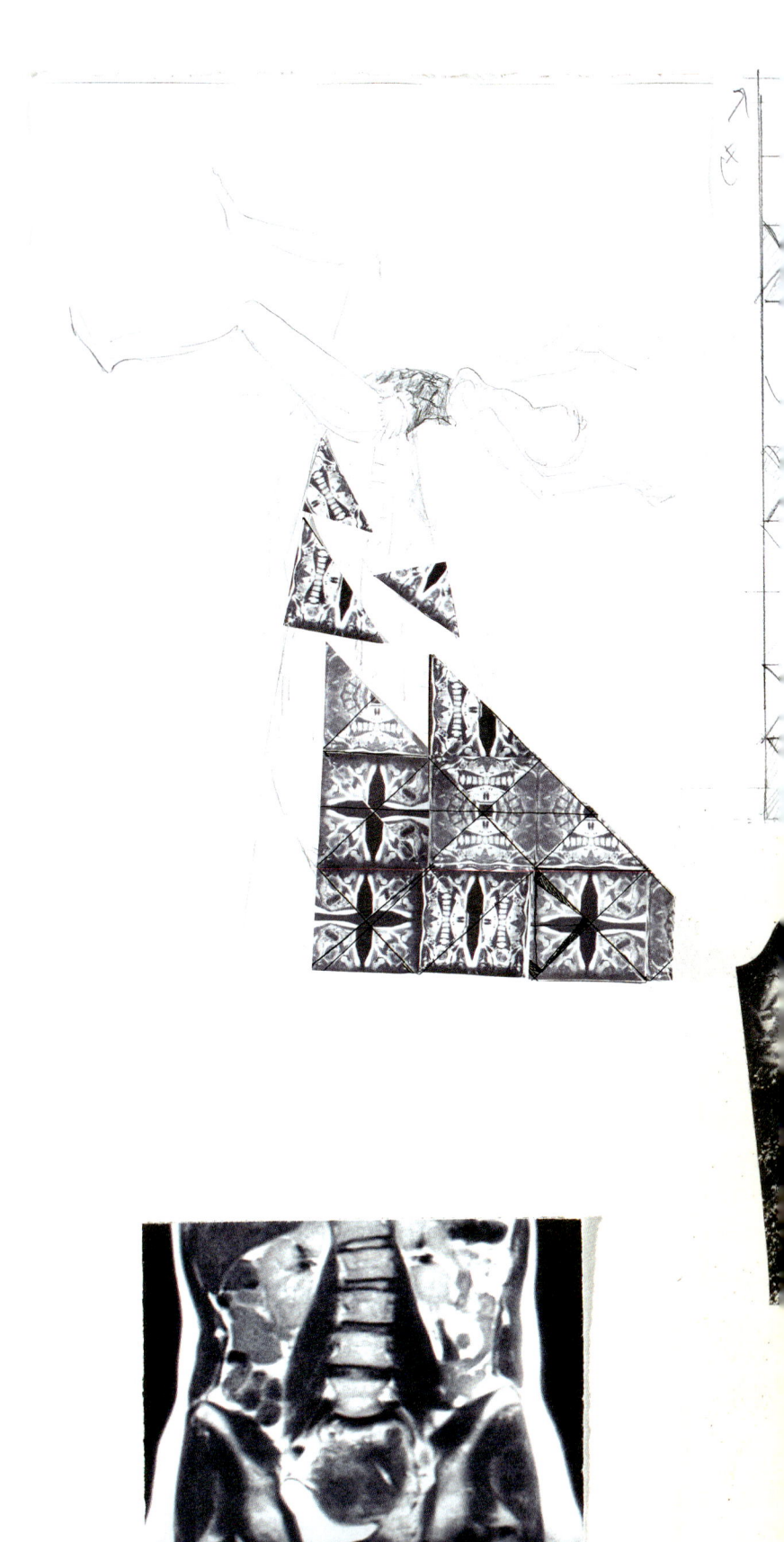

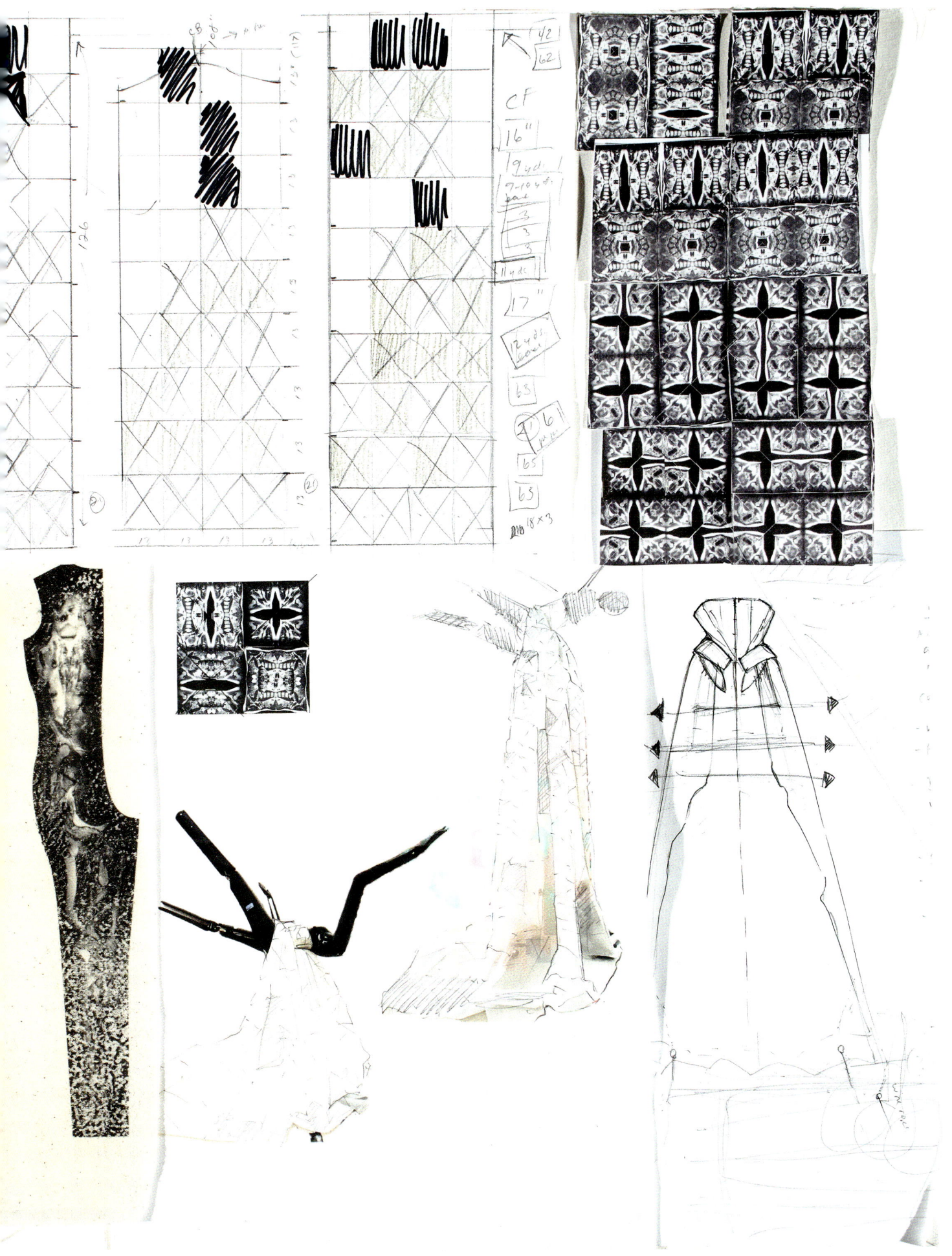

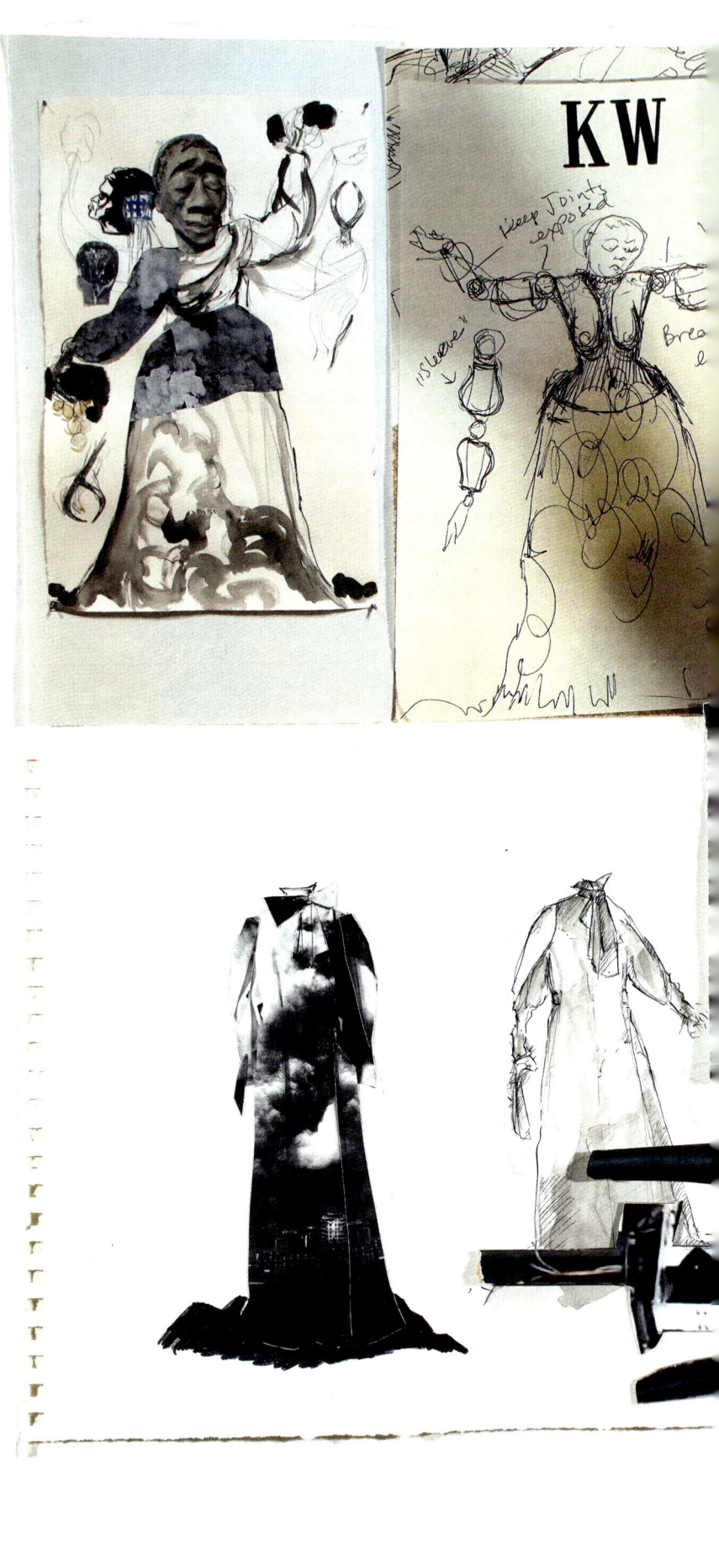

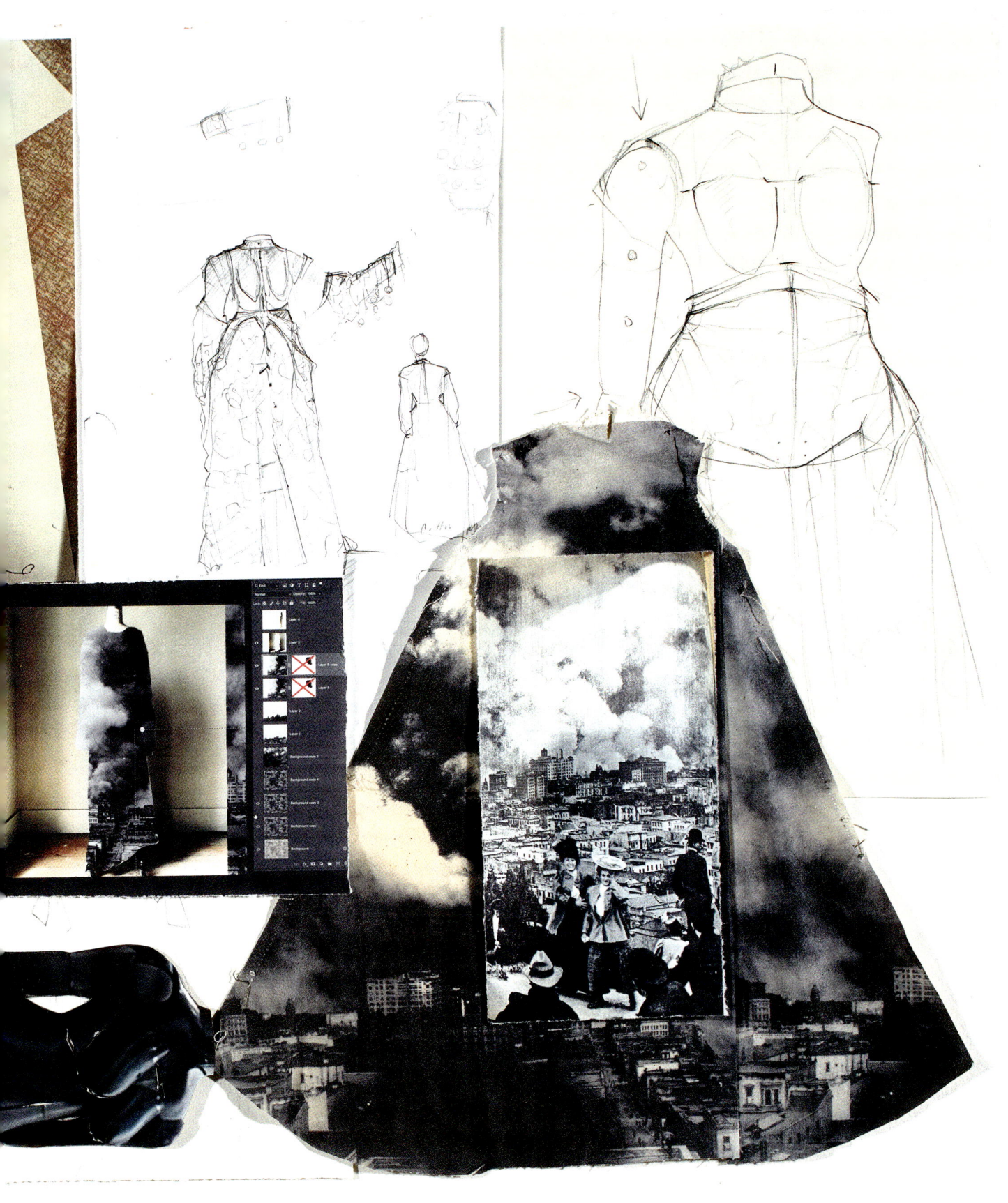

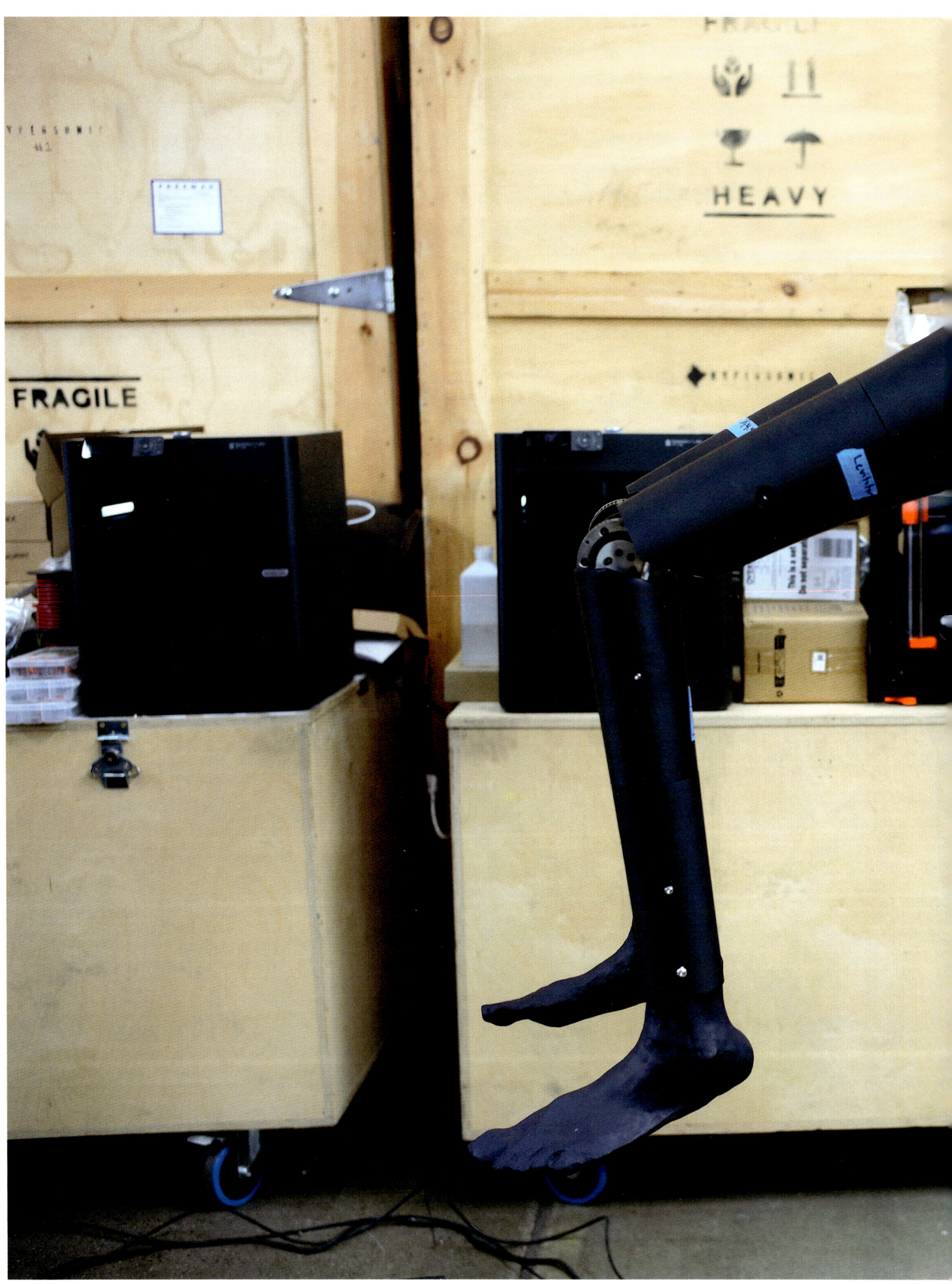

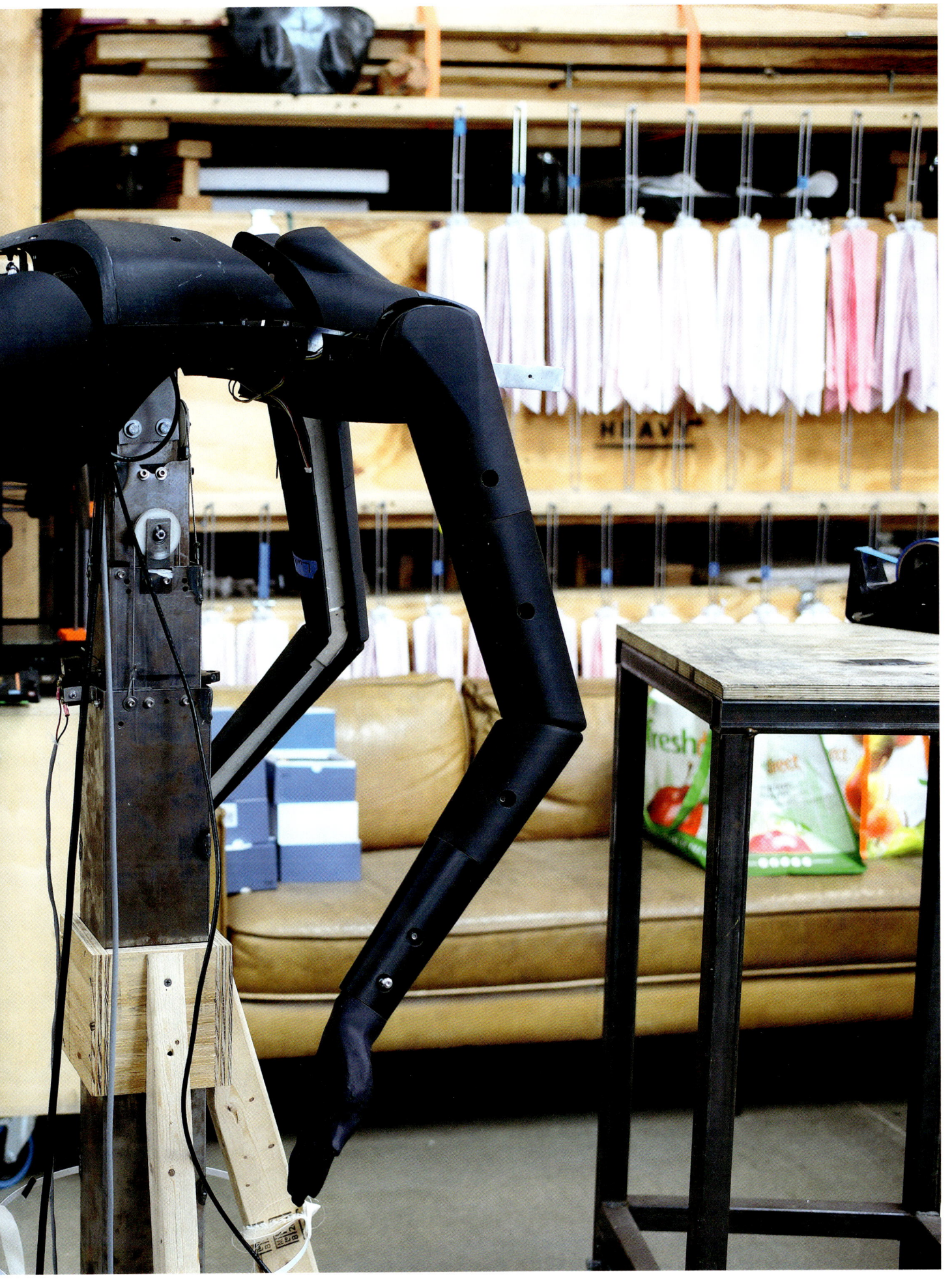

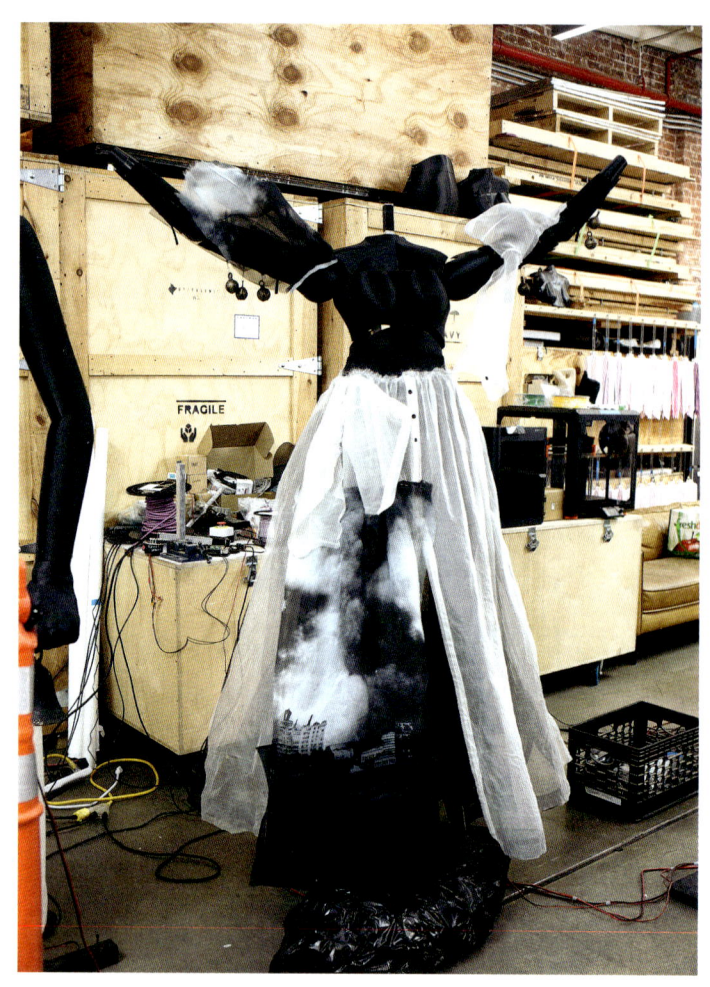

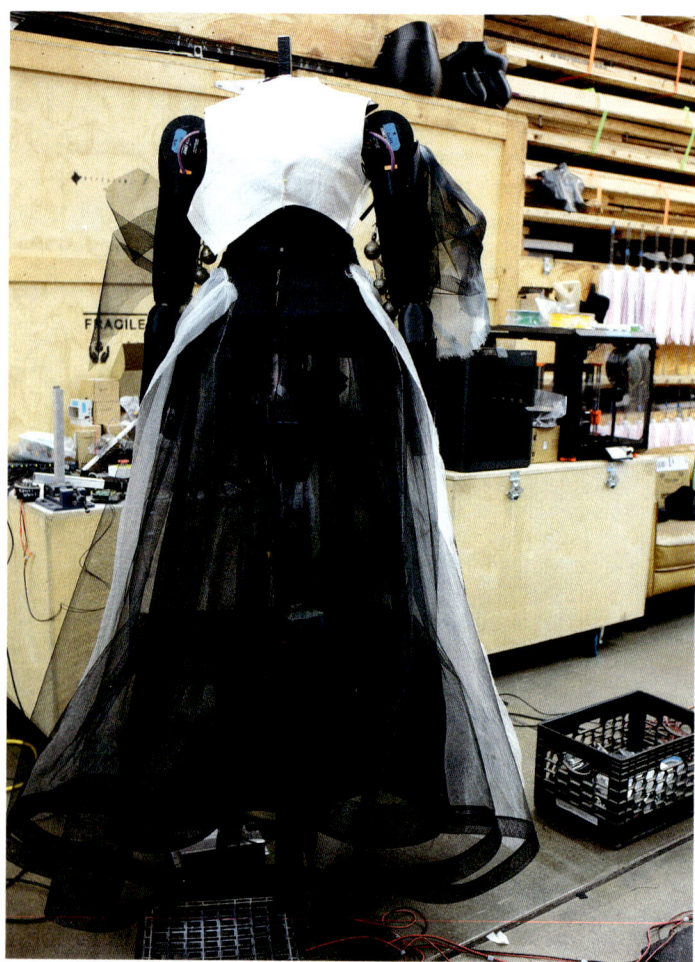

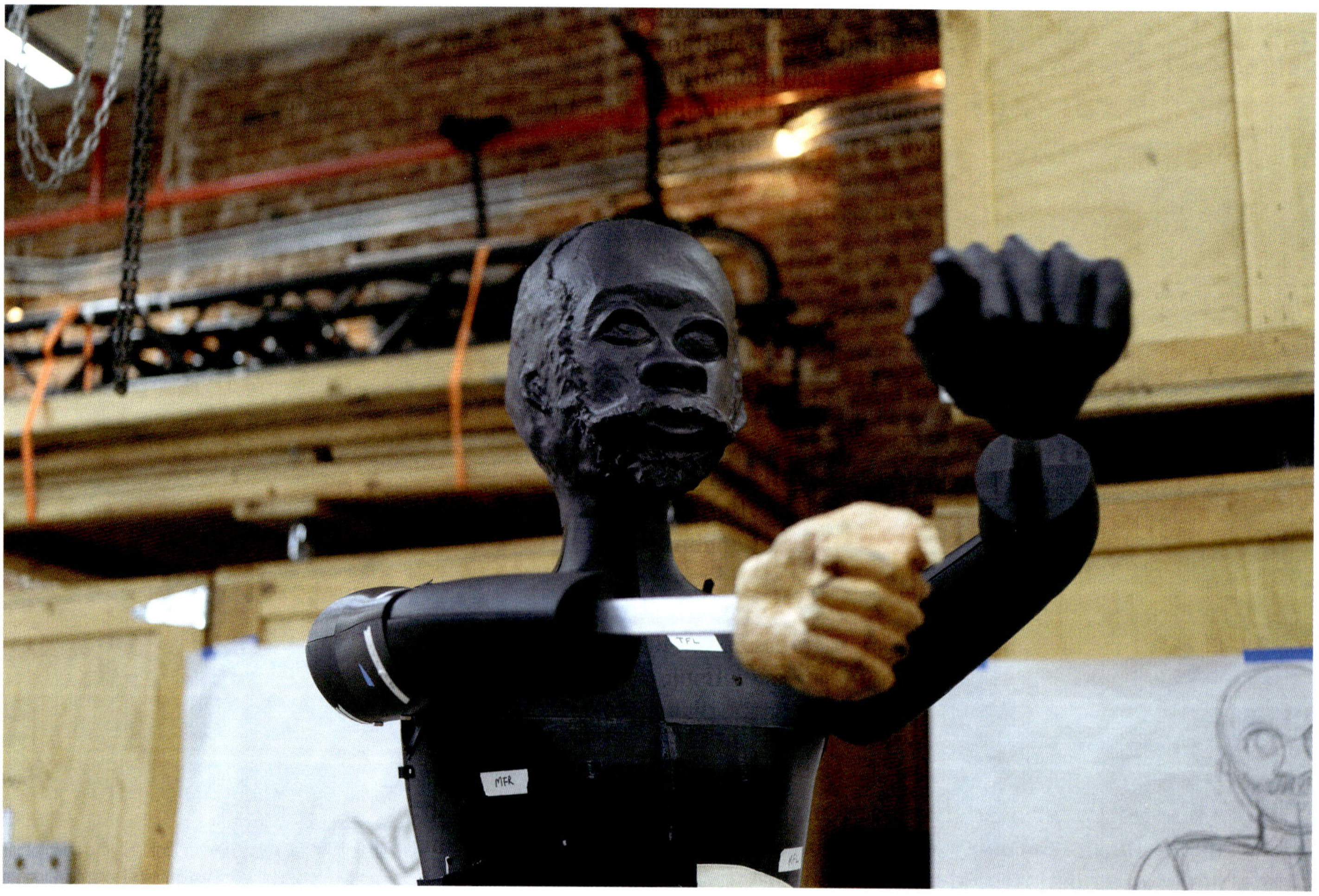

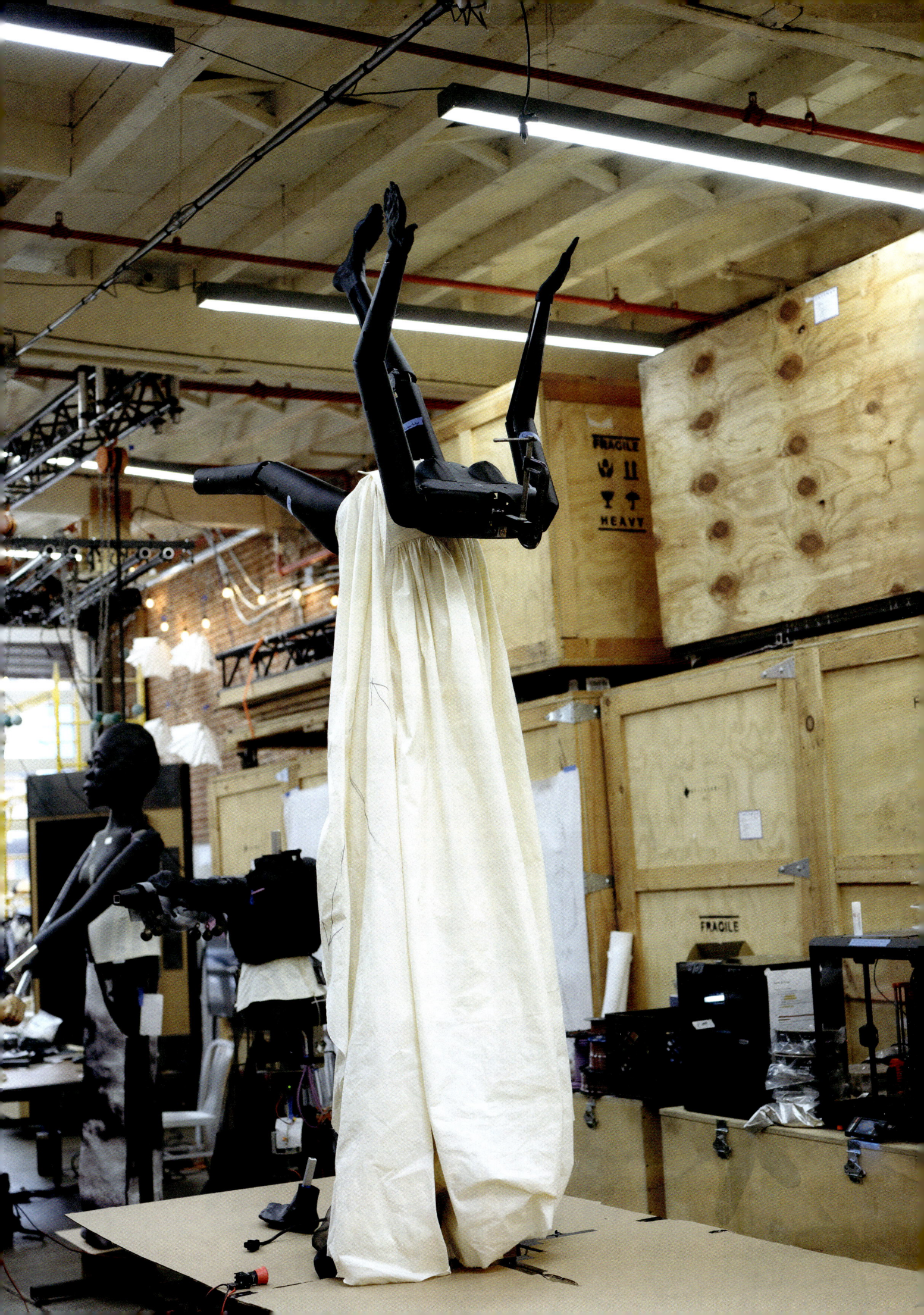

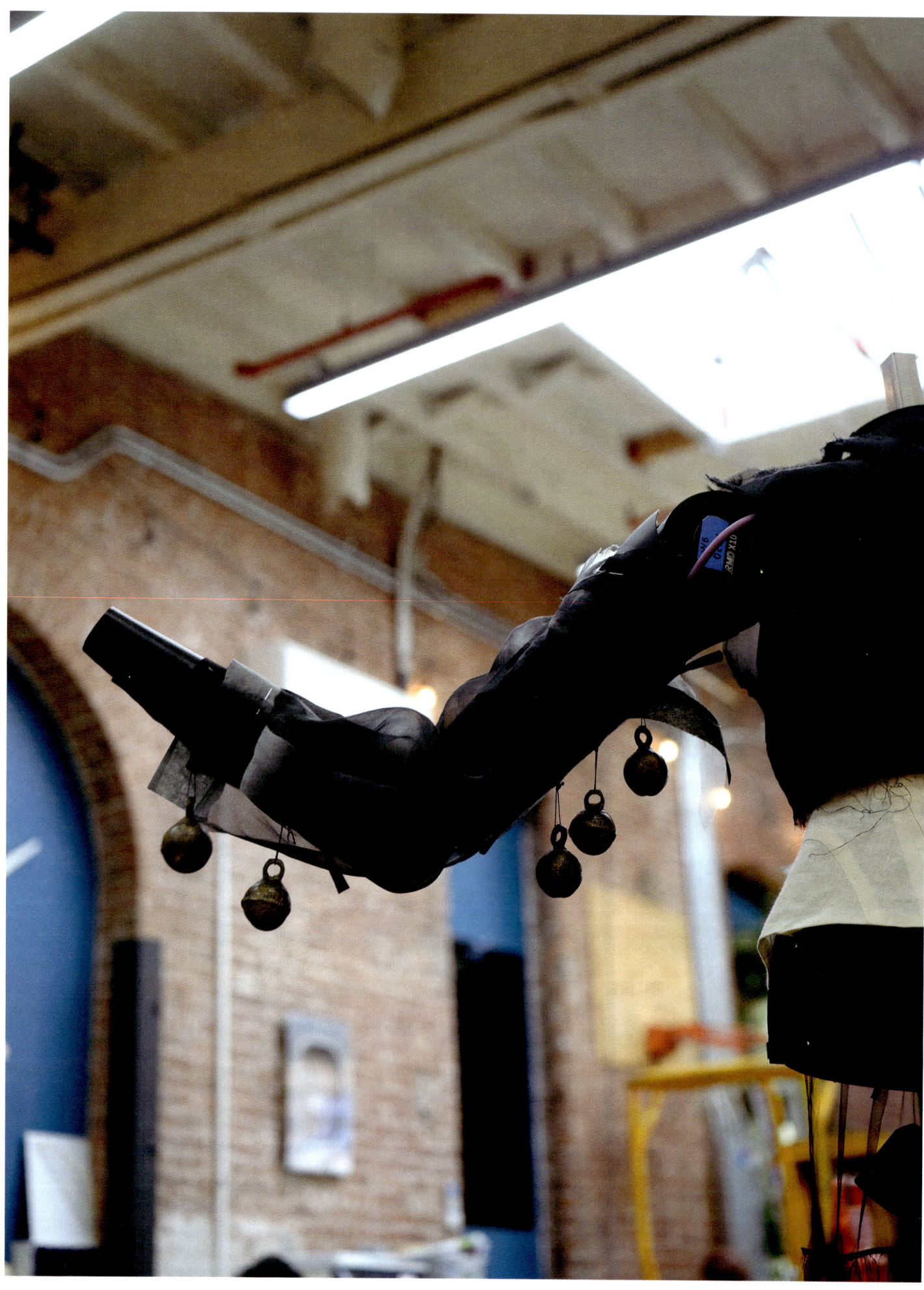

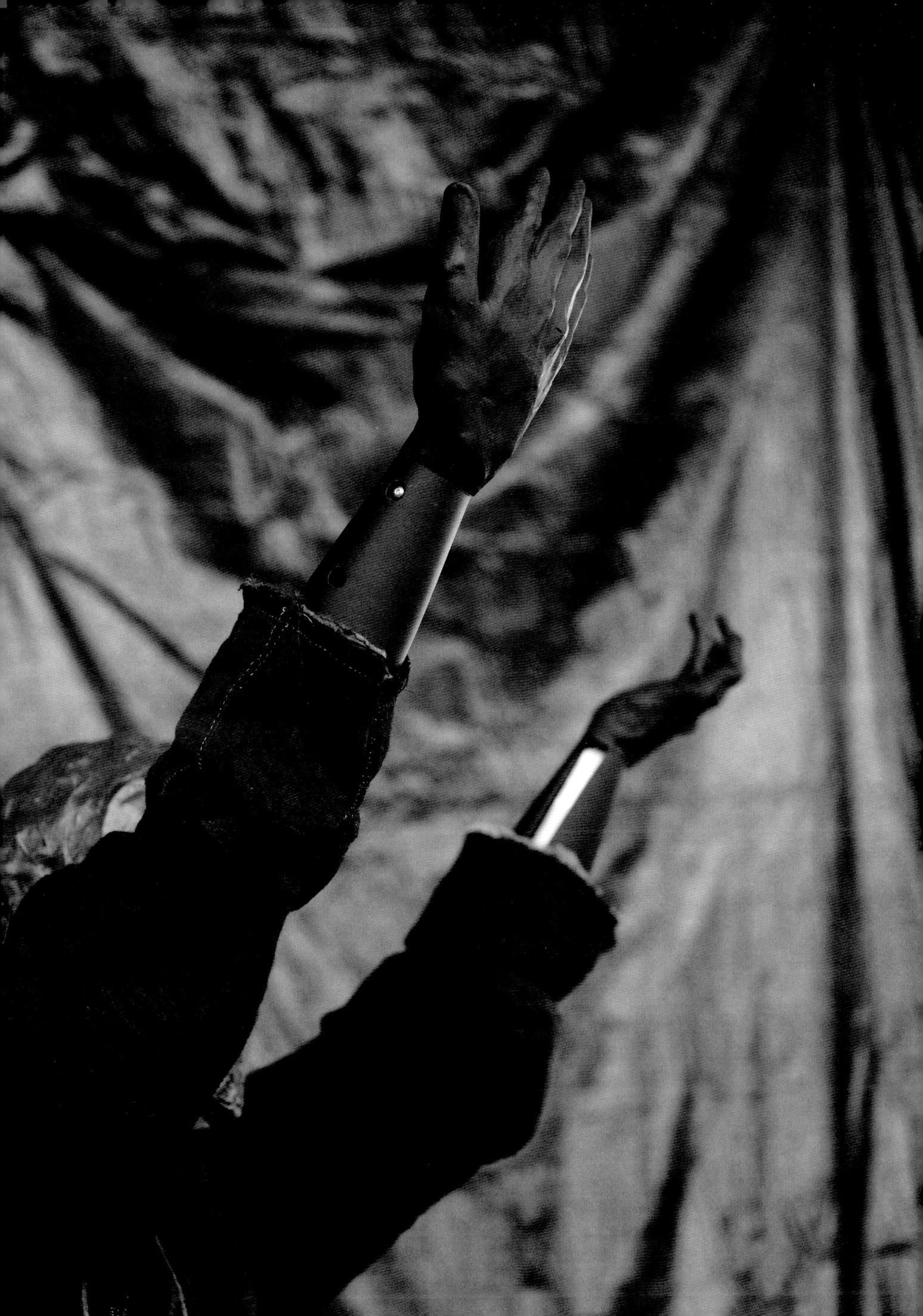

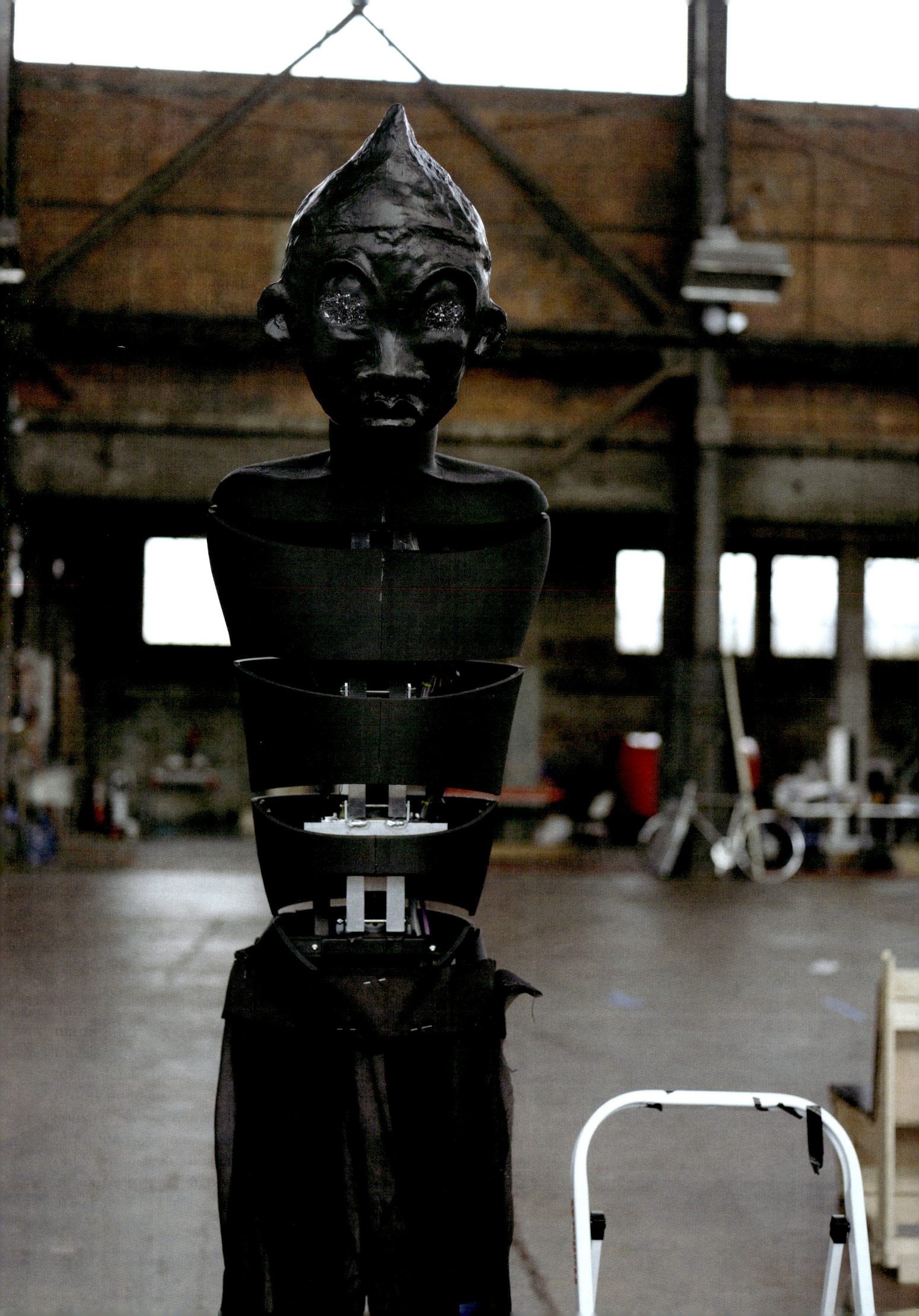

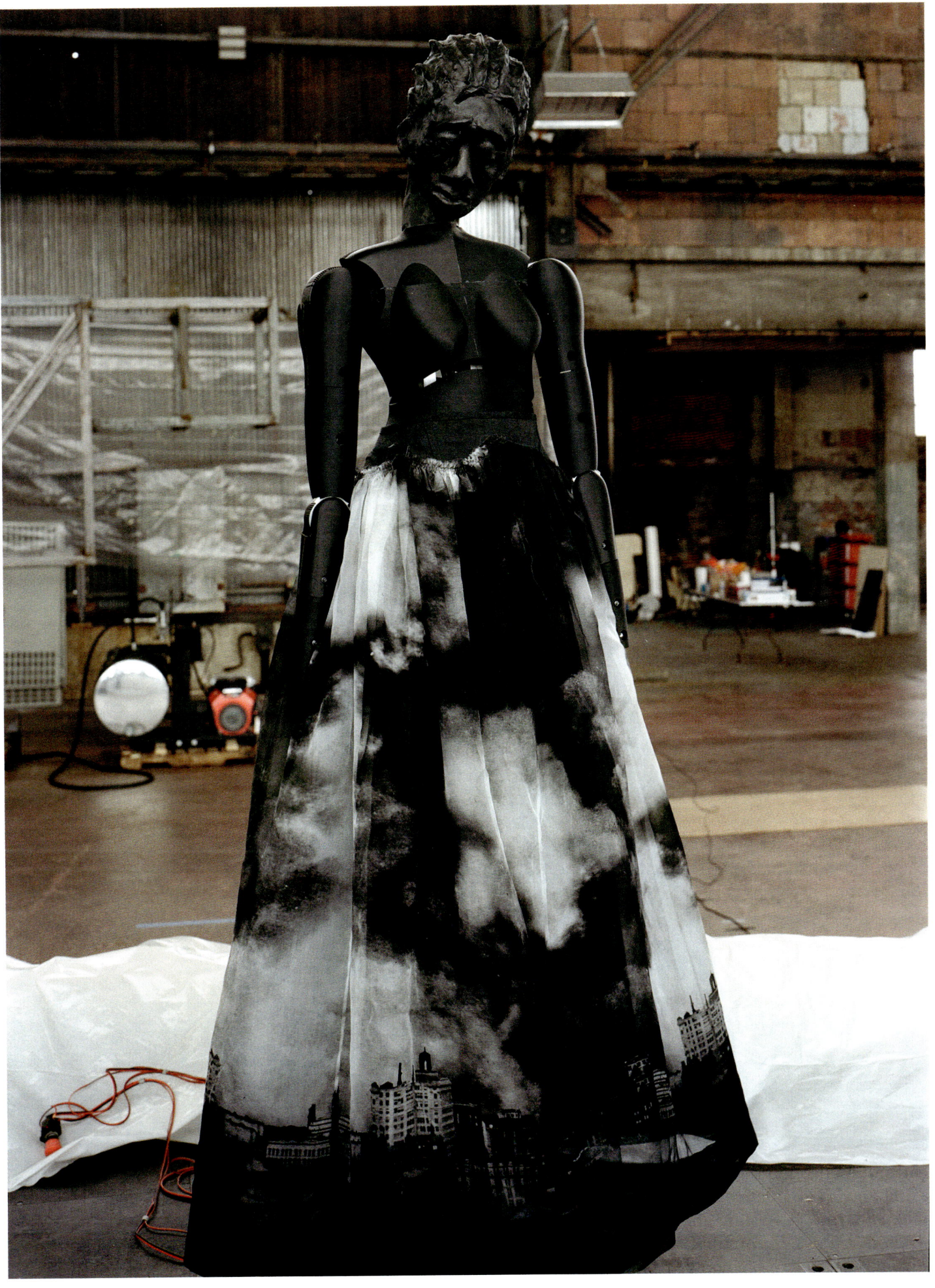

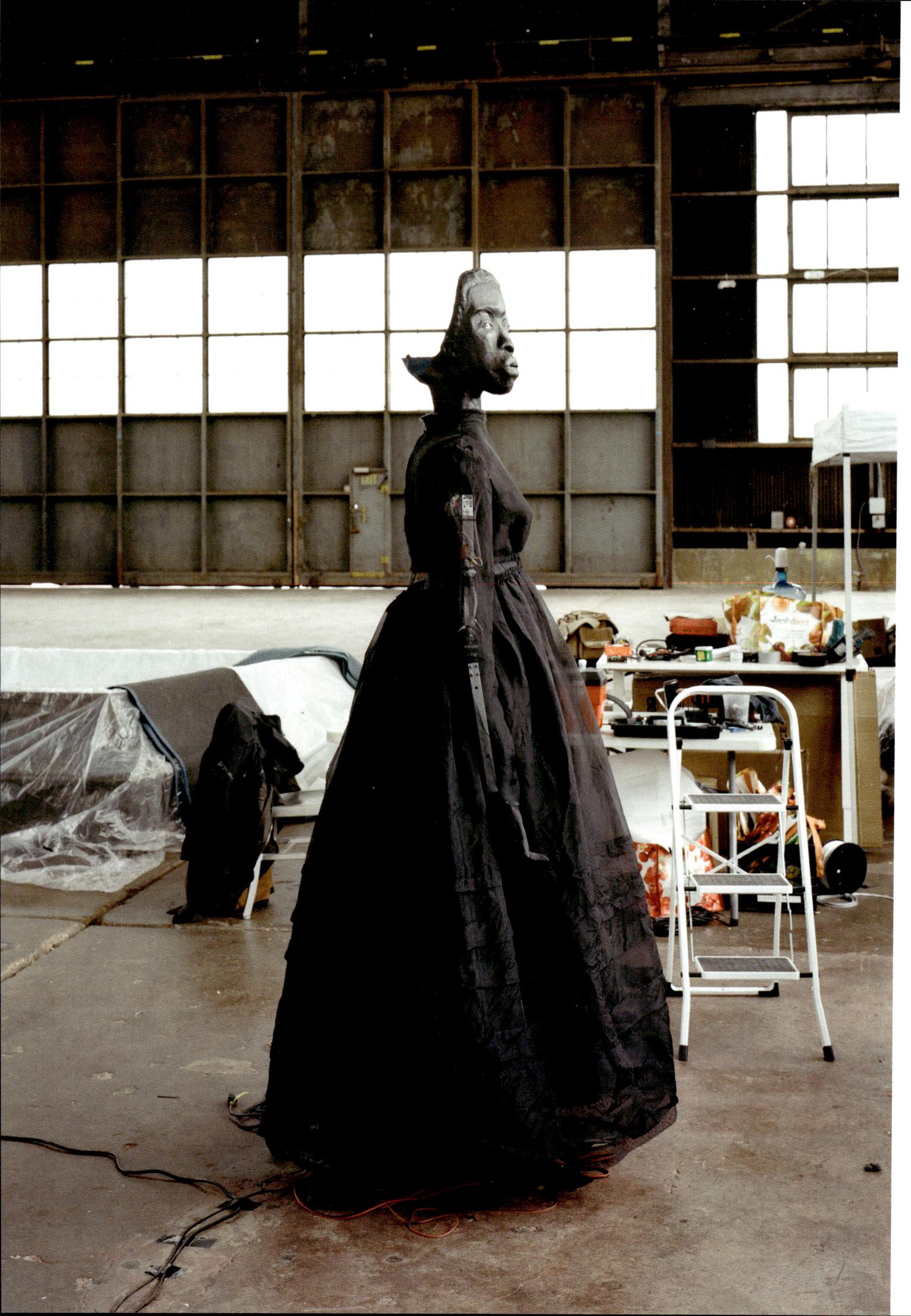

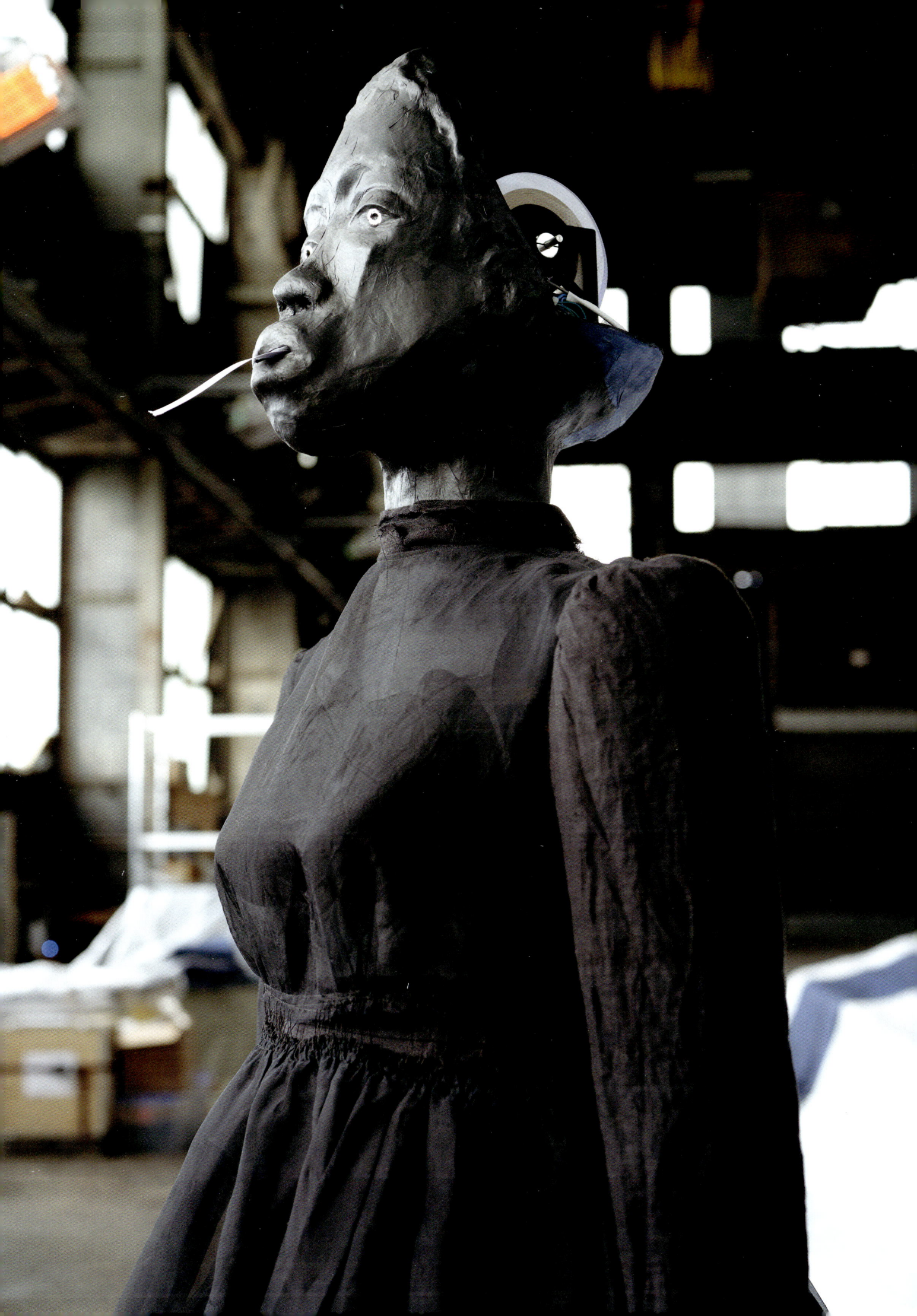

RACE AND THE UNCANNY VALLEY: NIGGERS, SLAVES, AND MACHINES
David A. M. Goldberg

The black, glassy eyes glittered with a kind of wicked drollery, and the thing [Topsy] struck up, in a clear shrill voice, an odd negro melody, to which she kept time with her hands and feet, spinning round, clapping her hands, knocking her knees together, in a wild, fantastic sort of time, and producing in her throat all those odd guttural sounds which distinguish the native music of her race; and finally, turning a summerset or two, and giving a prolonged closing note, as odd and unearthly as that of a steam-whistle, she came suddenly down on the carpet, and stood with her hands folded, and a most sanctimonious expression of meekness and solemnity over her face, only broken by the cunning glances which she shot askance from the corners of her eyes.

—Harriet Beecher Stowe, *Uncle Tom's Cabin*[1]

We are all cyborgs now.

—Kara Walker[2]

The Black automatons of Kara Walker's *Fortuna and the Immortality Garden (Machine)* evoke the Black cybernetic subjectivities, plantation informatics, and repositories of White Supremacist source code that bind Black being(s) and allowed such an atrocity as P. T. Barnum's purchase in 1835 of Joice Heth, an old and infirm Black woman he exhibited as George Washington's 161-year-old wet nurse. Advertised as a living relic from the nation's birth, Heth launched Barnum's career, and audiences were captivated by her monstrously gaunt appearance and accounts of raising a Founding Father. When public interest inevitably waned, Barnum harnessed an increasing fascination with all things mechanical and promoted Heth not as a living being but as a sophisticated automaton made of whale bone, leather, and India rubber. Upon her death, the showman staged a pay-per-view autopsy that gathered the gullible, the skeptical, and the outraged for one last time.[3] This event extracted any remaining value from Heth, whose humanity had been doubly denied: first by being enslaved, and second by her purported status as an automaton. This last bit of grotesque Victorian American entrepreneurialism is closely related to the spiritual through lines and brutal ambiguities of Walker's most ambitious silhouette-based installations; the expanded functionality of the shadow puppetry

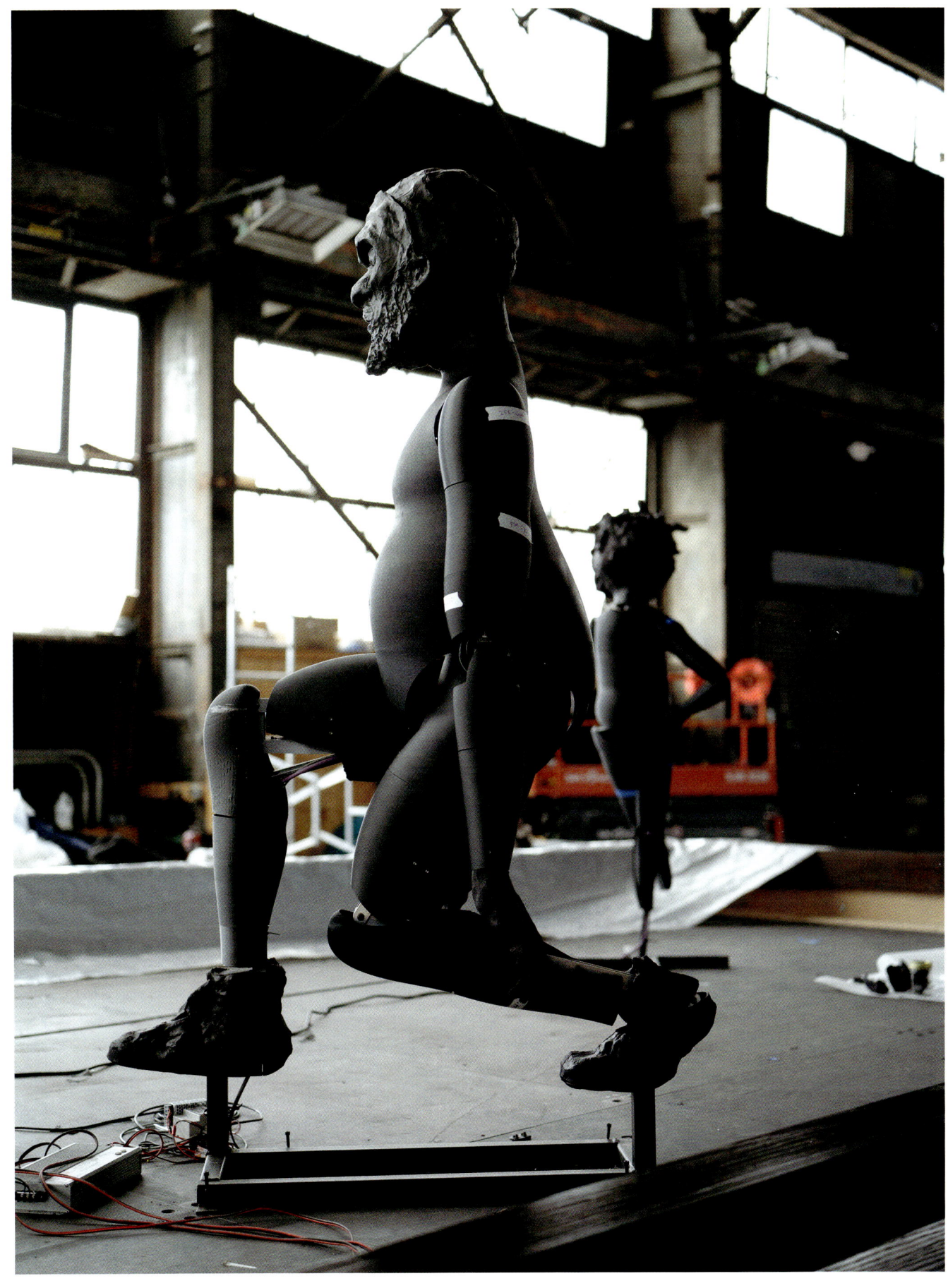

she introduced in the moving pictures of *8 Possible Beginnings or: The Creation of African-America* (2005); and the design, execution, and response that is *Fortuna and the Immortality Garden (Machine)*.

Barnum's profitable humbug is just one access point to the deep archive of raced and racist technology, philosophy, and engineering that Walker's latest work defiantly engages. Escape from anti-Blackness remains impossible, but using twenty-first-century tactics she takes advantage of the brief and narrow window of opportunity for self-definition that opens when Black folks gain representational control of a medium. By moving into spaces of digital (re)animation, Walker continues to erode, reconfigure, and possess stereotypes and archetypes that flourished in older media, including her own work. The figures of *Fortuna and the Immortality Garden (Machine)* are products of computer-aided design software, 3-D printing, and contemporary robotics engineering, and they are mobilized by electric motors and the Python programming language. The motion-capture data that choreographs Walker's quasi-living Black automatons is also composed of her own Black body and intellect, and acts of self-interpolation (reference poses and figurative representation) supported by narrative reflections, drawings, lower-tech prototypes, costuming, and hand-sculpted visages and limbs.

The work's history also includes references to the montage of less-articulated nineteenth- and twentieth-century racist toys, banks, and gizmos that Spike Lee assembled for the end credits of *Bamboozled* (2000); Don Pedro Colley's magical Negro hologram from George Lucas's *THX 1138* (1971); a cyborg Will Smith reapplying his Blackness in *I, Robot* (2004); and Keith Piper's *Robot Bodies* (2001–2017), an interactive installation exploring Blackness and Black alienation in terms of anthropomorphic machines, the false flesh of the android/gynoid that passes for human, and the cyborg's integrations of biology, mechanism, and computing. Walker's Black automatons are not meant to be taken for actual Black beings or autonomous mechanisms, of course; but because 99 percent of anti-Blackness is based on 100-percent fictional representations, they can be understood as conceptual hunting decoys, like the molasses children of her 2014 installation *A Subtlety* at the Domino Sugar Factory in Brooklyn and the tar babies set out to trap the Br'er Rabbits of early Black diasporan folklore.

With Walker in the role of a trickster working on behalf of Black being(s), anti-Black algorithmic biases become a minor threat compared to the larger issue of Black culture's algorithmic automation—

what one could call the Joice Heth scam executed at scale—and a corresponding, ever-intensifying threat of obsolescence. The information science of the Atlantic slave trade compressed the rich and diverse lifeways of captives from Western Africa's Abron, Bakongo, Igbo, Fon, Fulani, Mbundu, Mende, Wolof, and Yoruba cultures into an interchangeable set of dehumanizing stereotypes. Chattel slavery optimized the resulting bio/logical format—Black life—to justify and characterize its violent protocols of biomechanical labor. As early as 1861, Black beings were recognized as robots or automatons, when formerly enslaved abolitionist author Harriet Jacobs wrote: "These God-breathing machines are no more, in the sight of their masters, than the cotton they plant, or the horses they tend."[4] She is describing a philosophy that turns living things into commodity objects and eighteenth-century strategies of control and representation that morphed into Immaculate Slavery[5]—a market-driven complex of digital trauma, psychological manipulation, and varieties of emotional and psychic violence that connects Africa's Gold Coast to California's Silicon Valley. Under new versions of the master's hyper-reductive sight, we digital citizens are processed by algorithms of surveillance, simulation, and mediation that leave us no less of a machine than the antebellum slave. As Walker puts it, "We are all cyborgs now," and though this is incredibly bad for everyone, it is an extra burden on those whose lives, suffering, and innovative survival strategies constitute Immaculate Slavery's training data. What Walker's Black automatons accomplish in their endless repetition—levitation, divination, timekeeping, et cetera—demonstrates and illustrates relevant aspects of a history and future of intelligent machines.

Someone reading Harriet Beecher Stowe's *Uncle Tom's Cabin* with no historical knowledge of chattel slavery could interpret the encounter between Miss Ophelia and Topsy (quoted above) as a work of surreal speculative fiction. Ophelia finds herself "paralyzed with amazement" by the spectacle of this machine-slave-animal—this *nigger*—that sings, pats juba, and pantomimes. Along with her rhythmic sounds and steam-whistle melodies, Topsy's "black, glassy eyes," "wicked drollery," and "cunning glances" communicate an ambiguous nonhuman affect that could be a function of programming or a demonstration of agency. Stowe's elaborate description emphasizes a profound social and biological gulf that White Supremacy's determinations and measurements of Black sentience produce and maintain. According to scholar

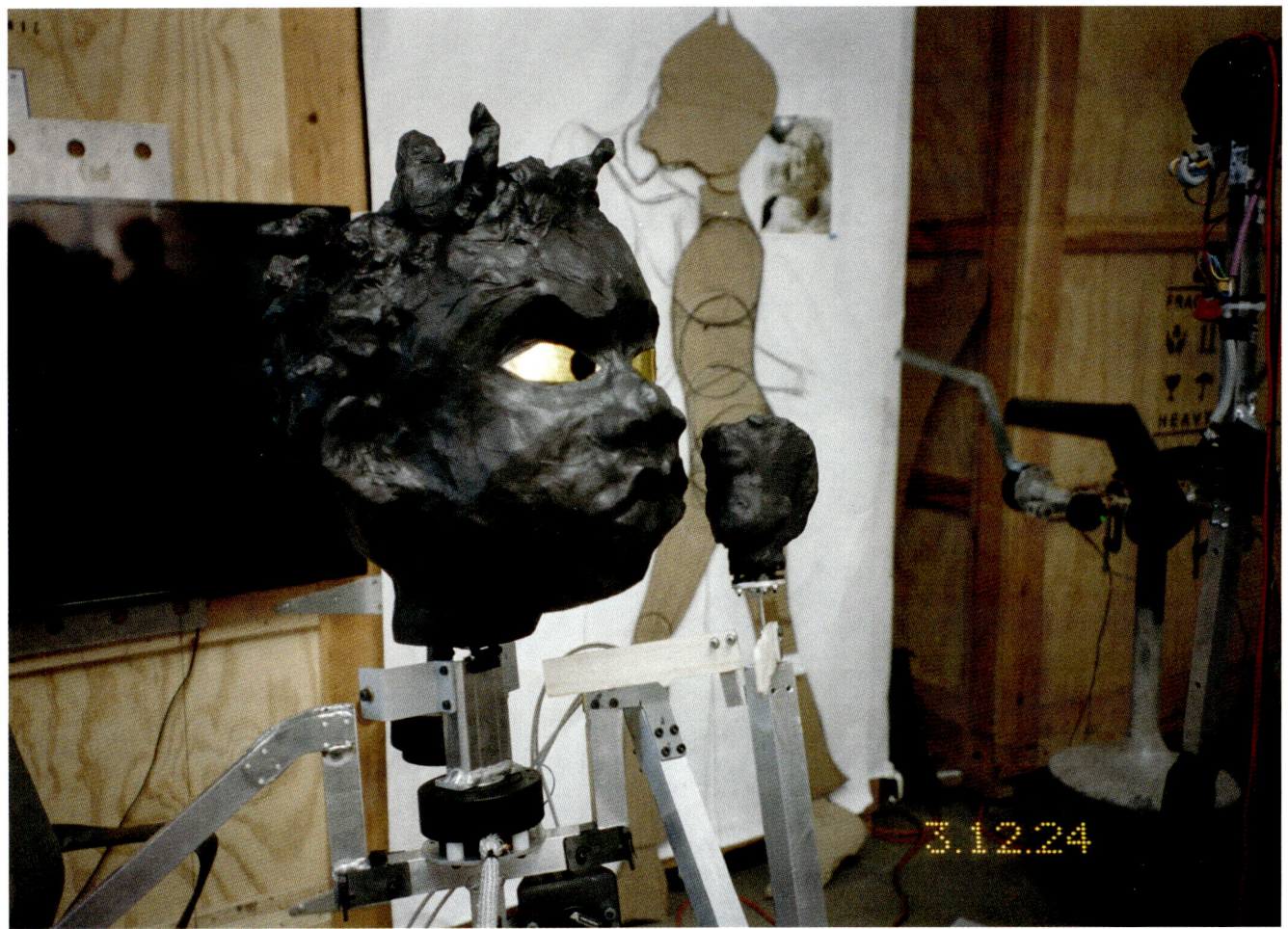

Stephen M. Best, Stowe feared that "Americans may never again be able to make 'clar' [clear] the distinction between persons and property" and that this animated "her further panic that there may be an afterlife to slavery."[6] Stowe's anxieties have since been borne out and confirmed in ways that are not restricted to chattel slavery's segue into the prison industrial complex and modern policing.[7]

Topsy is an ancestral humanoid artificial intelligence that can be found dancing along the curve of robotics theorist Masahiro Mori's Uncanny Valley, somersaulting at one end of popular computing advocate Theodor H. Nelson's spectrum of resistance to the totalitarian Machine, and outperforming the highly advanced robots featured in Boston Dynamics' promotional media. Walker's work illuminates such examples because it demonstrates how White Supremacy's influence on technological development is almost invisible when it is at its Blackest.

In 1970 Mori anticipated a world in which the responsibilities, behaviors, and external appearance of people and anthropomorphic machines would become indistinguishable.[8] So he invented a two-dimensional spectrum with human likeness measured on the horizontal axis and the degree of affinity on the vertical (fig. 1, right). The Healthy Person is at one end of highest affinity and likeness, while the Industrial Robot is at the other. Between them is a curved distribution of relative resemblance and receptivity based on physical attributes such as skin color and texture, qualities of motion, the presence or absence of prosthetics, and expressive capacities. Significantly, the Industrial Robot does not represent the worst of the nonhuman, as Mori's curve is characterized by a steep and narrow dip that is relatively close to human likeness but also maximizes negative affinity. This is the Uncanny Valley, where the signs of healthy life can be crudely pantomimed or are entirely absent, and the strongest negative reactions correspond to encounters with entities like the Corpse/Zombie.

This is also the realm of poorly fitting or mismatched artificial limbs, mutilated-but-living bodies, glass eyes, and incompetent or attenuated mechanical and visual representations of humans. One has to climb out of the Valley to encounter Humanoid Robots, an automaton such as Fortuna, and the automated limbs of optimized factories and assembly lines. Such entities are less shocking than the Corpse or Zombie, first because they are in the category of tools, systems, and servants—the enslaved—and second because they are not meant

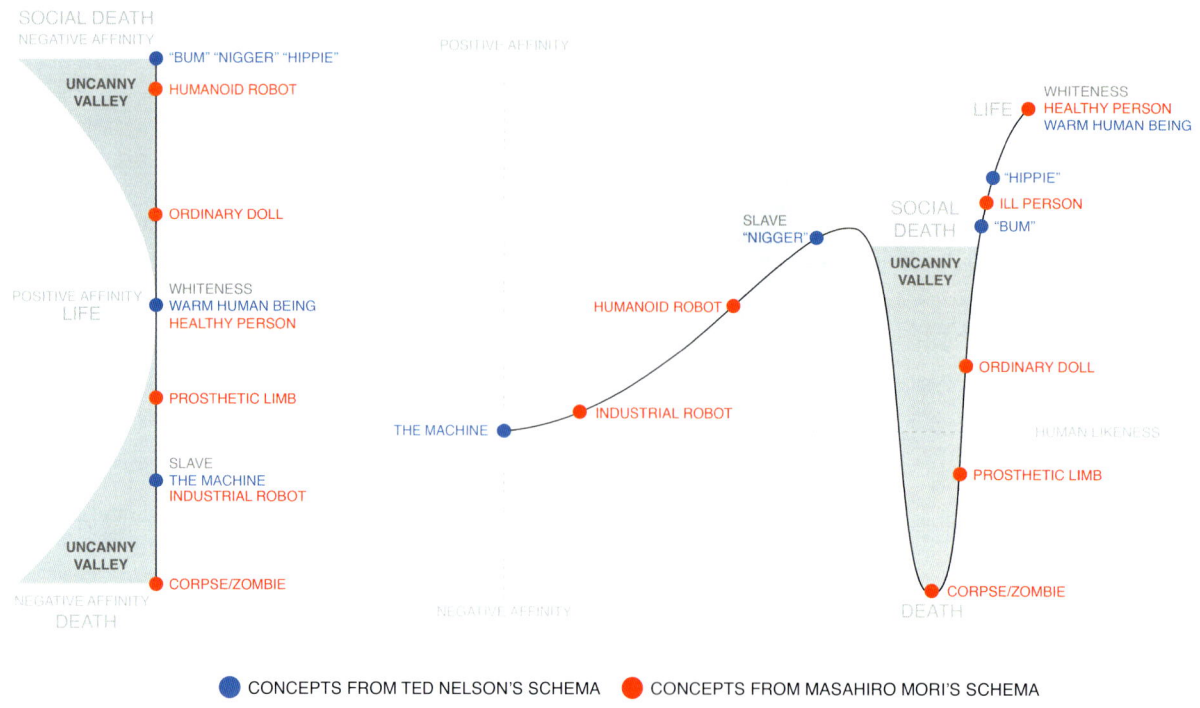

SOCIAL DEATH
NEGATIVE AFFINITY
POSITIVE AFFINITY

"BUM" "NIGGER" "HIPPIE"
UNCANNY VALLEY
HUMANOID ROBOT

WHITENESS
HEALTHY PERSON
WARM HUMAN BEING
LIFE

"HIPPIE"
SOCIAL DEATH
ILL PERSON
"BUM"
UNCANNY VALLEY

ORDINARY DOLL

SLAVE
"NIGGER"

POSITIVE AFFINITY
LIFE
WHITENESS
WARM HUMAN BEING
HEALTHY PERSON

HUMANOID ROBOT

ORDINARY DOLL

HUMAN LIKENESS

PROSTHETIC LIMB

THE MACHINE
INDUSTRIAL ROBOT

PROSTHETIC LIMB

SLAVE
THE MACHINE
INDUSTRIAL ROBOT

UNCANNY VALLEY

NEGATIVE AFFINITY
DEATH

CORPSE/ZOMBIE

NEGATIVE AFFINITY

CORPSE/ZOMBIE
DEATH

● CONCEPTS FROM TED NELSON'S SCHEMA   ● CONCEPTS FROM MASAHIRO MORI'S SCHEMA

Graphical interpolation by David A. M. Goldberg, based on schemas by Nelson and Mori

Figure 1. An interpolation of Mori's Uncanny Valley graph (right) sets up a range of human likeness and affinity distributed on a curve between the Healthy Person and the Industrial Robot. Mori's original graph included curves that distinguished static and moving entities, but I have combined them for simplicity. What I call Nelson's "Machine Myth" axis (left) also schematizes a split opposition with a Warm Human Being centered between the Machine at one end and "Bum," "Nigger," "Hippie" at the other. Where Nelson explicitly locates the "Nigger" and acknowledges racist bias, no such entity exists for Mori. However, concepts from one schema can easily be mapped to the other, thereby revealing the position of the dehumanized slave in relation to the warm, healthy, and white master. Nelson's concepts are represented by blue markers and text, while Mori's are in red. Walker's *Fortuna and the Immortality Garden (Machine)* makes Black being(s) the center or height from which expressions of artificial or prosthetic life are measured, but because we are excluded from the category of the (warm, healthy) human, we must contend with a separate, uncharted Uncanny Valley while still being embedded in the one visualized here.

to pass as a Healthy Person. Mori understood that phenomenological assessments and affective reactions were based on how people, monsters, and machines look and behave, but Stowe and Jacobs understood how chattel slavery had already mapped the Uncanny Valley and positioned enslaved Black beings—shrill, glassy-eyed, fantastically dexterous machines like Topsy—with robots on its far side.

In 1974, writing in the wake of the civil rights and antiwar movements and at the dawn of personal computing, Nelson wanted people to free themselves of their fear of the Machine that is "Taking Over the World."[9] Like Mori, Nelson schematized the relationship between people and technological systems in terms of a relative polar opposition. He positioned the Warm Human Being (equivalent to Mori's healthy one) at a center point between two extremes: that of the Machine at one end, and the charged antisocial stereotypes of the "Bum," "Nigger," and "Hippie" at the other (fig. 1, left). He imagined that some people feared or hated the Machine because they did not want to be subjected to mindless cruelty, injustice, and dehumanization: the same forces that governed Karl Marx's infernal machines, the factories of Chicago, and the plantations

of chattel slavery. Nelson compared the fear and superstition of racists, squares, and other social conservatives to those who reacted similarly to computers and other advancing technologies. Unfortunately, Nelson sets up the figure of the "Nigger" in polar opposition to the Machine, thereby excluding it from the category of the Warm Human Being and ignoring the historical circumstances, social structures, and racist hallucinations that turned living Black beings *into* machines and "niggers."

It is unlikely that Mori or Nelson had a Black being like Topsy in mind when they imagined the essential human attributes of health and warmth as the degree zero or privileged center of human-cyborg relations, but they likely would have regarded Stowe's Miss Ophelia as whole and wholesome without thinking about her whiteness as a prerequisite. As sociologist Orlando Patterson informs us, the White Supremacist logic of chattel slavery locates the "nigger" outside of civil society, beyond the master's sight in the (non)space and presumed darkness of social death.[10] For Mori, metaphysical and biological death is the gap or valley that separates life from animation, automation, prosthetics, and puppetry. Nelson conceived of the Machine as social death writ large, but the equivalence of the "nigger" and the Machine established by chattel slavery destabilizes the opposition of his allegorical avatars. Because the "Hippie" is no longer a viable antisocial stereotype and terms like "unhoused" have humanized the "Bum" to a degree, positioning the Warm Human at a midpoint becomes redundant, and what remains of Nelson's schema is already accounted for in Mori's. Ophelia gazes across the Uncanny Valley at Topsy, at a "thing" created by the Machine of chattel slavery that is obviously not human but evidently too cunning and entertaining to be dismissed as cotton, livestock, or industrial robot—she/it is utterly fascinating but cannot be trusted. Nelson likely would have understood his era's mistrust of computer-driven bureaucracies and the machinic managers that deferred to them as a contemporary version of Ophelia's feelings for and about Topsy.

Nelson wanted people to engage with personal computers with the same affinity and affect they could show for similarly intimate technologies like automobiles, bicycles, and cameras. He imagined a techno-utopian difference between *the* Machine and *your* Machine, where the latter serves us and amplifies our capacities. Such anthropomorphic feelings for things represent a paternalistic investment in mastery, ownership, and enjoyment that we refer to casually as love (as in "I love my phone / my car / my computer"). This love is rooted in White Supremacist protocols that justify the exploitation of Black being(s) at all levels of intimacy: from chattel slavery's anonymous labor to the indispensable "personal assistance" the owned provided the owners in carriage houses, parlors, kitchens, nurseries, and bedrooms.

As I consider the anxiety produced by Ophelia's negative affinity for and fascination with Topsy's inhuman performativity, I find comparable reactions among contemporary viewers of Boston Dynamics' robot demonstration videos. A late 2020 clip features several humanoid, quadruped, and two-wheeled robots doing a choreographed dance routine to the Contours' 1962 single "Do You Love Me?" As Billy Gordon pleads "Do you love me, now that I can dance?" the robots perform classic Black social dances like the Mashed Potato and the Twist with mathematical, absolutely unfunky precision.[11] Obviously, these robots are not representations or caricatures of Black performers, but the company's attempt to cross the Uncanny Valley using Black music and Black dance—in the tradition of blackface minstrelsy—makes them political and cultural proxies for Black beings. Top comments beneath the video express a sardonic dismay

that is particular to our era; many quips frame the dance performance in terms of an anticipated robot uprising, while others sarcastically express fears of miscegenation, replacement, or obsolescence. But Topsy "knocking her knees together, in a wild, fantastic sort of time" had the same shocking but hypnotic effect on Ophelia that witnessing Boston Dynamics' grooving robots has on us. One can imagine that Ophelia and her creator were both hit with future shock caused by having to possibly widen their circles of empathy for such creatures. It is no accident that musicality and artistic expression are potential means of doing so.

Other Boston Dynamics demonstration videos feature robots running, climbing, and doing acrobatics, but dancing set to music invites the viewer to make intuitive and aesthetic assessments of the company's technological prowess. To demonstrate the sophisticated articulation that their robots can achieve, engineers programmed them with movements that require different parts of the anthropomorphic form (hips and shoulders, elbows and knees, for example) to move in independent rhythmic cycles. Such challenging motions are the expressive hallmarks of dance in Western Africa, and they are the foundation of most popular dances in the United States, as seen in blackface minstrel shows, *American Bandstand*, *Soul Train*, MTV's *The Grind*, *Fortnite*, every animated GIF you find funny, and countless TikTok videos. By programming these machines to do things that racism advertises as being not only natural to Black beings but stereotypically unachievable by whites, Boston Dynamics is doing the "impossible" in a twofold gesture.

The choreography performed by these robots is technically impressive, but without music its impact would be diminished considerably. The specific song selection and use of choreographed dance make more explicit Boston Dynamics' effort to close or fill the Uncanny Valley. On a practical level, music masks what is likely an extremely loud orchestra of electromechanical noises produced by these robots when they are in motion. But on the perceptual level, synchronized sound also produces a naturalized sense of wholeness that is meant to defer immediate considerations of artifice. The engineers could have choreographed a ballet routine and used Johann Strauss's "Blue Danube Waltz" to riff on *2001: A Space Odyssey*. Instead, they used "Do You Love Me?" which, in this context of dancing robots that might otherwise be rejected because they are just machines programmed to pretend, I read as an elaborate pun that turns a

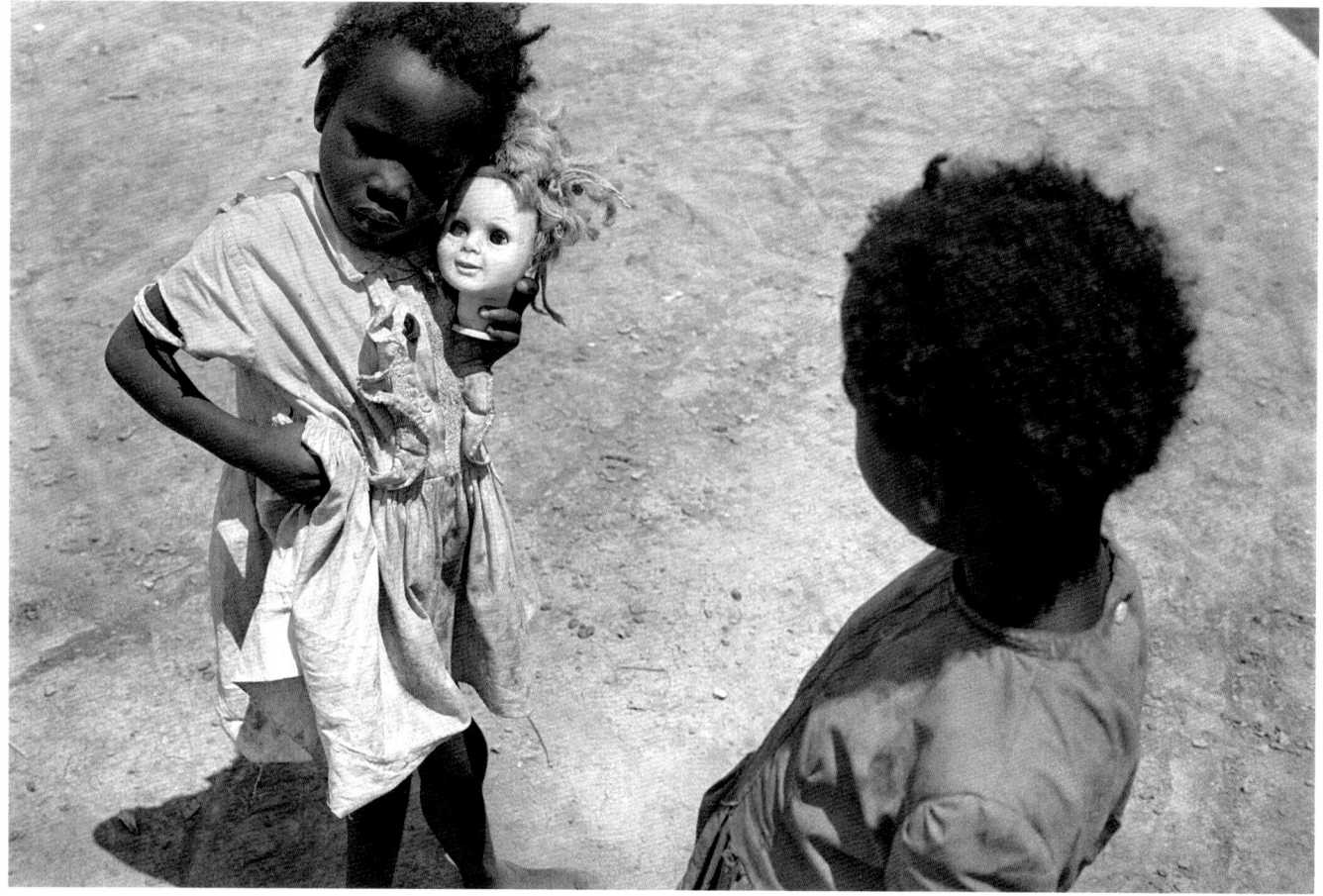

Eugene Richards, *Broken Doll*, Hughes, Arkansas, 1970, printed 2017. Gelatin silver print. Image: 14 ⁵⁄₈ × 21 ¹³⁄₁₆ in. (37.2 × 55.5 cm), sheet: 19 ¹⁵⁄₁₆ × 23 ¹³⁄₁₆ in. (50.6 × 60.5 cm). Nelson Atkins Museum, Gift of Eugene Richards. 2018.19.1

romantic suitor's flirtatious question into a metaphysical plea for acceptance: *Do you love me now that I can dance?*

I am not asserting that Boston Dynamics is a White Supremacist organization. Rather, I am speculating that there might not be a Boston Dynamics without chattel slavery, at least not one that could promote its products with such an effective configuration of cultural appropriation. Their use of Black art and expressivity to animate their robots does not reinstate chattel slavery, but it does reveal and highlight the complexity of its afterlife. To contemplate Walker's *Fortuna and the Immortality Garden (Machine)* is to occupy a similar position, but from a perspective of Black being(s) that can only be fully rendered if the work's engines of historical continuity are brought fully online. Boston Dynamics synthesizes Blackness in the form and content of their robots' choreographed movements, and by doing so reintroduces a racialized performance that is as old as encouraging enslaved or incarcerated Black beings to sing while laboring. The Black being that dares to claim the tenuous and ever-contested position of health and warmth sees Walker's Black automatons dancing their way out of Mori's Uncanny Valley with moves that come from a Black past that

began among those who were born on or banished to its far side—*this* is the "separate but equal" Uncanny Valley I am concerned with.

Stowe, Mori, Nelson, and Boston Dynamics embrace the Black automaton by fetishizing it (Stowe and Nelson), ignoring it (Mori), or exploiting it by appropriating and replicating the cultural inventions of Black beings (Boston Dynamics). As a result, the Black automaton remains palatable (and profitable) because it continues to perform to the specifications of the stereotype and threatens actual Black beings with obsolescence. For actively White Supremacist or MAGA-compliant beings in this position, there is no possibility for integration with those who sought to evade or escape the Machine because those types will and were always meant to be one with it. Everyone else is beginning to recognize that we pay for access to databases, algorithms, software, and networks that we don't own or control in order to do the majority of the things we can, must, and want to. We are all objects of Immaculate Slavery now, but some of us will embrace a new version of Blackness expressed through artificial systems that have been trained on the previous centuries' exploitation of Black musicality, athleticism, creativity, criminality, and resistance.

Any actual Black being(s) among us who survive this new Middle Passage will face yet another fundamental threat to our existence. Fortunately, we have Kara Walker with us for this iteration, and she is attempting to forestall our obsolescence with her consistently unflinching approach that necessarily indicts beings on both sides of this Uncanny Valley that separates—but doesn't disconnect—Black and white, life and (social) death, and the "nigger" from human being(s).

1. Harriet Beecher Stowe, *Uncle Tom's Cabin* (Cambridge, MA: Belknap Press of Harvard University Press, 2009), 310.
2. See Walker's essay in the present volume, page 12.
3. Benjamin Reiss, *The Showman and the Slave: Race, Death, and Memory in Barnum's America* (Cambridge, MA: Harvard University Press, 2001).
4. Harriet Jacobs, *Incidents in the Life of a Slave Girl* (New York: Penguin Books, 2000), 10.
5. I am indebted to Elaine Katzenberger of San Francisco's City Lights Bookstore for this term. She was in turn riffing on Elizabeth "Betina" Martinez's concept of immaculate dictatorship: "Ours is an immaculate dictatorship, with no visible blood on its hands." Martinez, "The Immaculate Dictatorship," *ZNet*, September 22, 2003, https://znetwork.org/znetarticle/the-immaculate-dictatorship-by-elizabeth-martinez.
6. Stephen M. Best, *The Fugitive's Properties: Law and the Poetics of Possession* (Chicago: University of Chicago Press, 2004), 3.
7. See, for example, George Jackson, *Soledad Brother: The Prison Letters of George Jackson* (Chicago: Lawrence Hill Books, 1994); Michelle Alexander, *The New Jim Crow: Mass Incarceration in the Age of Colorblindness* (New York: New Press, 2010); Robert Perkinson, *Texas Tough: The Rise of America's Prison Empire* (New York: Picador, 2010); Simone Browne, *Dark Matters: On the Surveillance of Blackness* (Durham, NC: Duke University Press, 2015); Ruth Wilson Gilmore, *Golden Gulag: Prisons, Surplus, Crisis, and Opposition in Globalizing California* (Berkeley: University of California Press, 2007); and KRS-One's single "Sound of da Police" (Jive, 1993).
8. Masahiro Mori, "The Uncanny Valley," trans. Karl F. MacDorman and Norri Kageki, *Robotics and Automation* (June 2012), https://spectrum.ieee.org/the-uncanny-valley. The original essay was written more than forty years before this widely circulated translation, which Mori authorized and reviewed.
9. Theodor H. Nelson, *Computer Lib/Dream Machine* (self-published, 1974), 9.
10. Orlando Patterson, *Slavery and Social Death: A Comparative Study* (Cambridge, MA: Harvard University Press, 1983).
11. Boston Dynamics, "Do You Love Me?," December 29, 2020, www.youtube.com/watch?v=fn3KWM1kuAw.

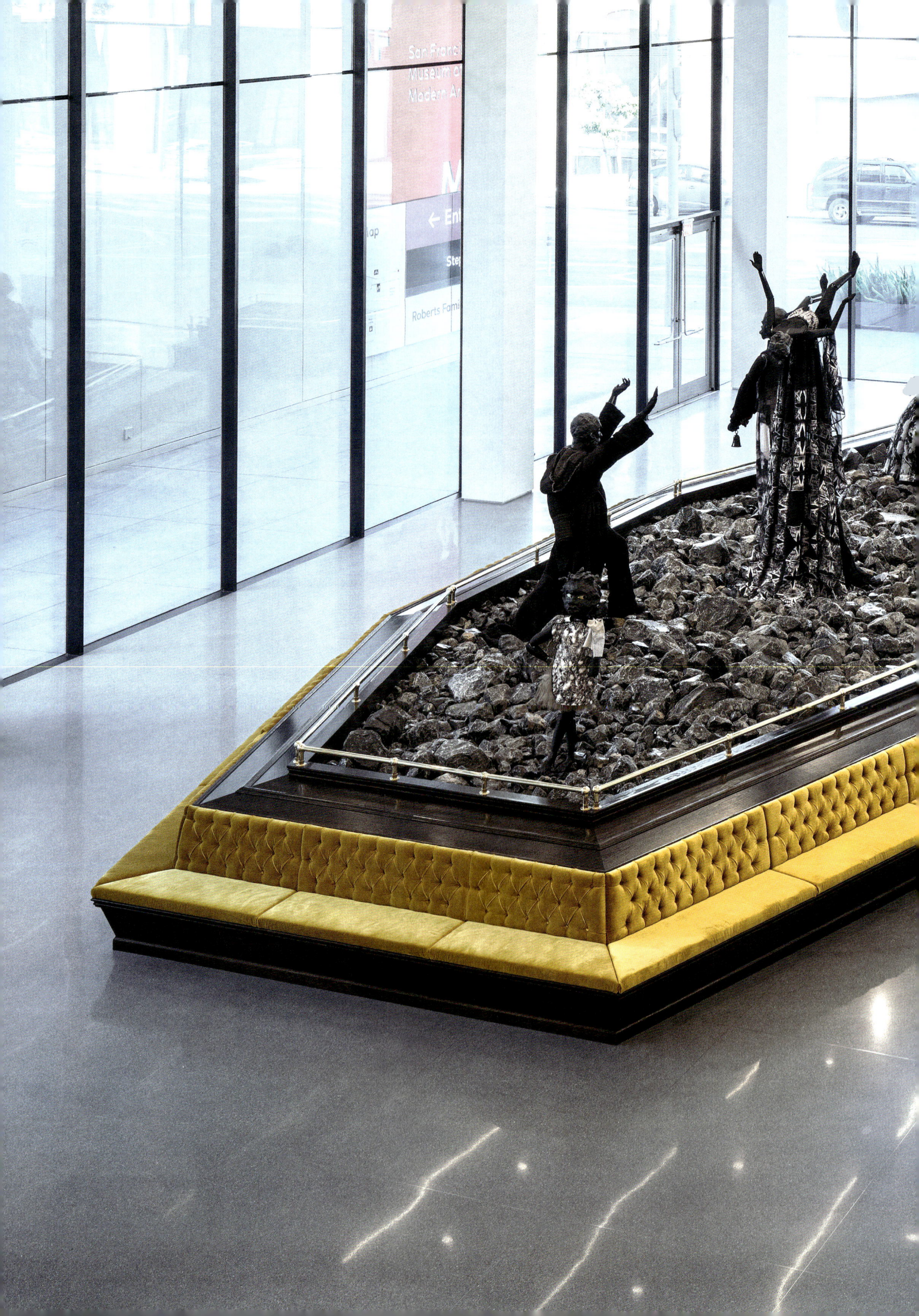

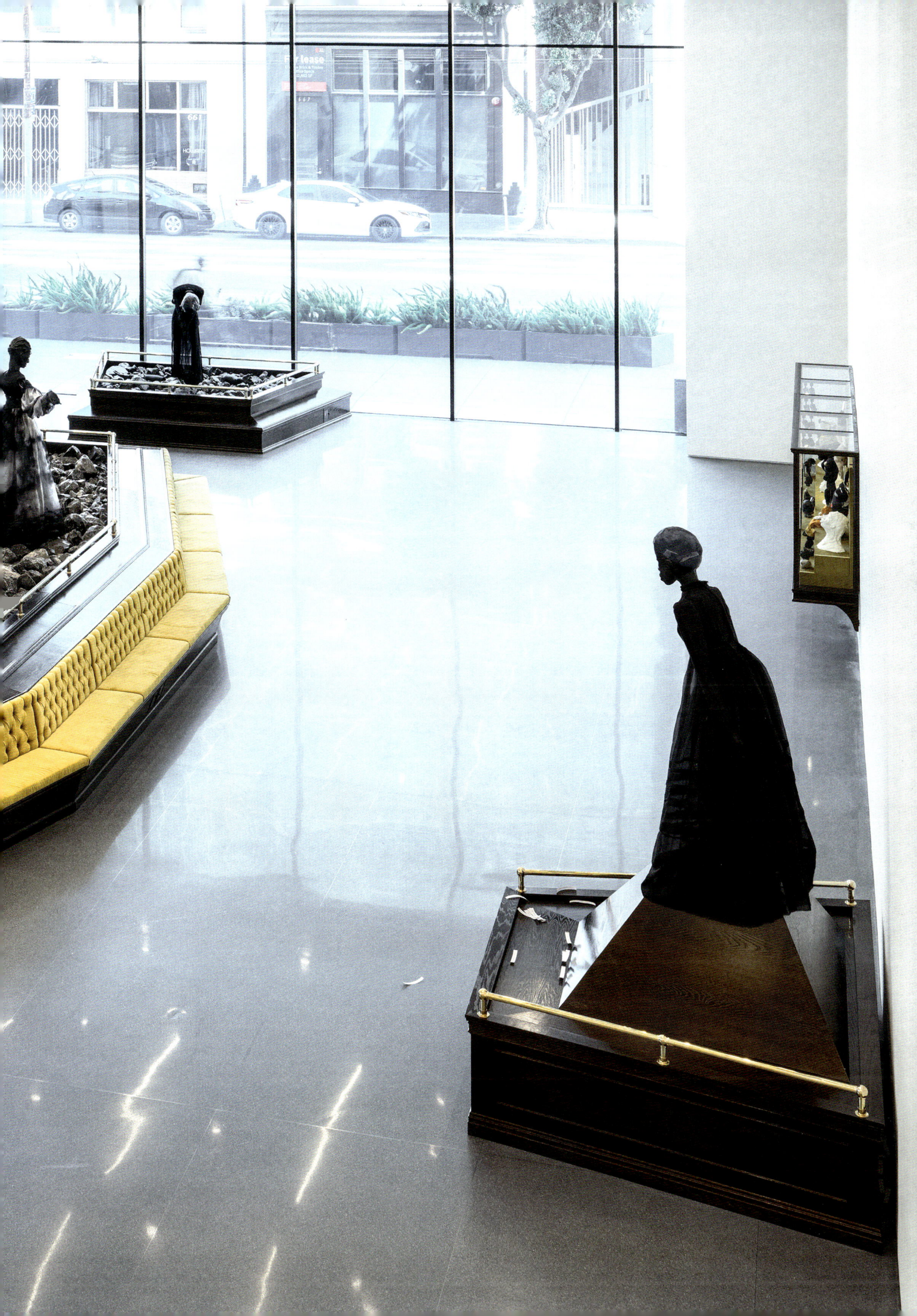

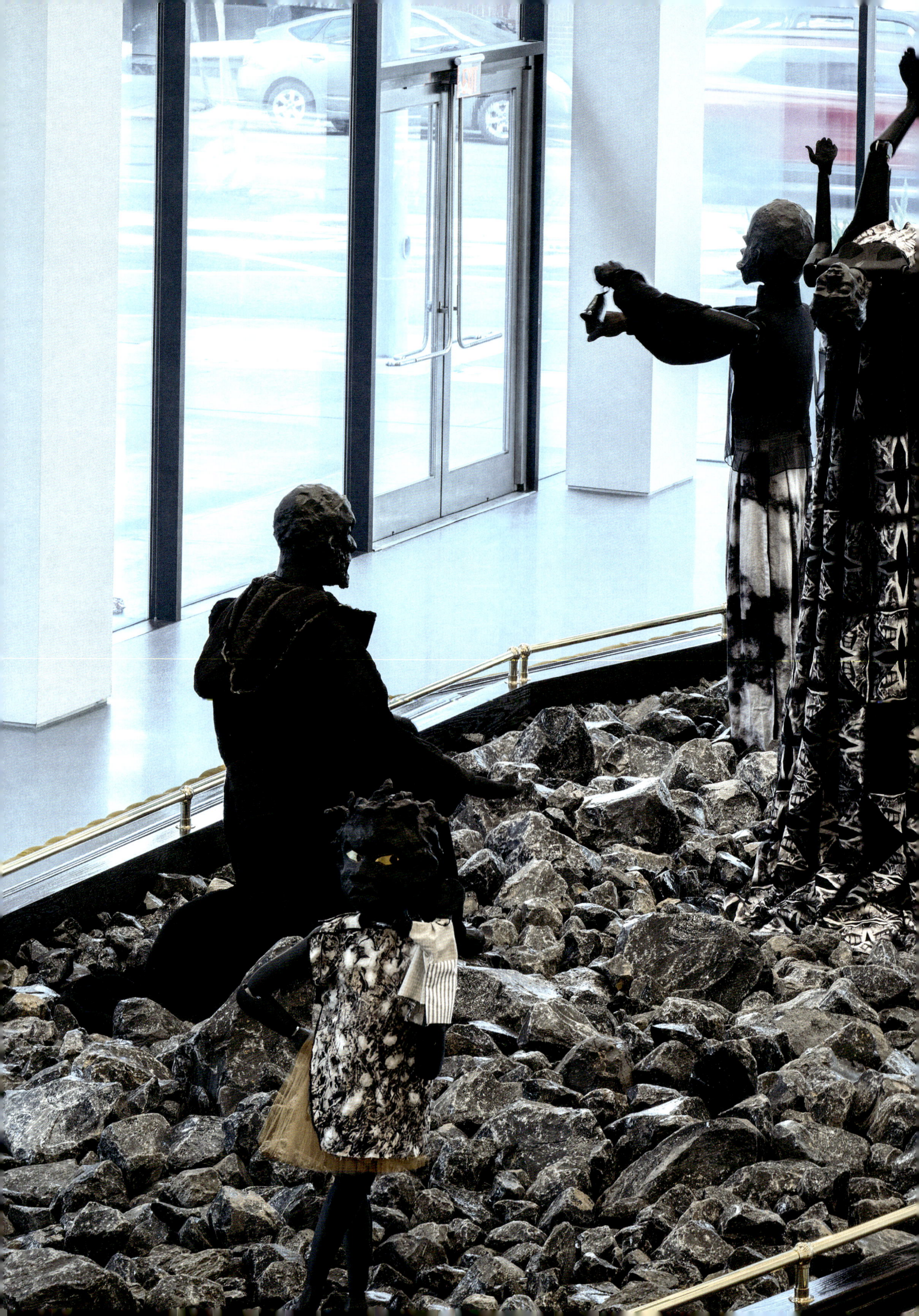

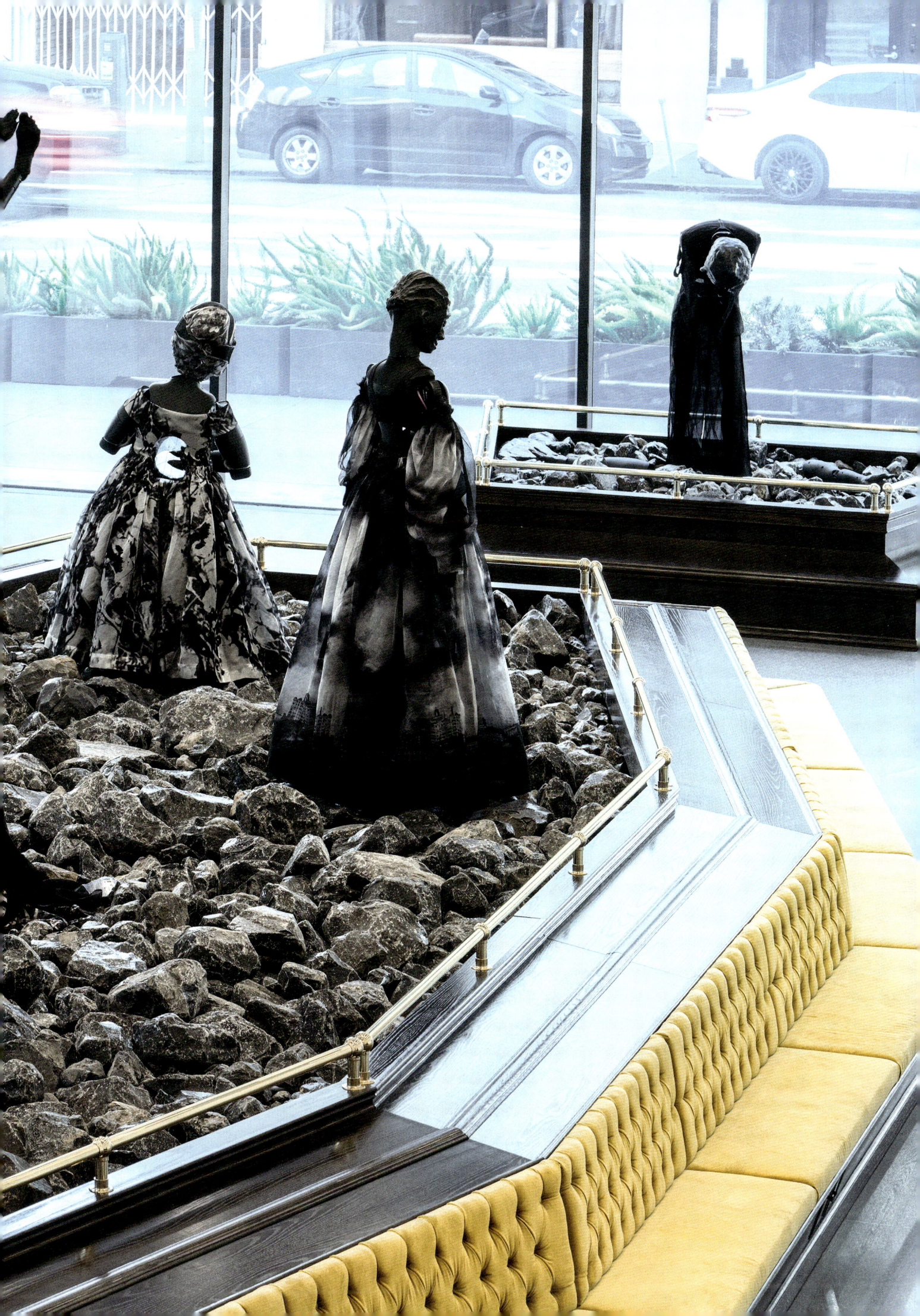

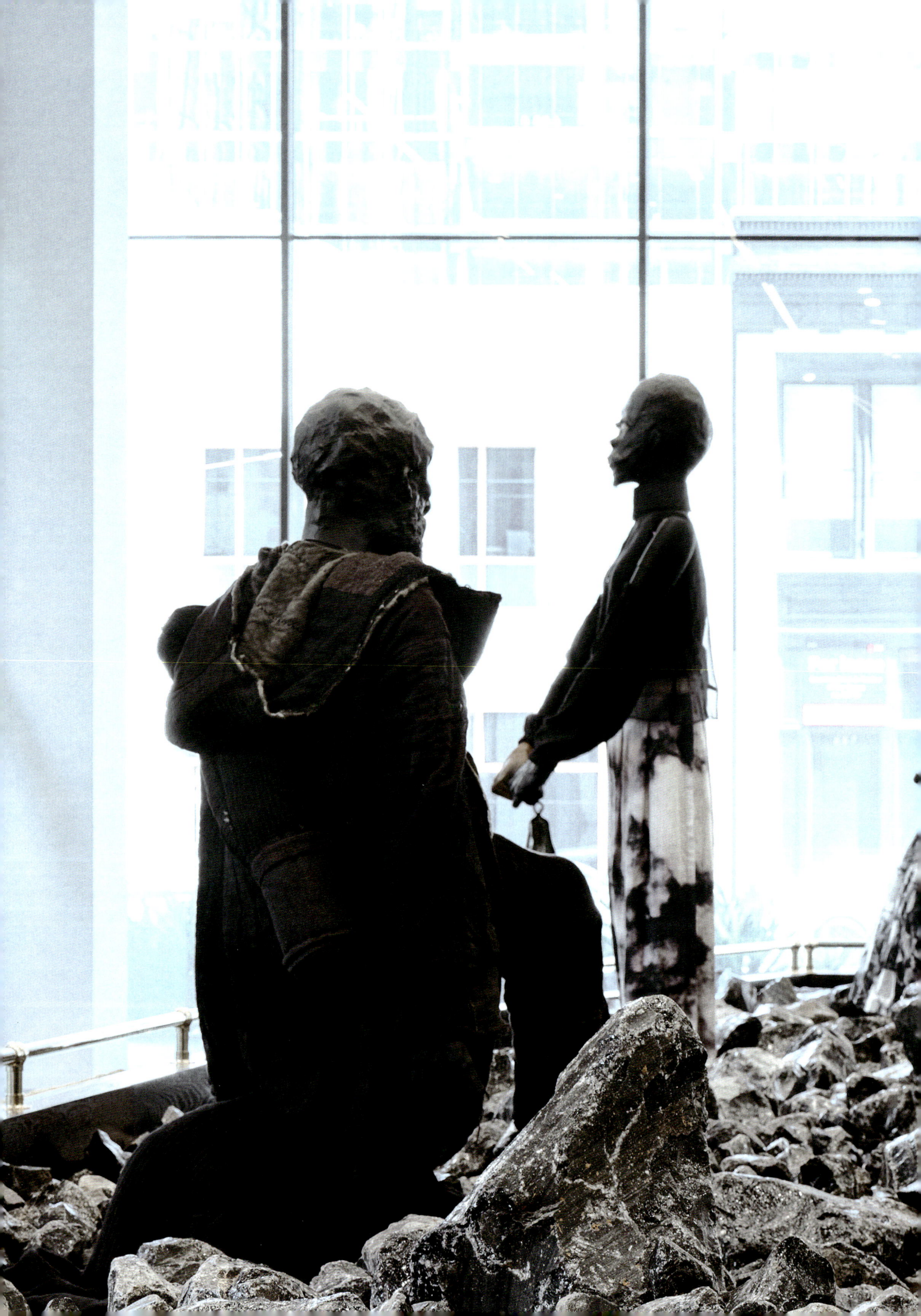

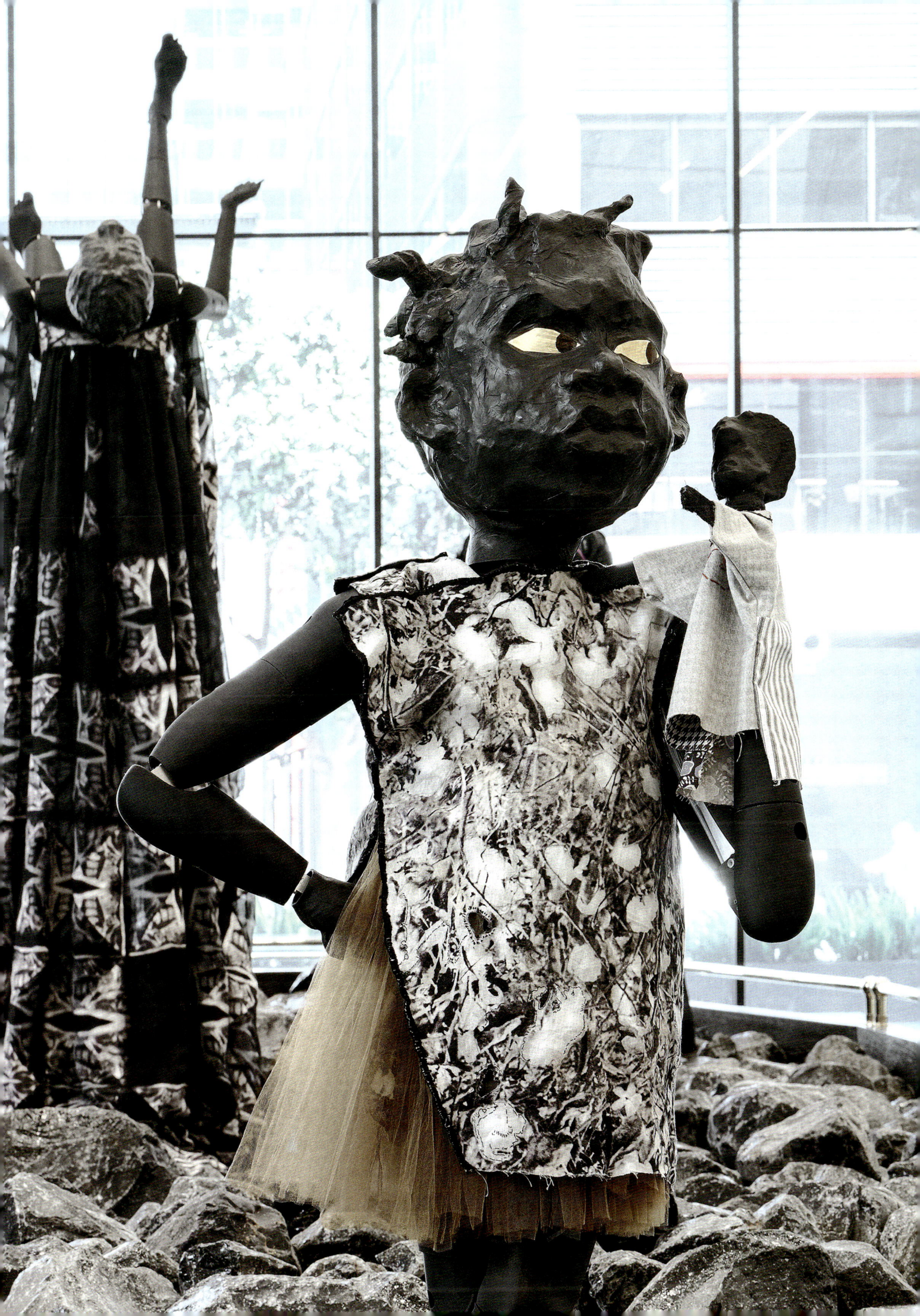

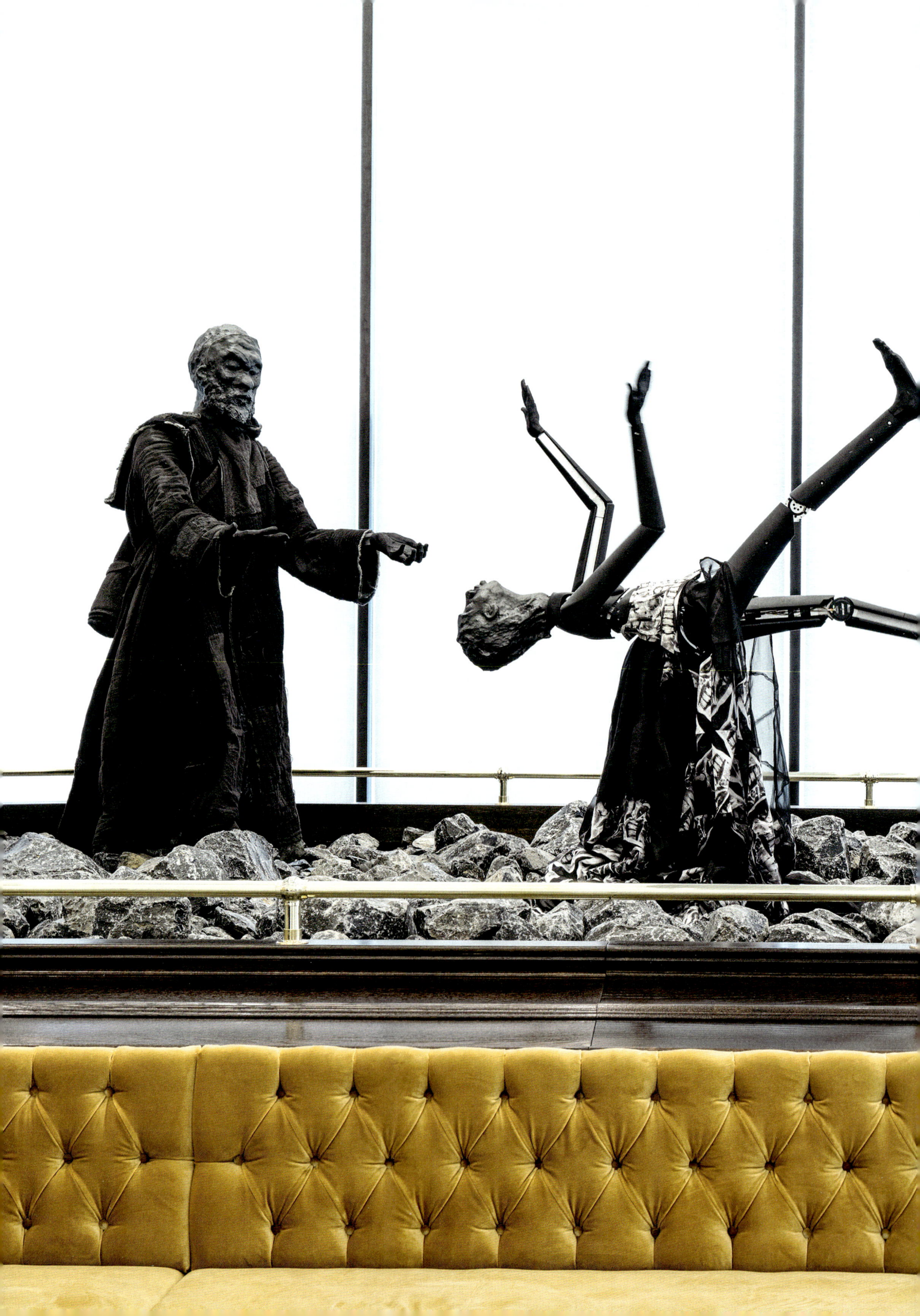

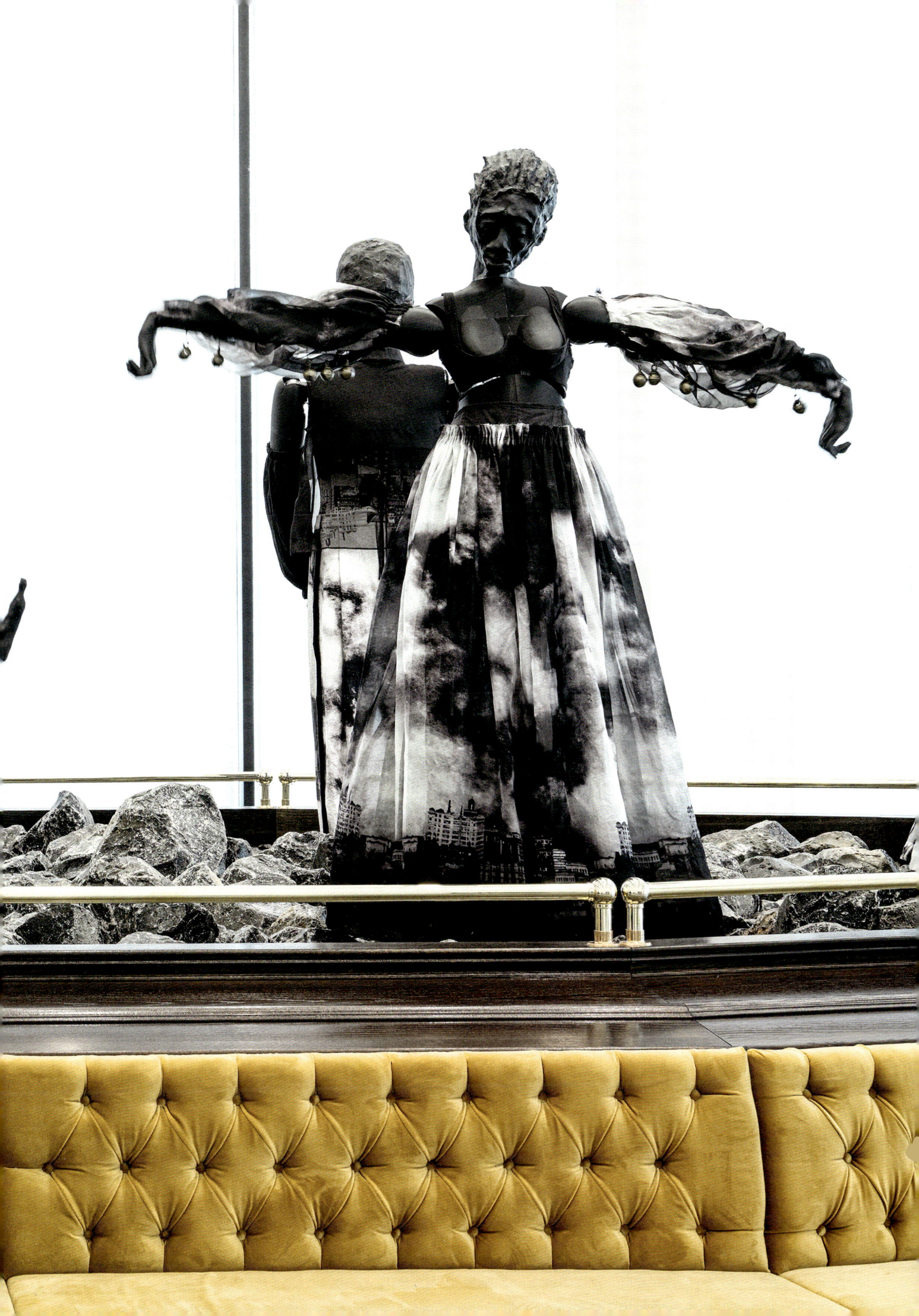

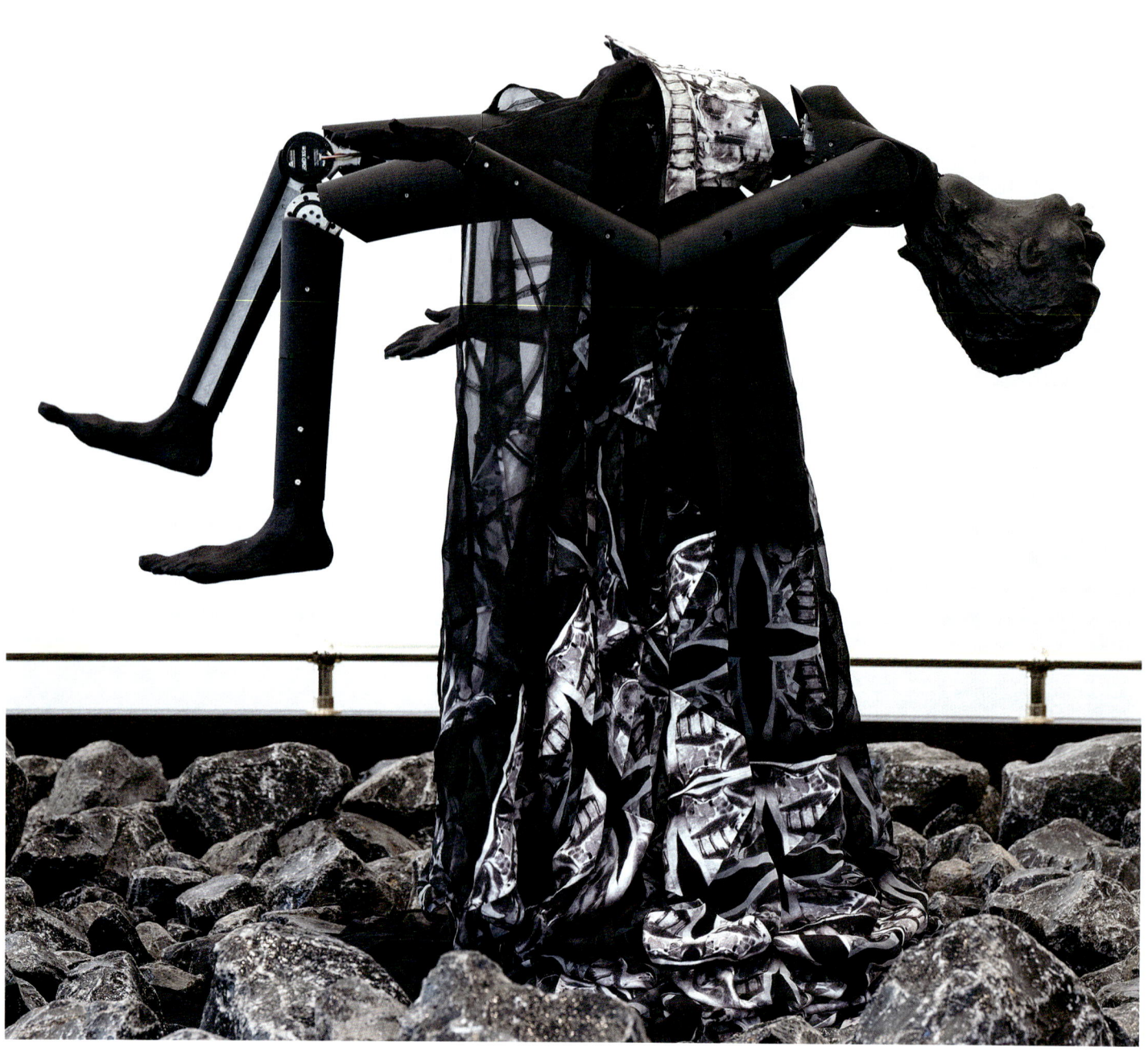

90

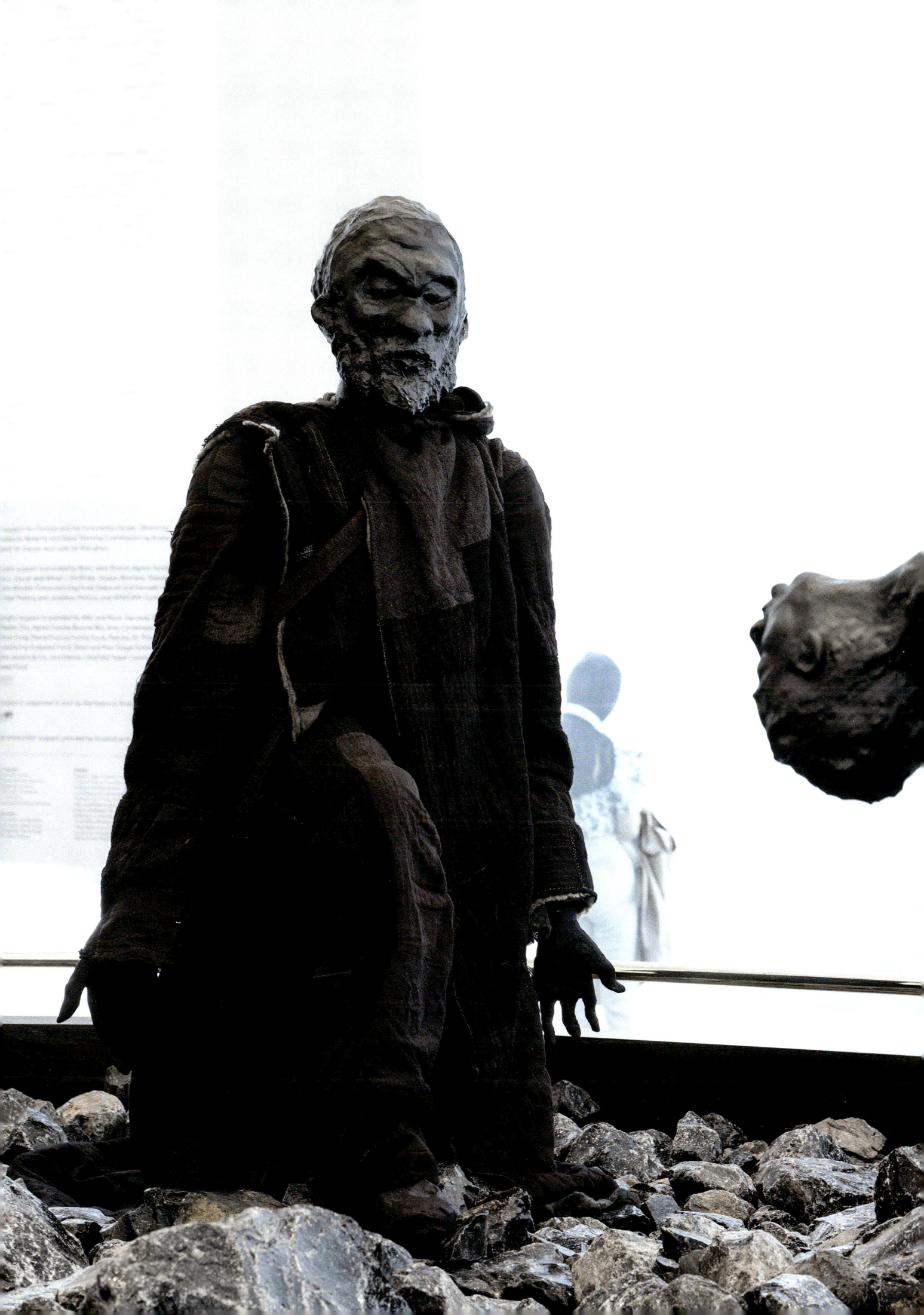

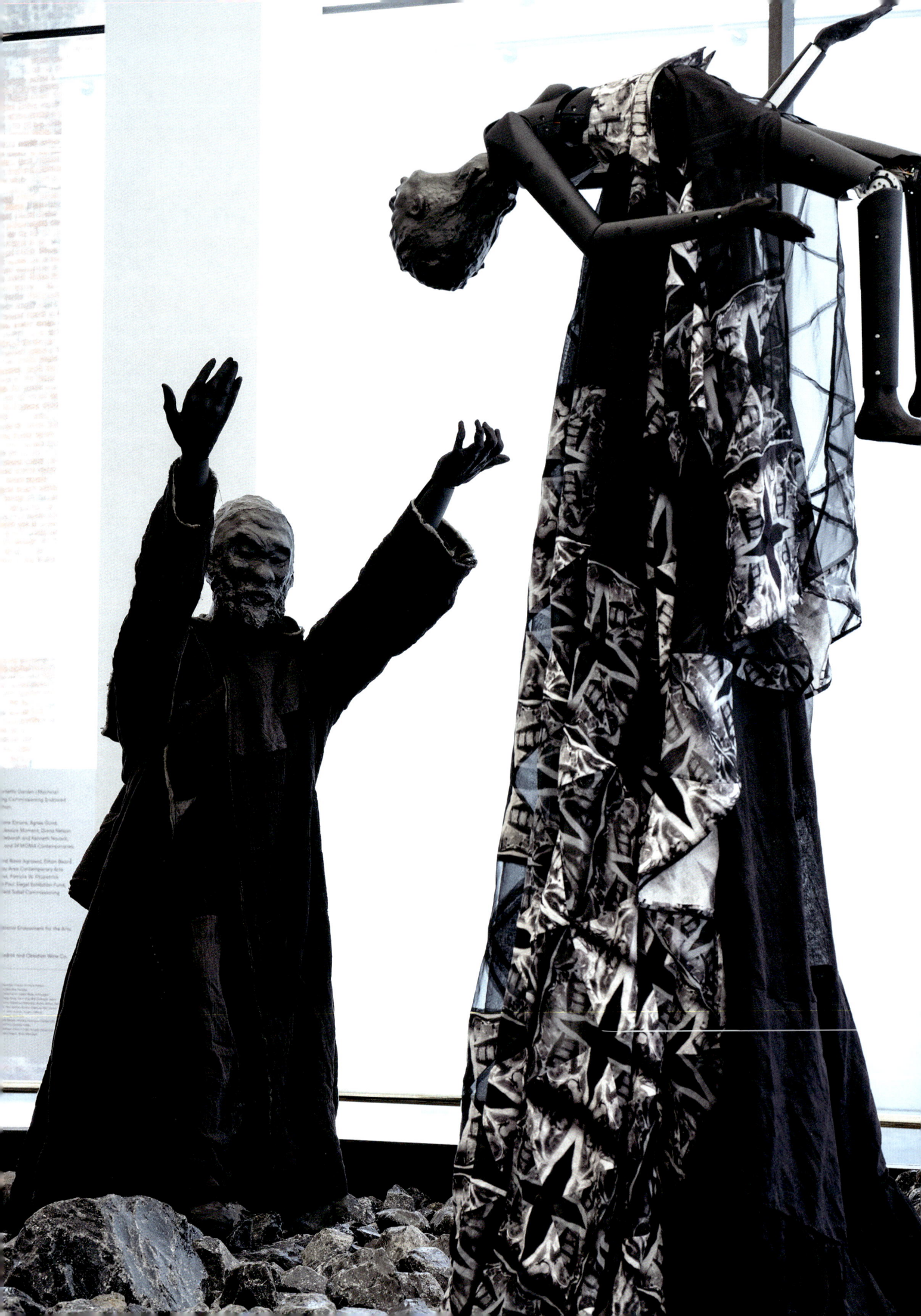

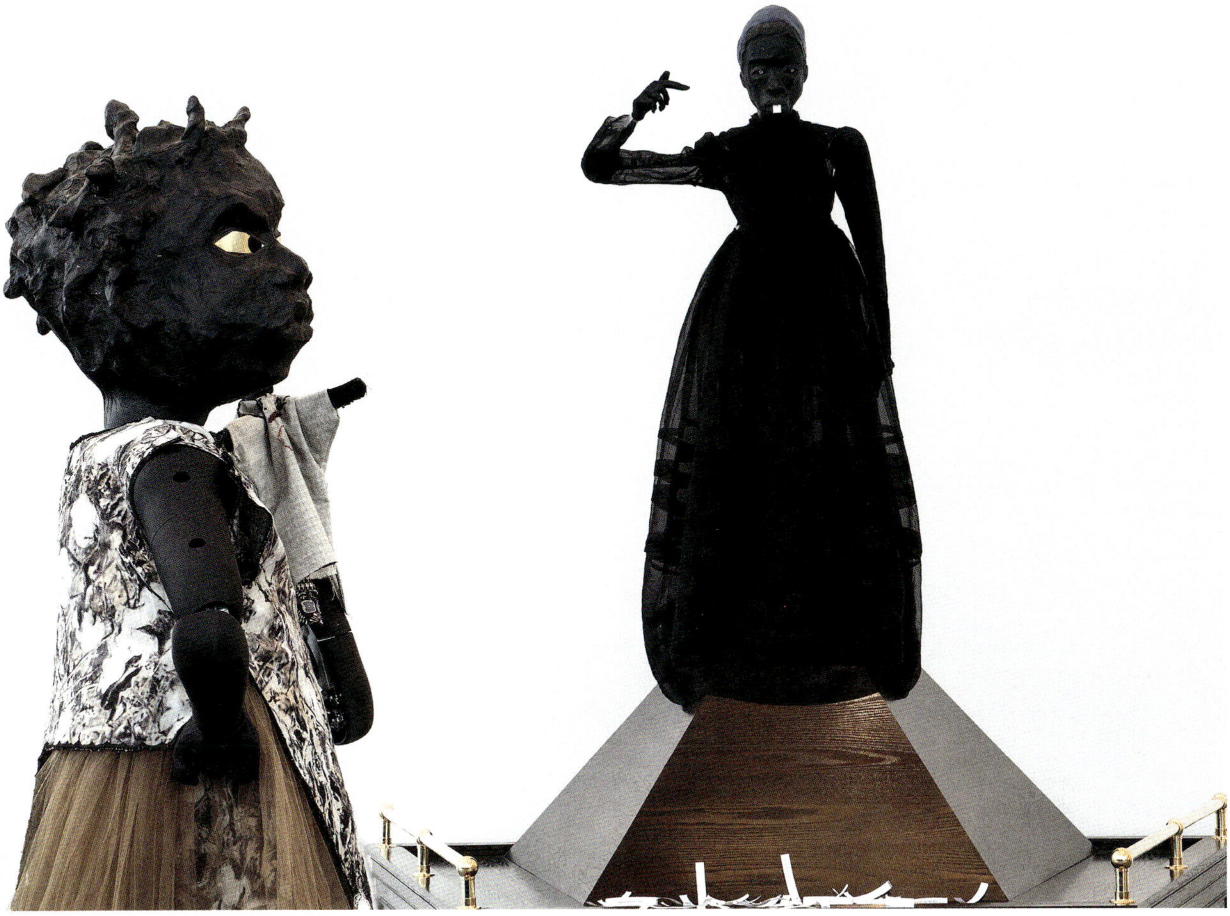

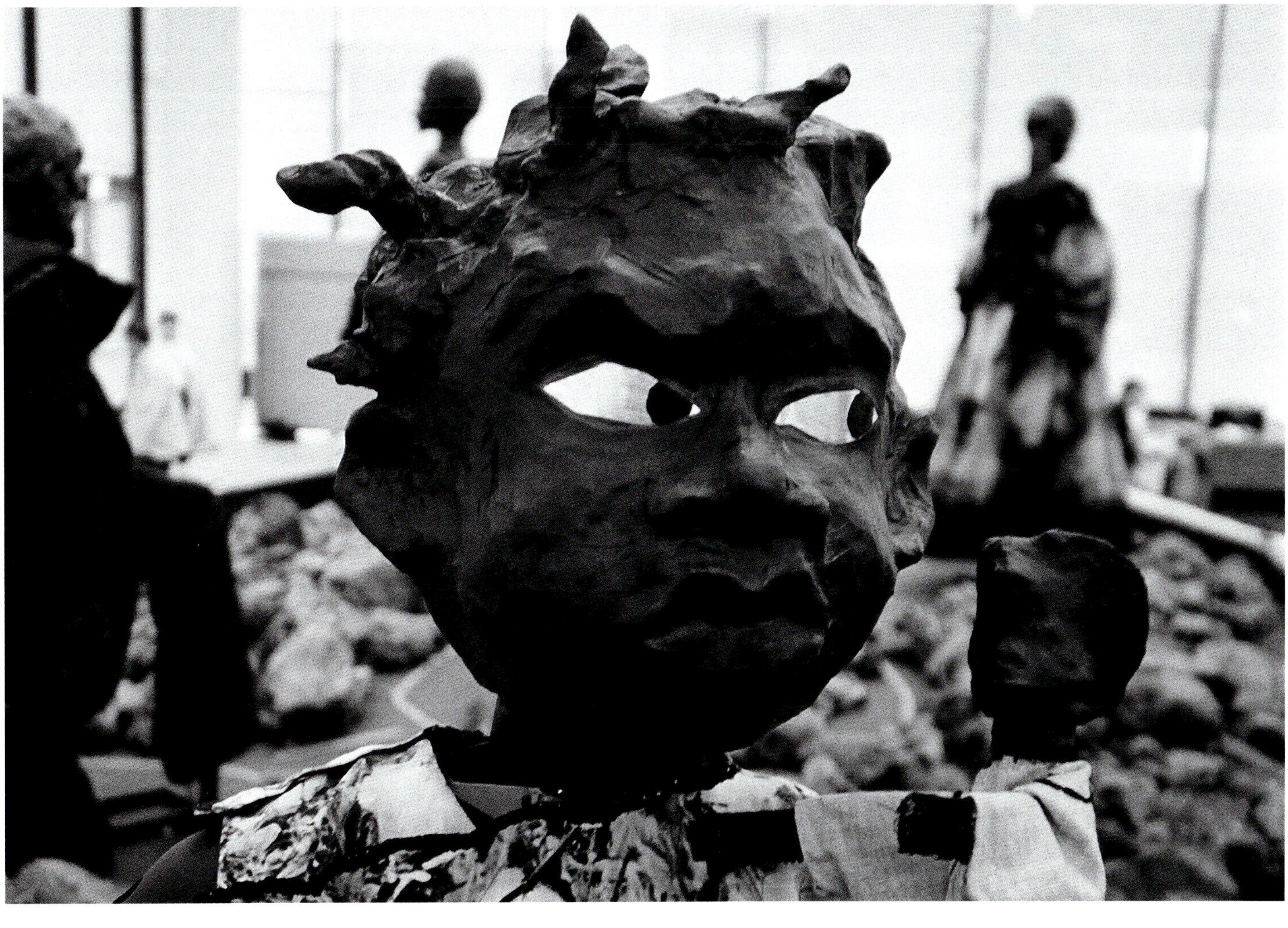

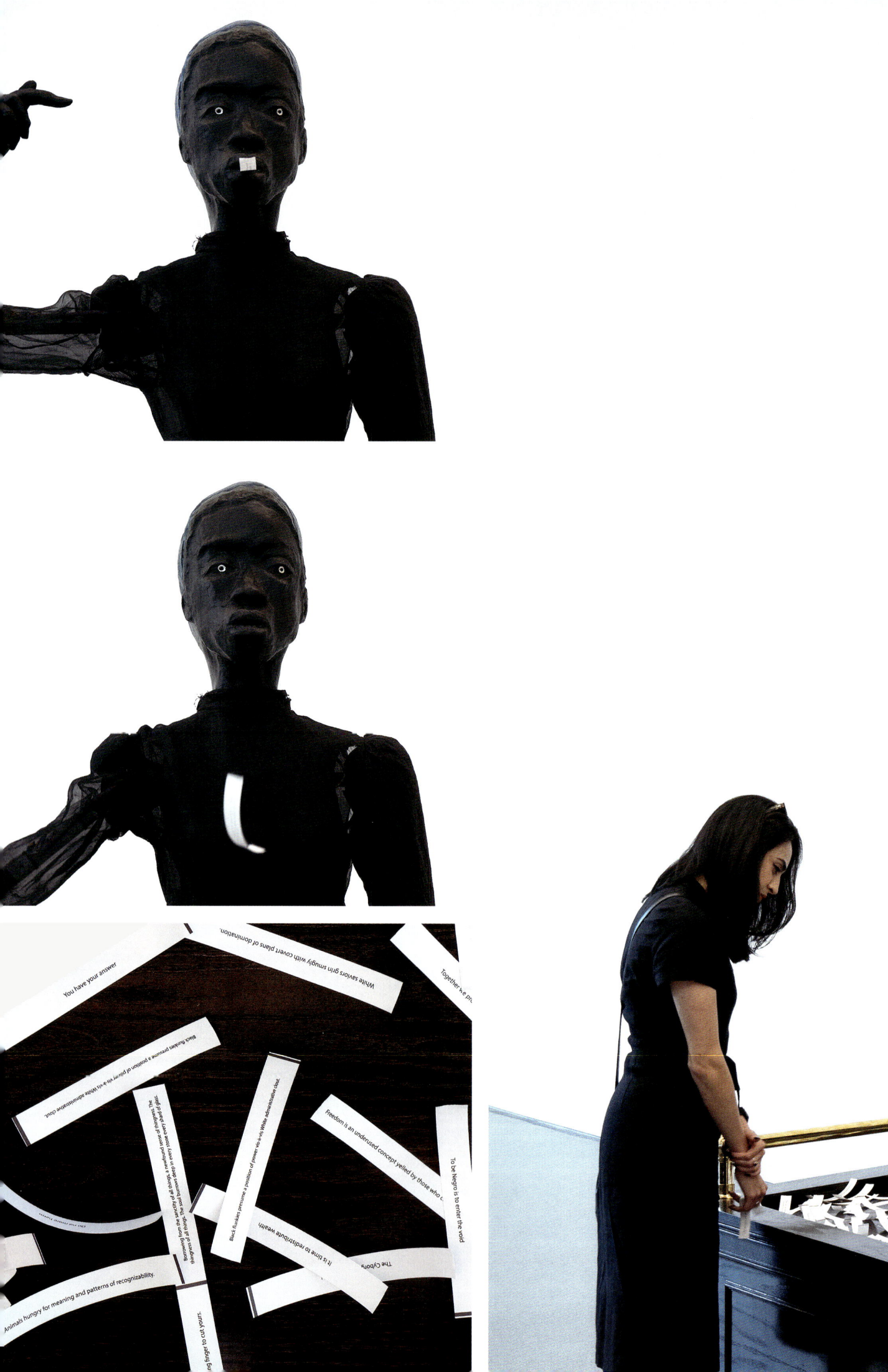

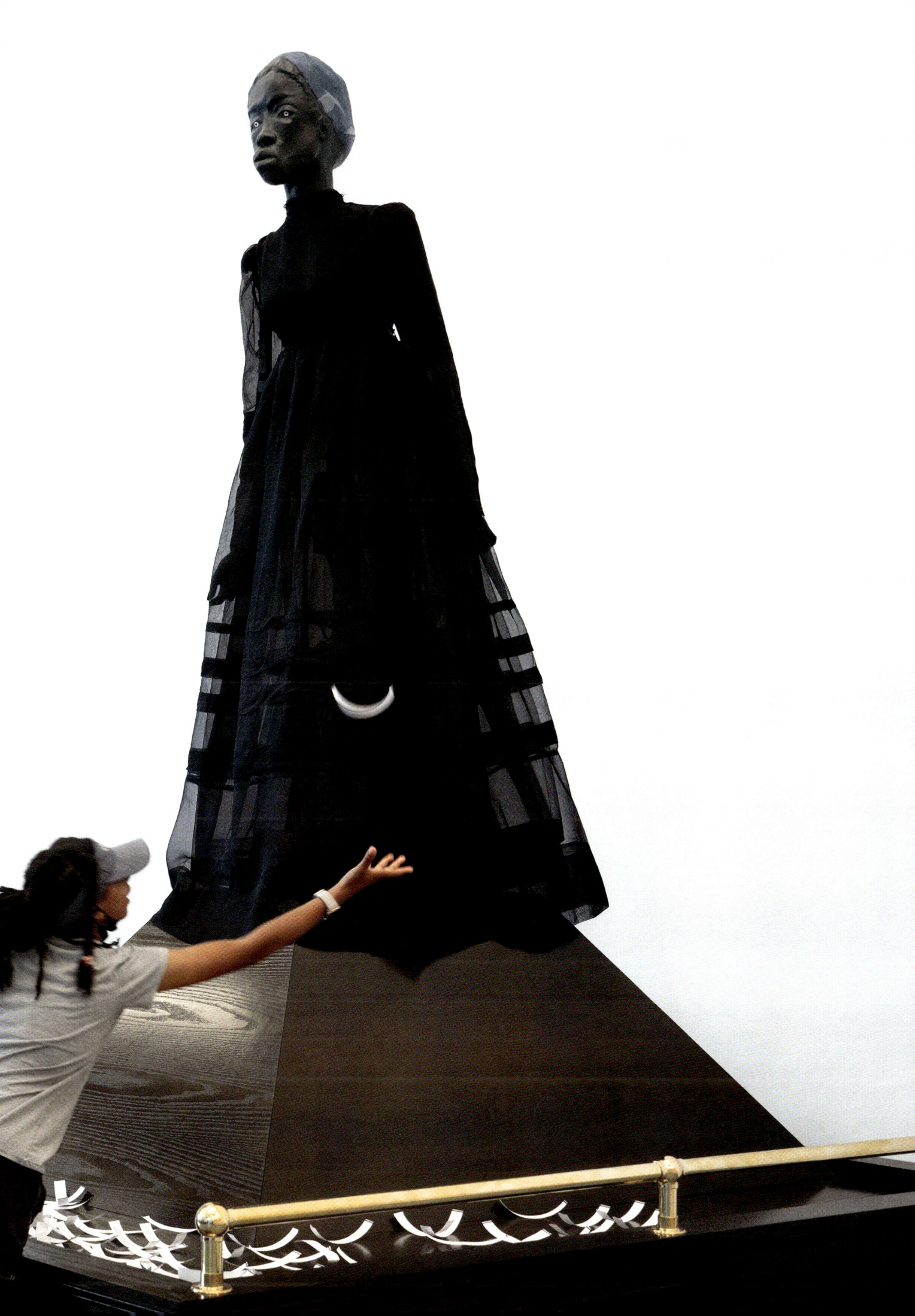

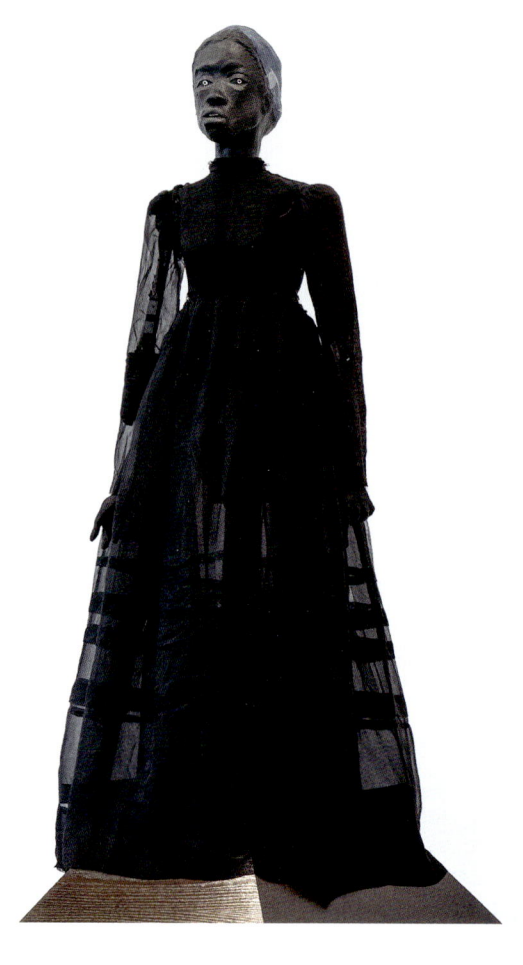
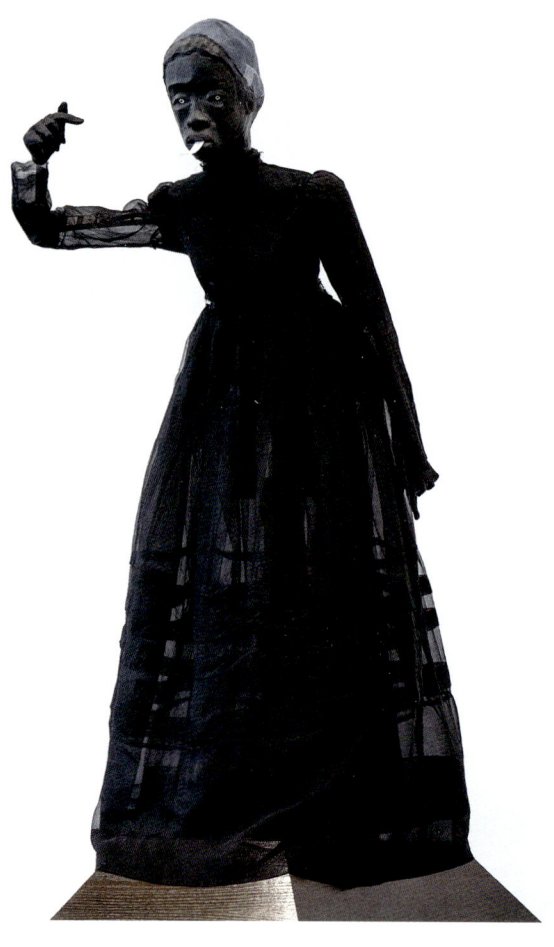
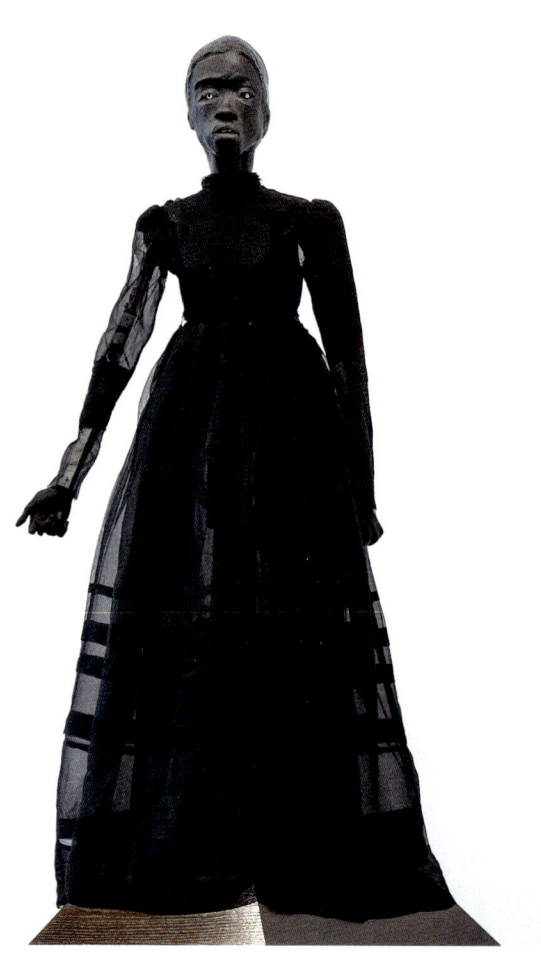
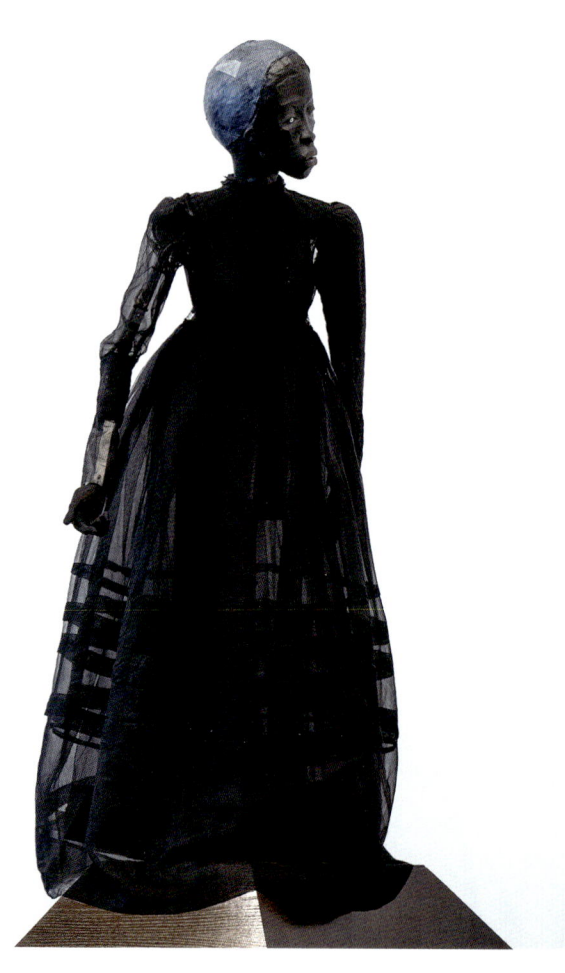

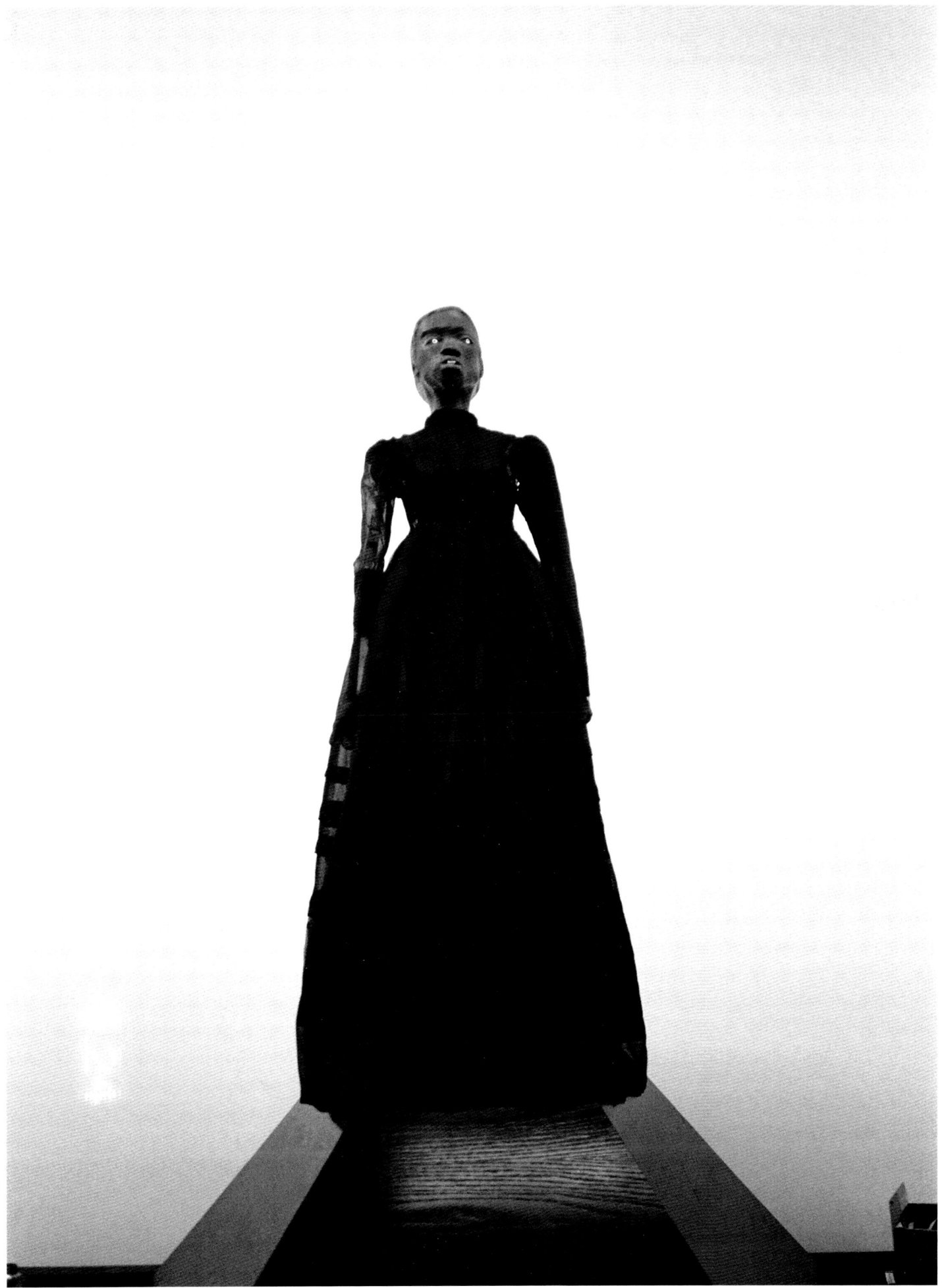

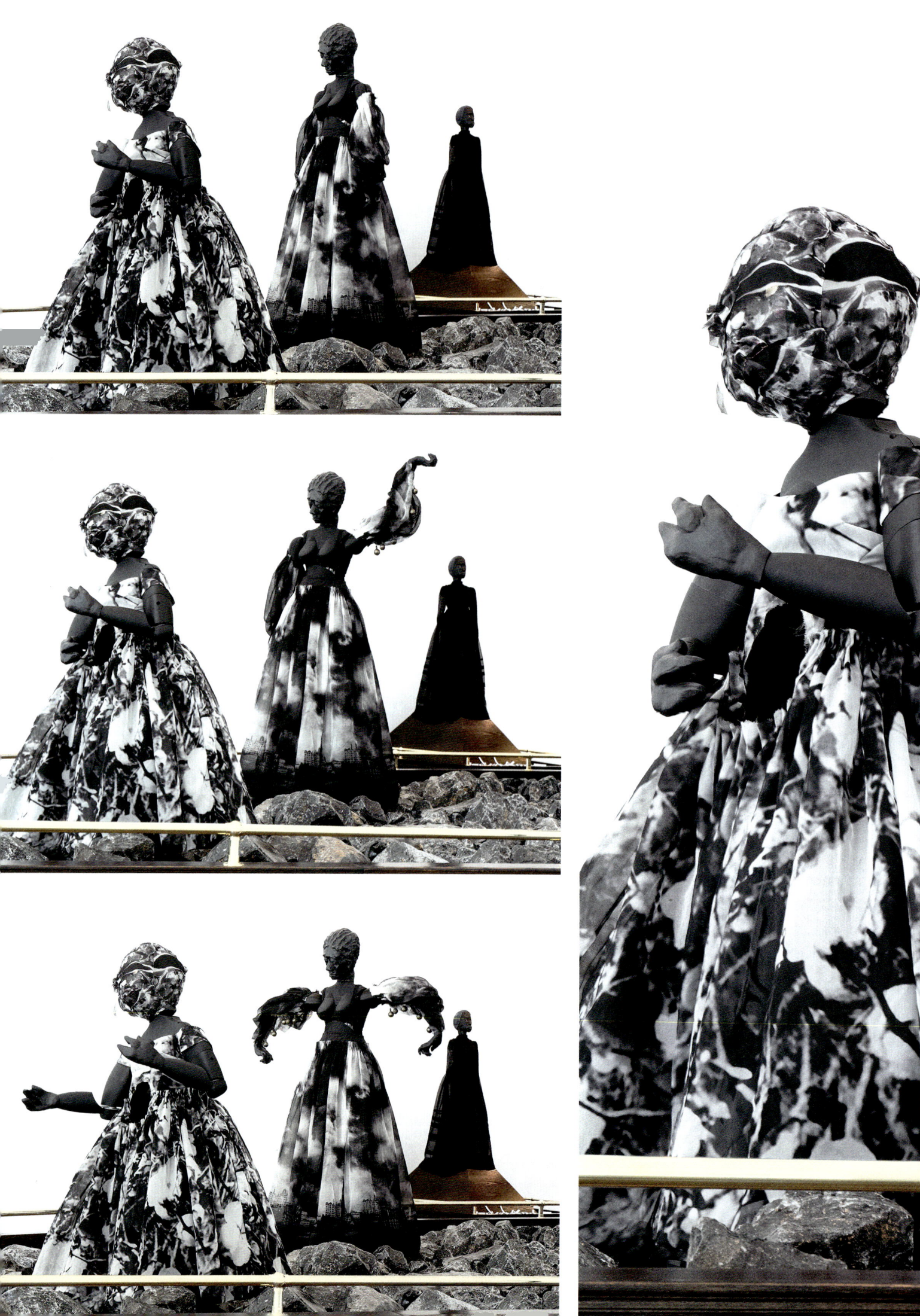

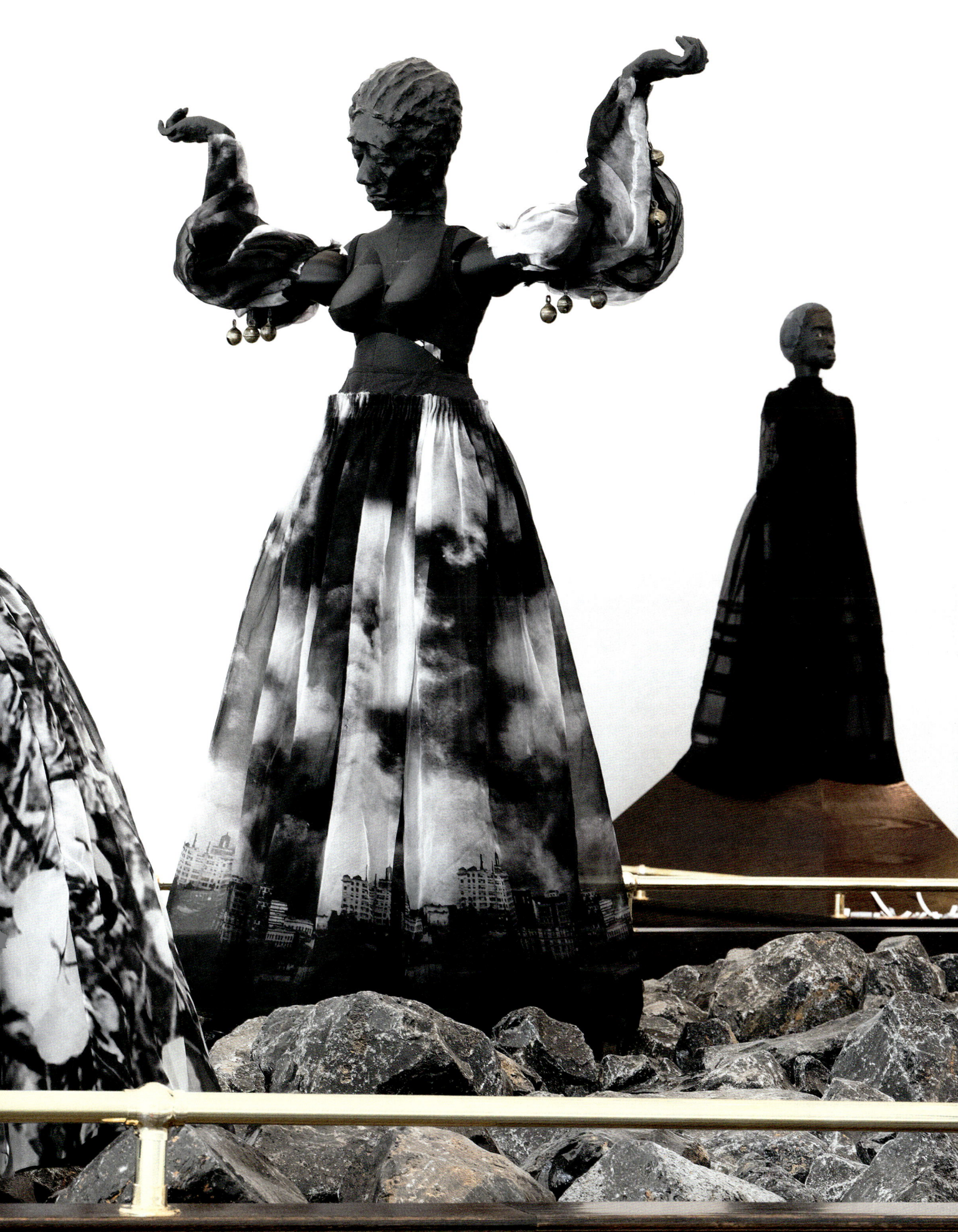

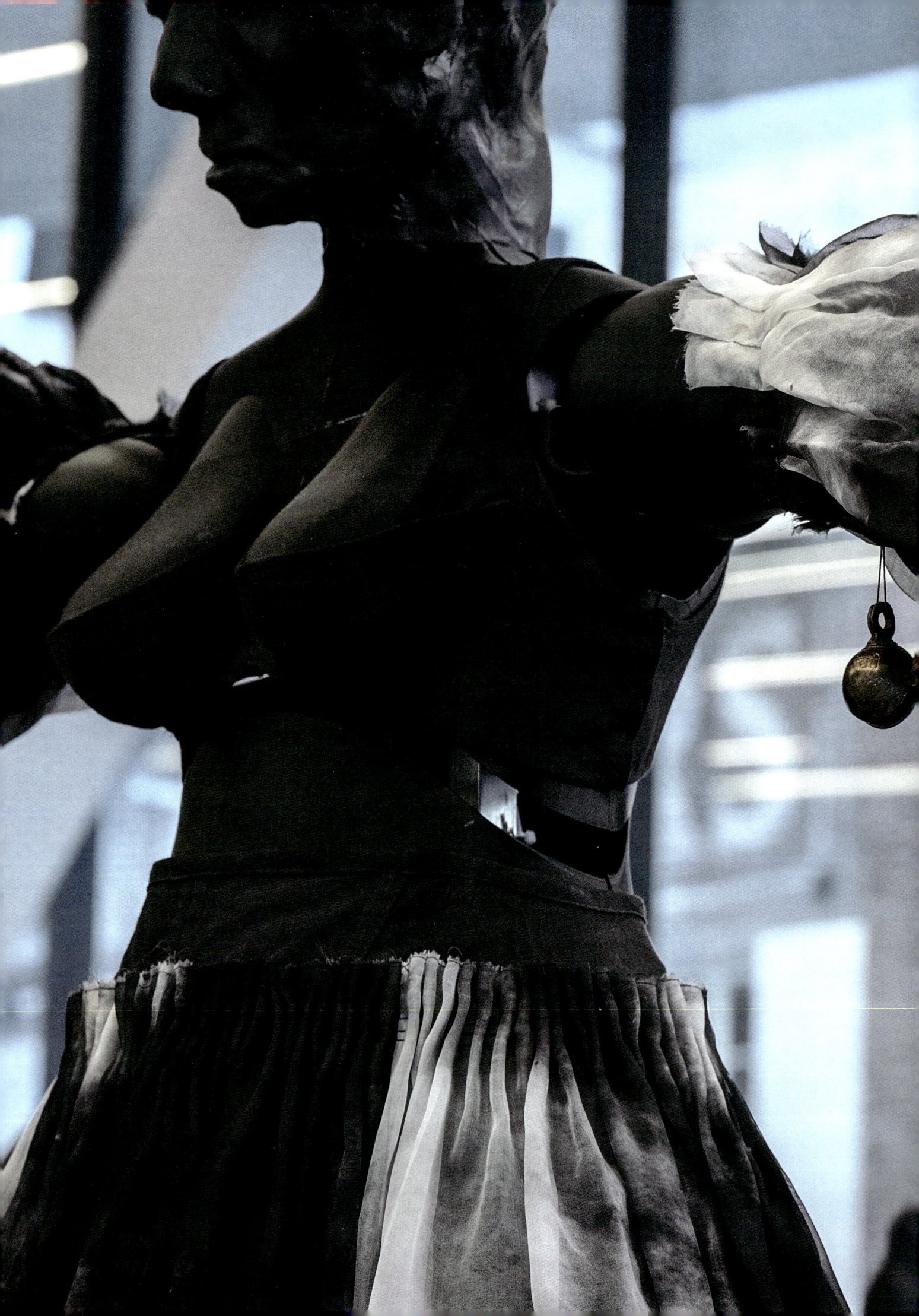

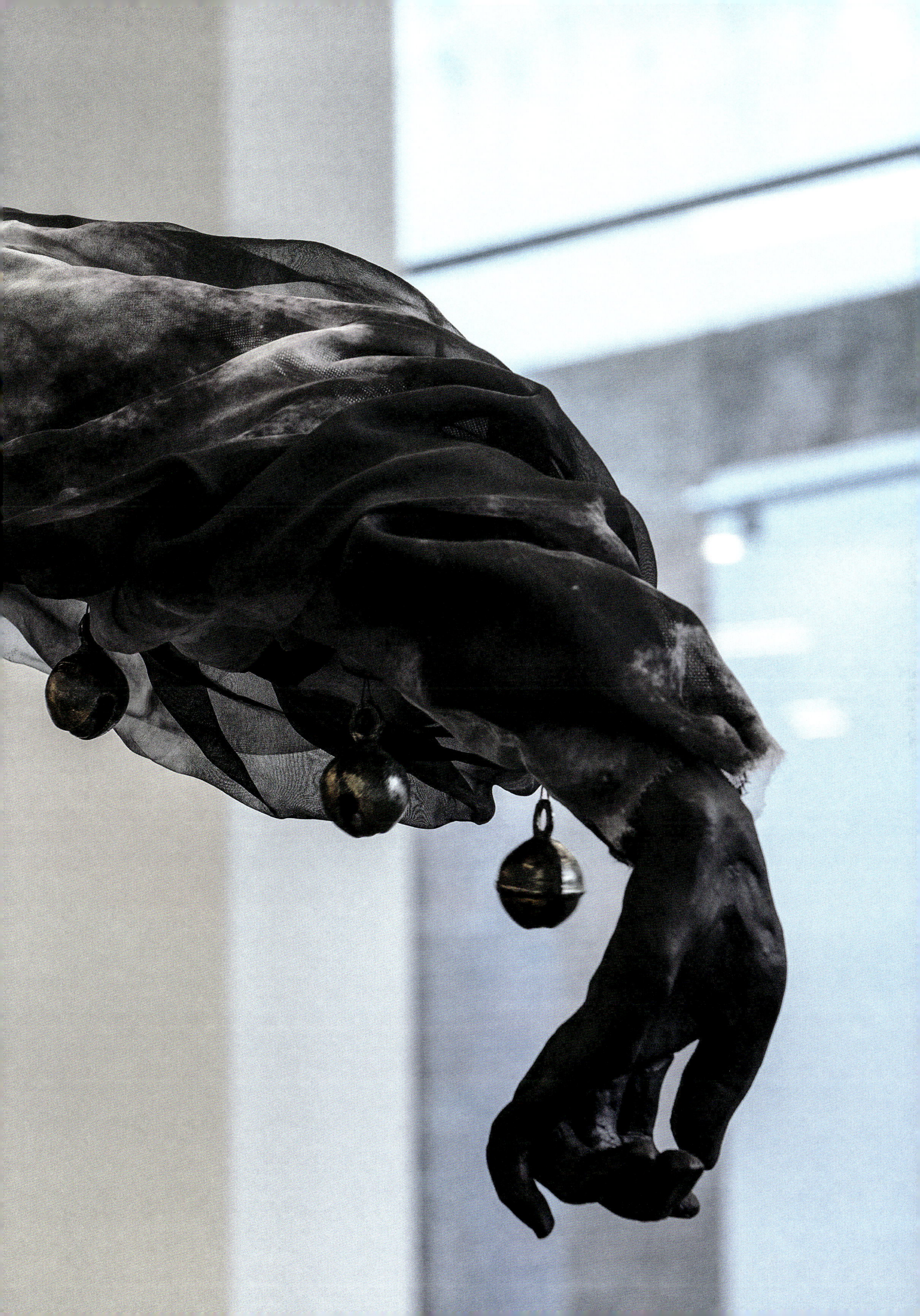

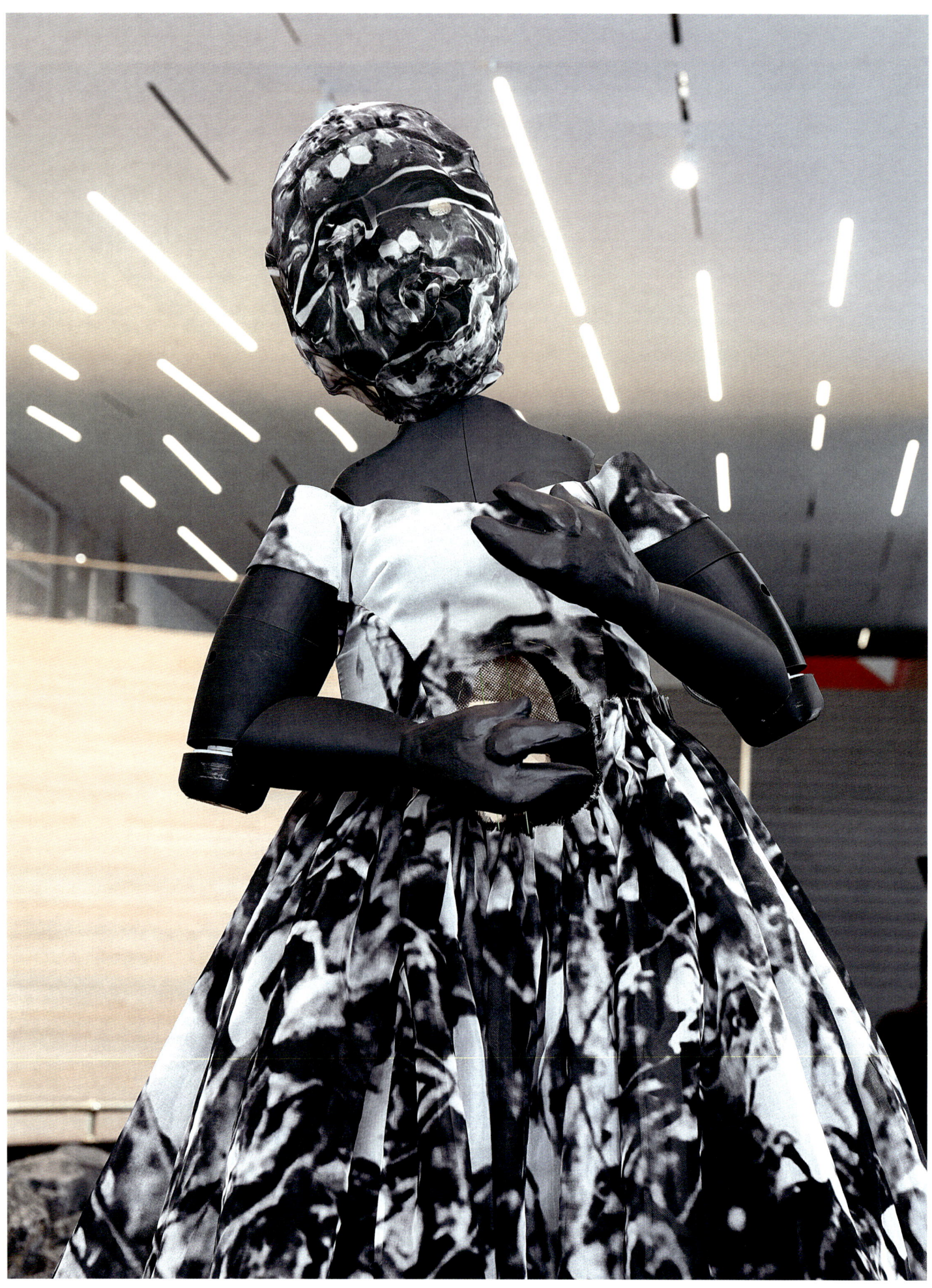

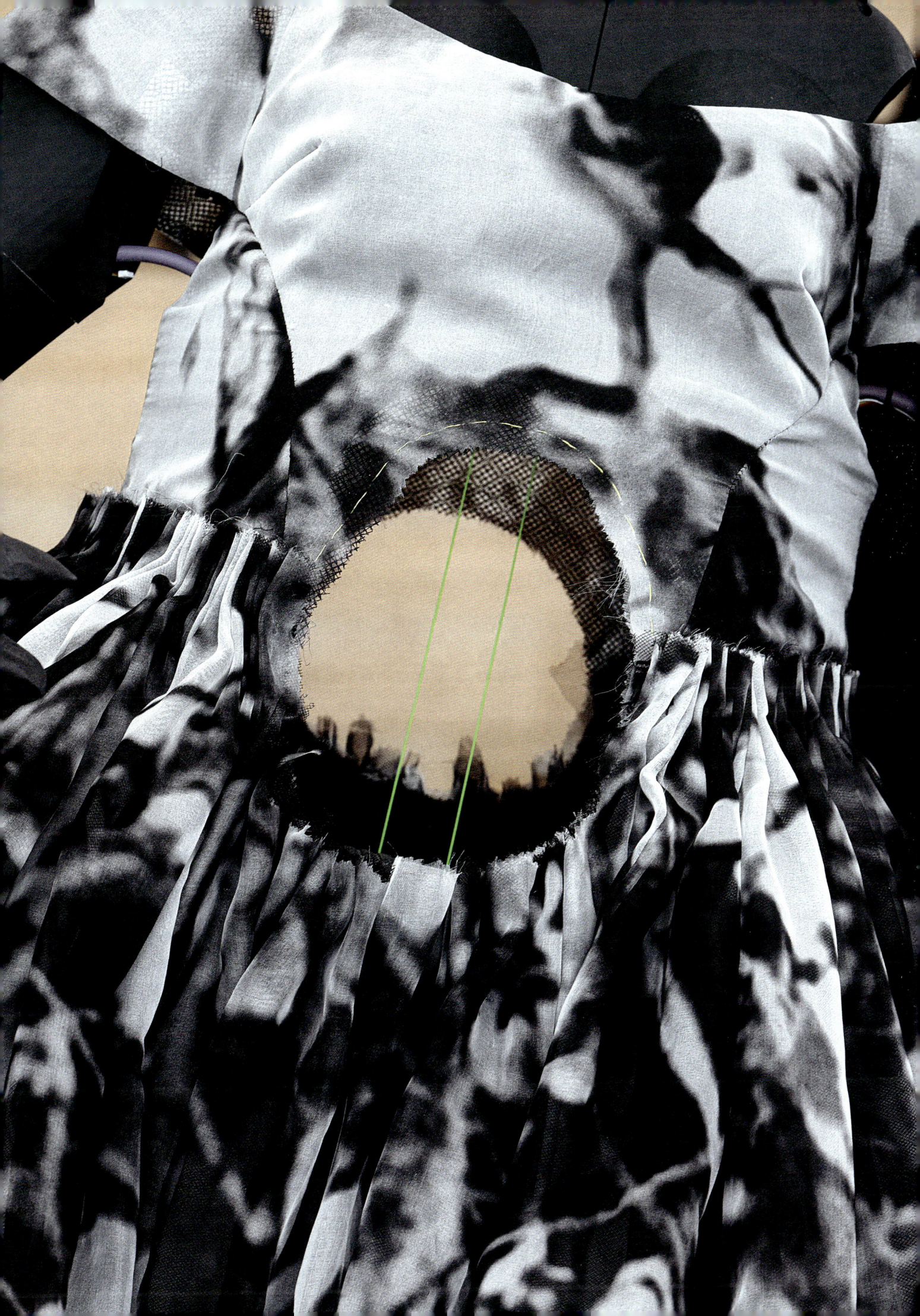

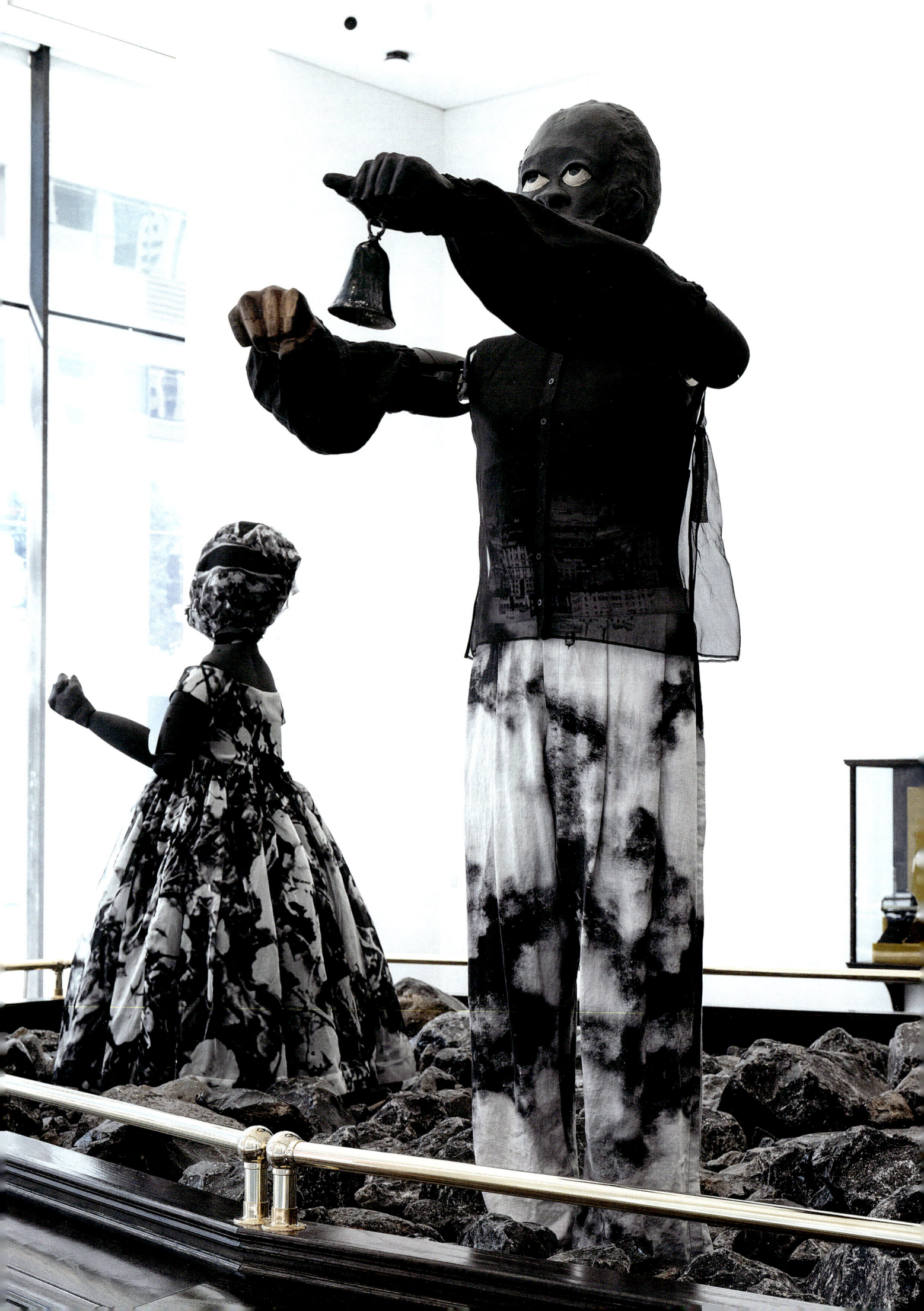

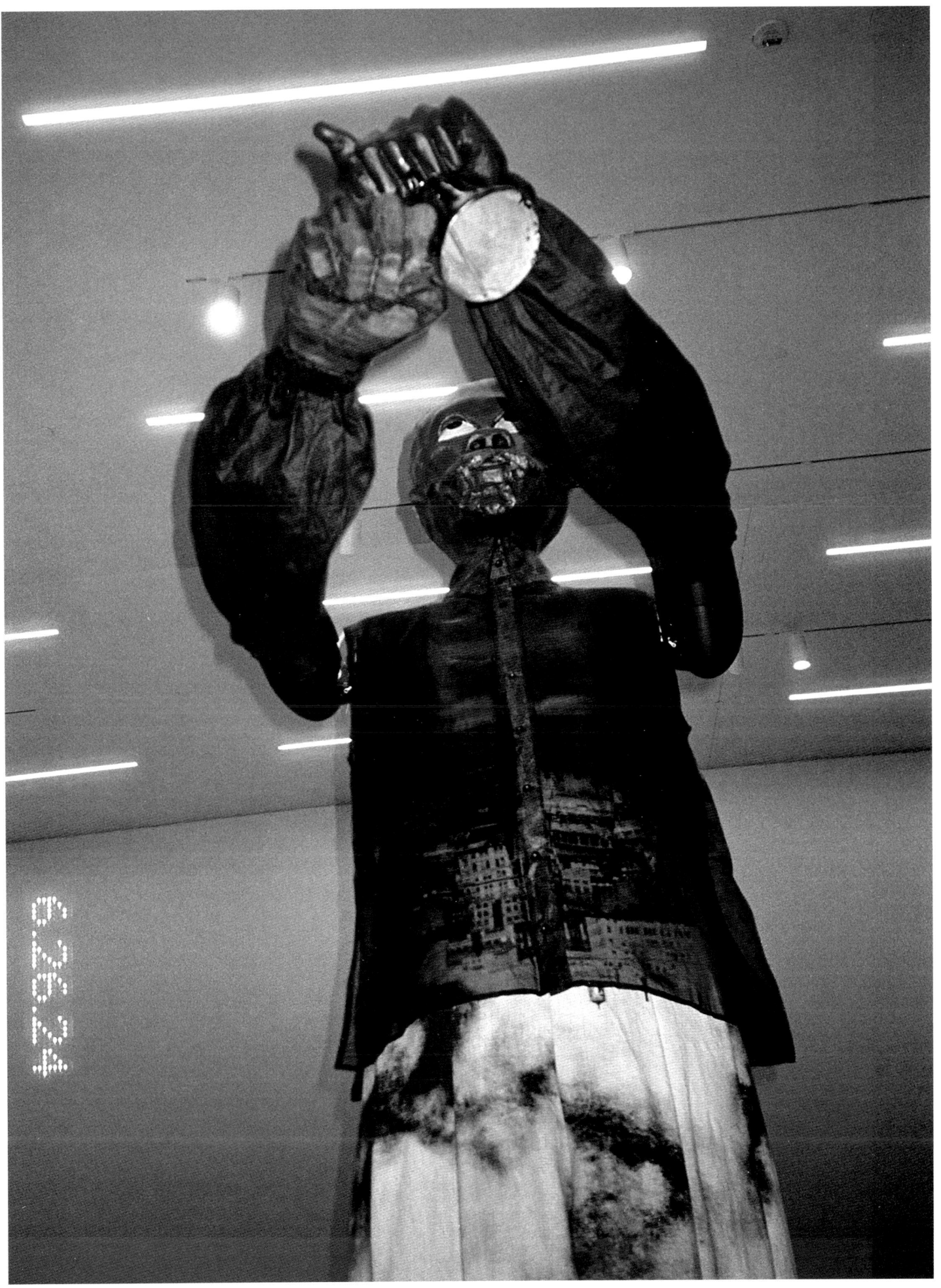

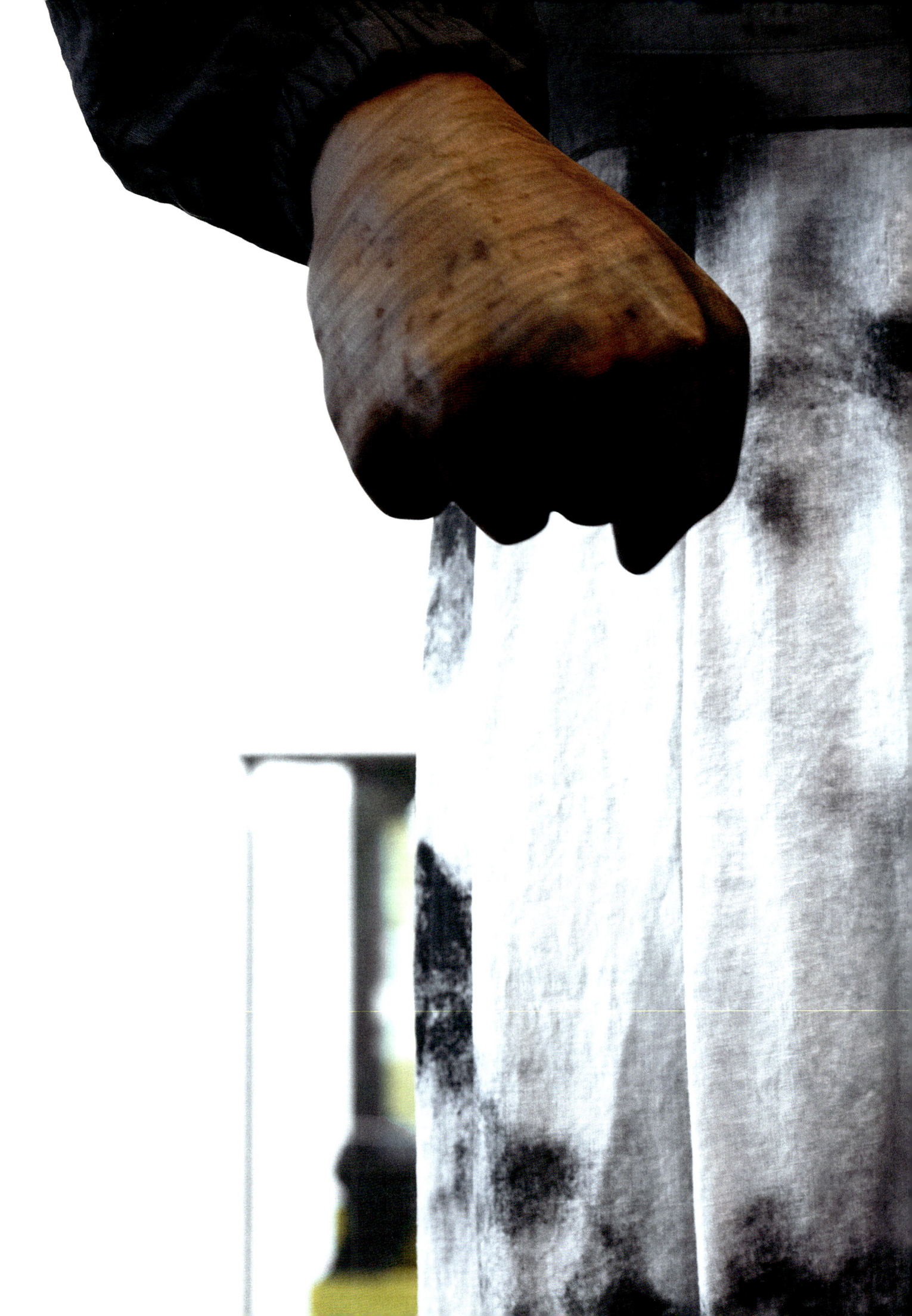

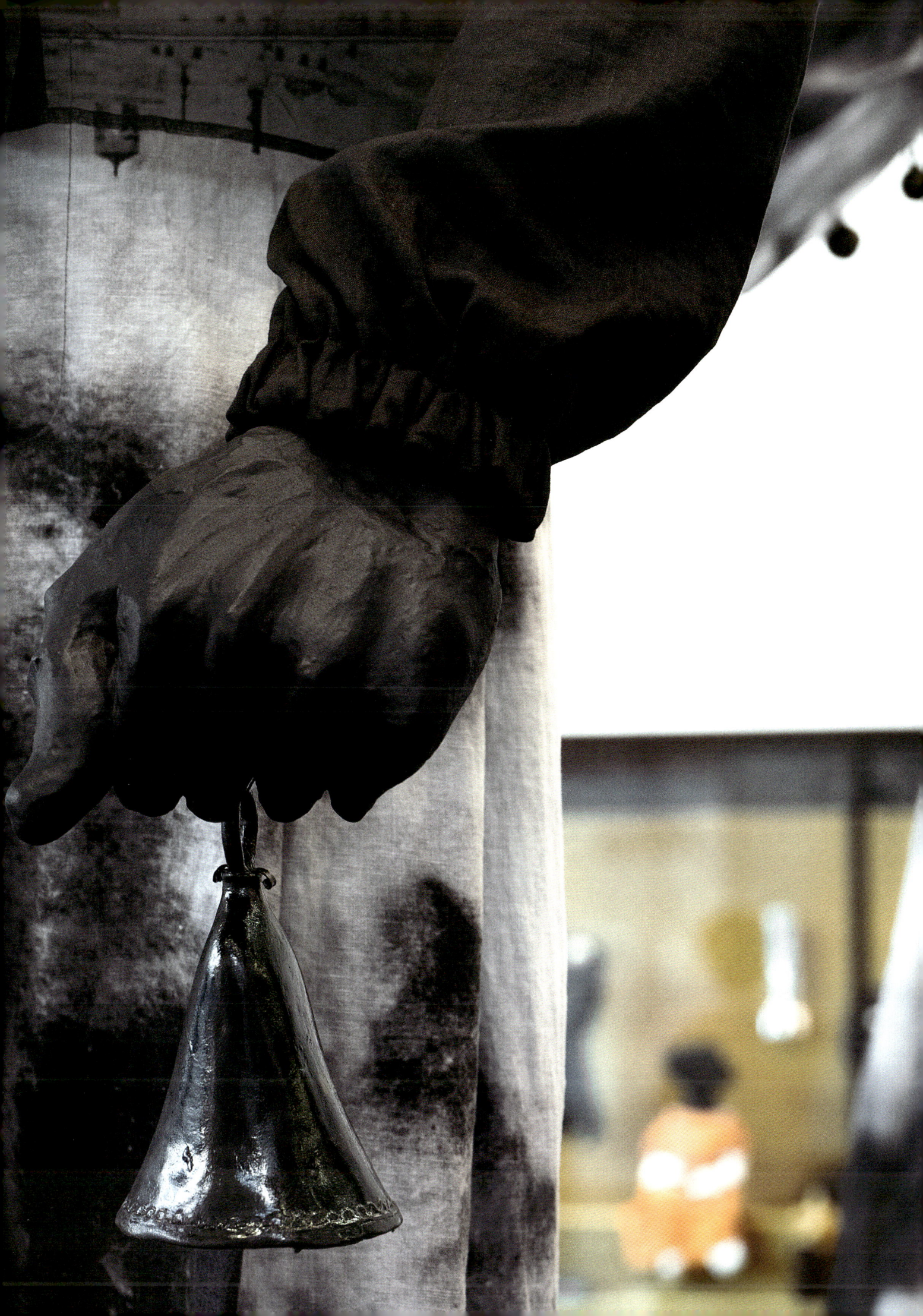

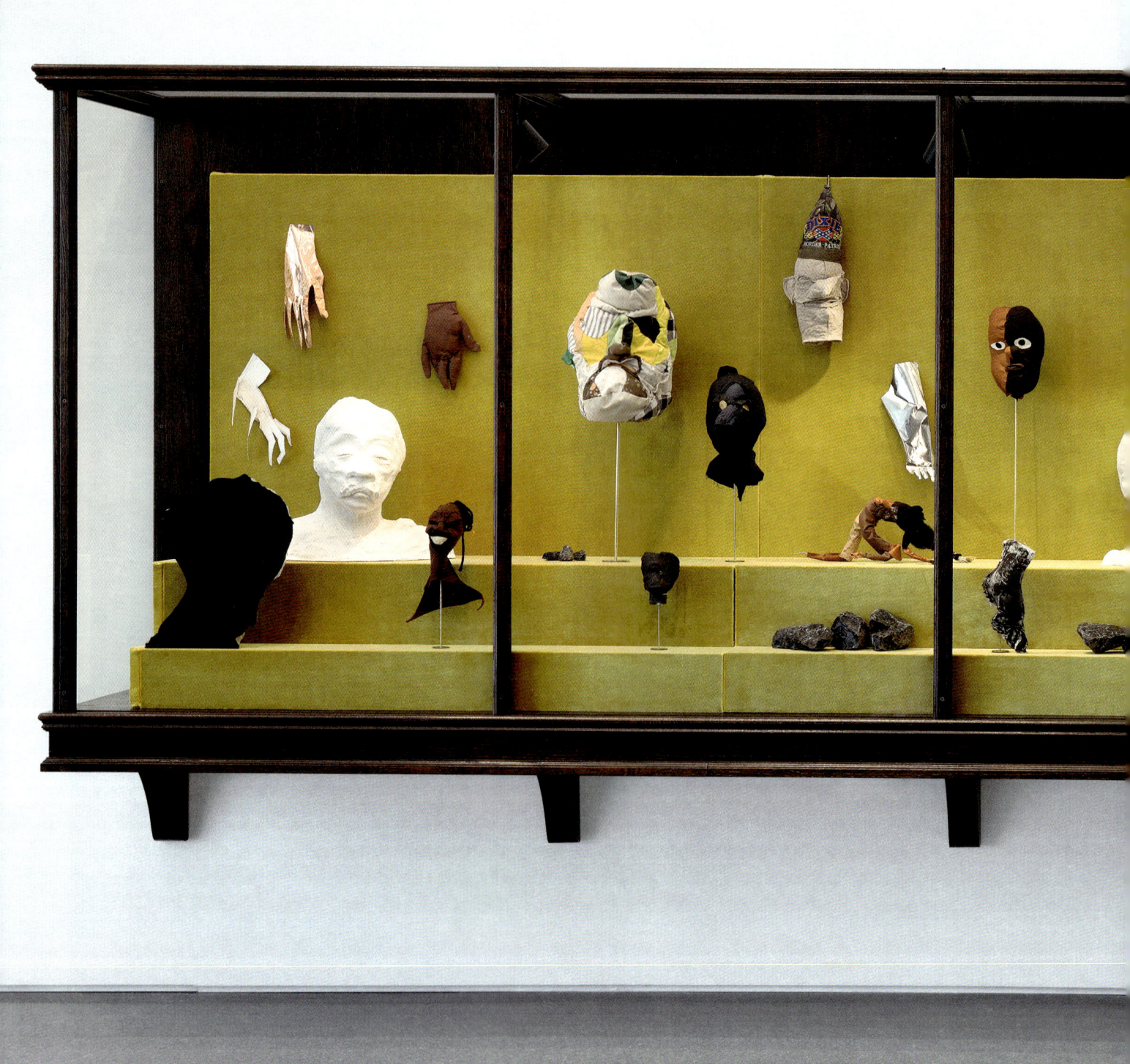

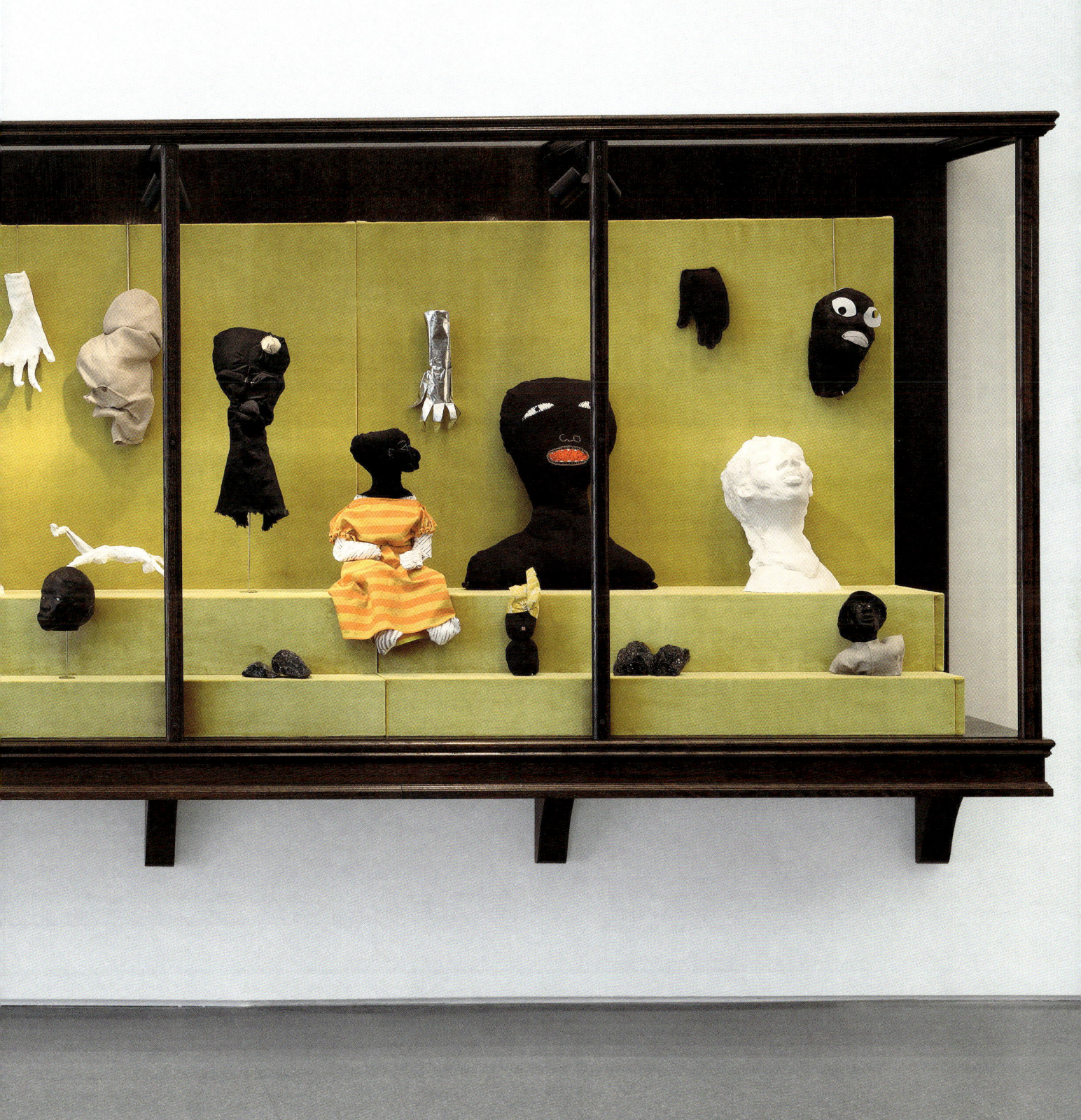

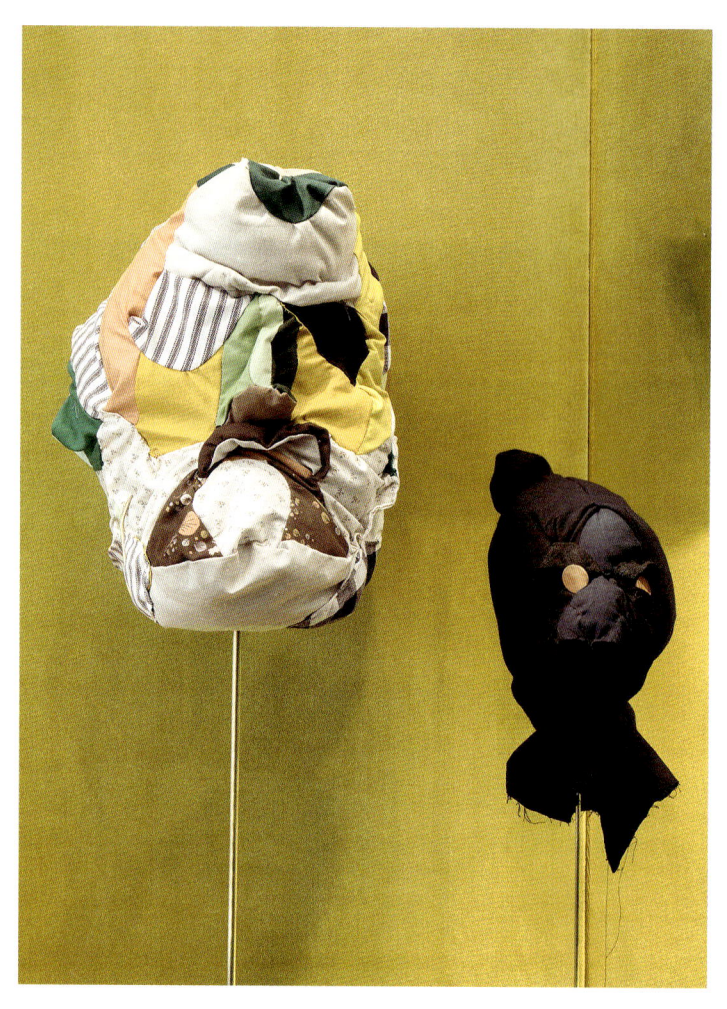
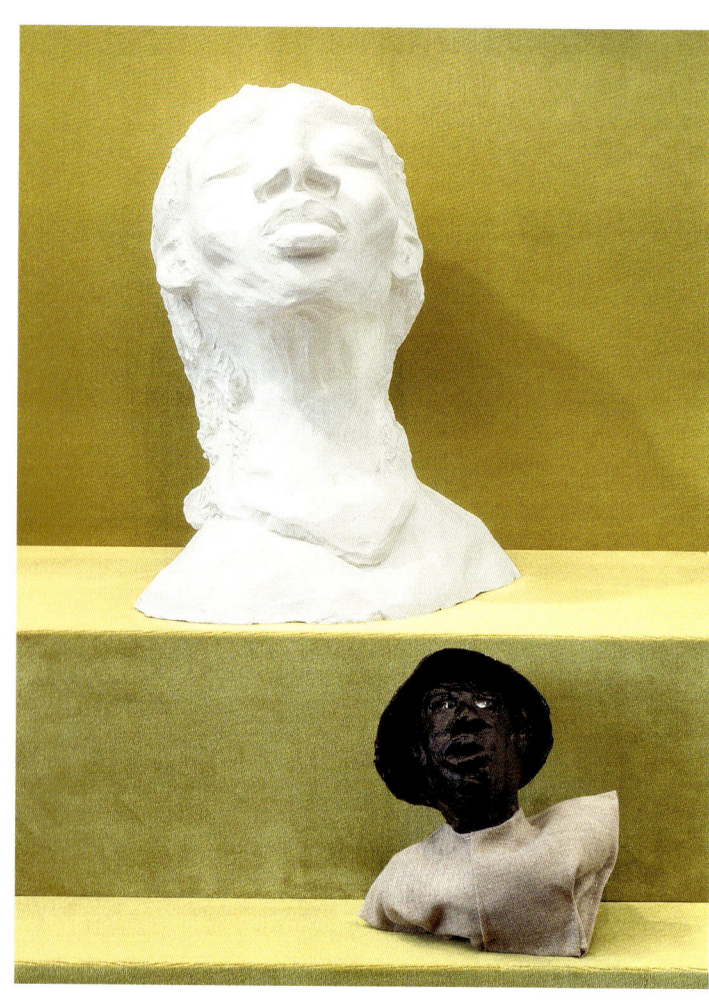
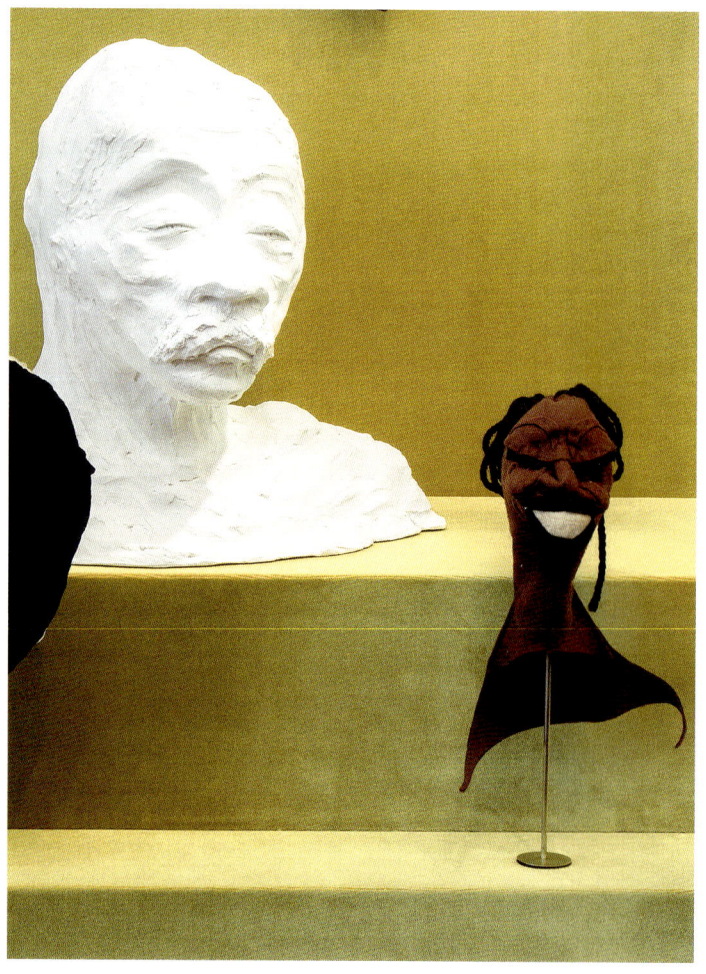
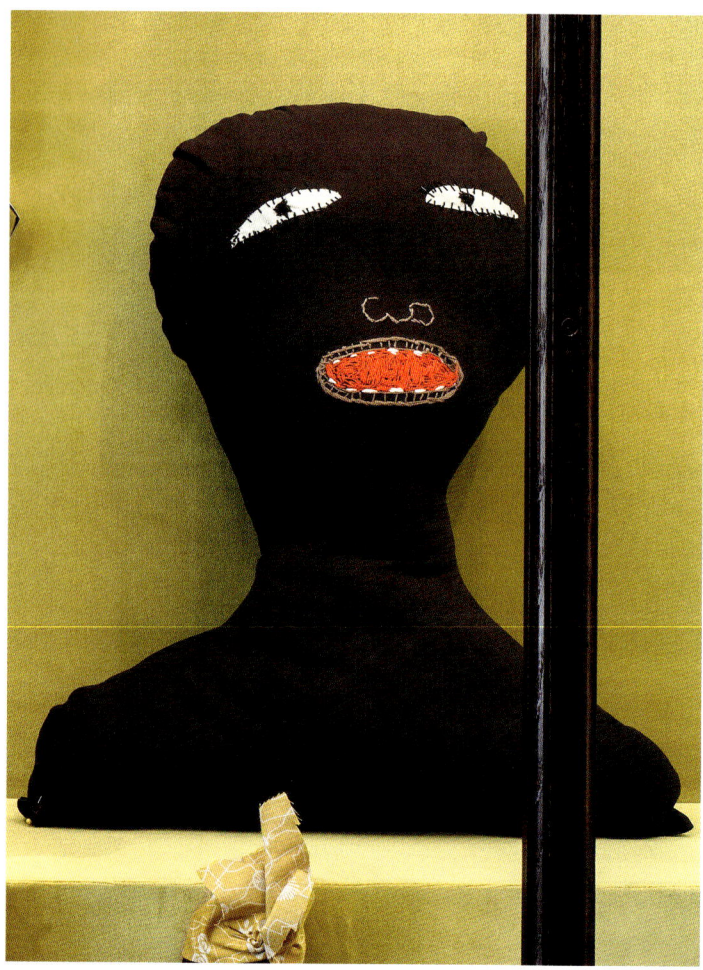

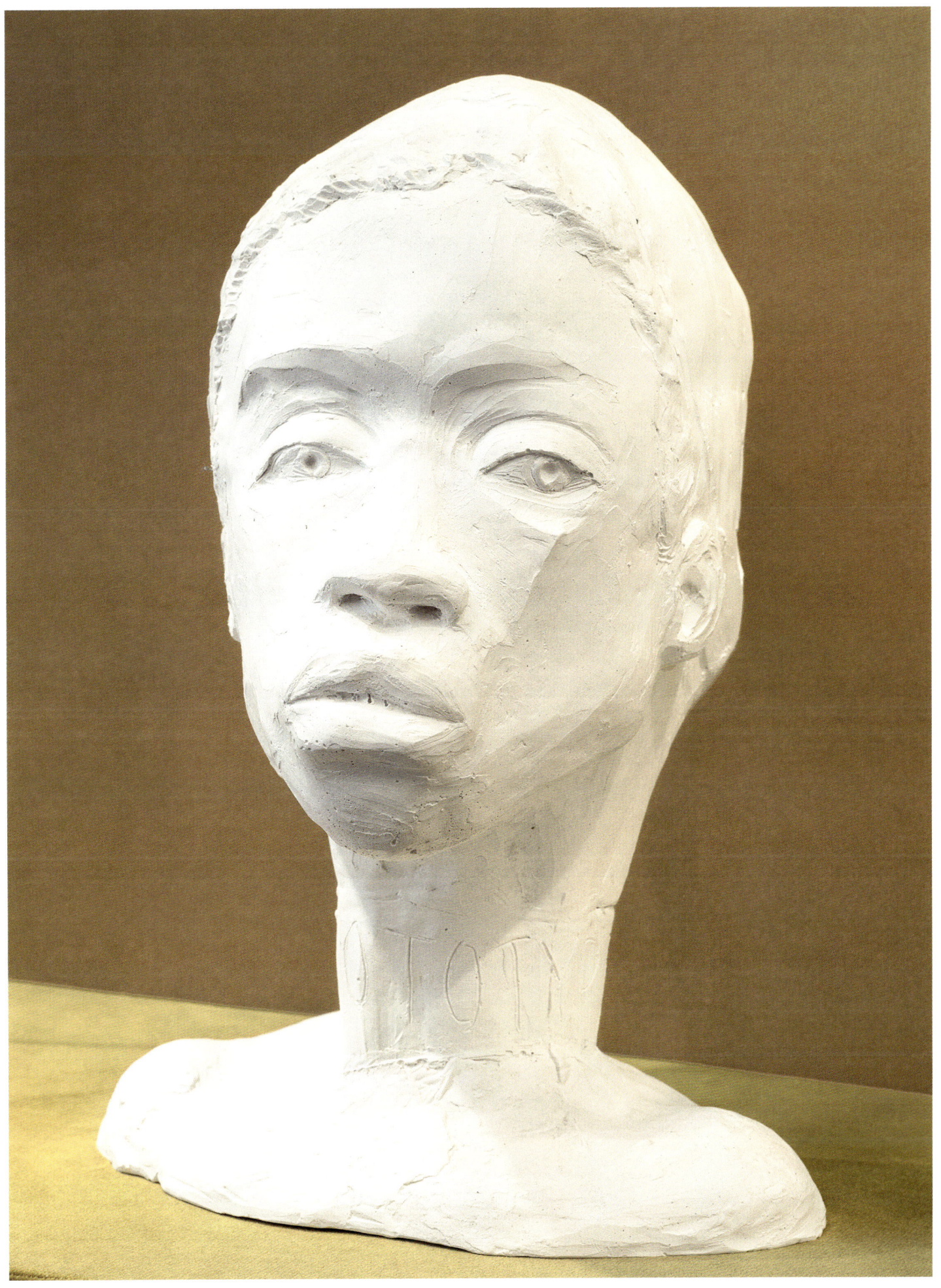

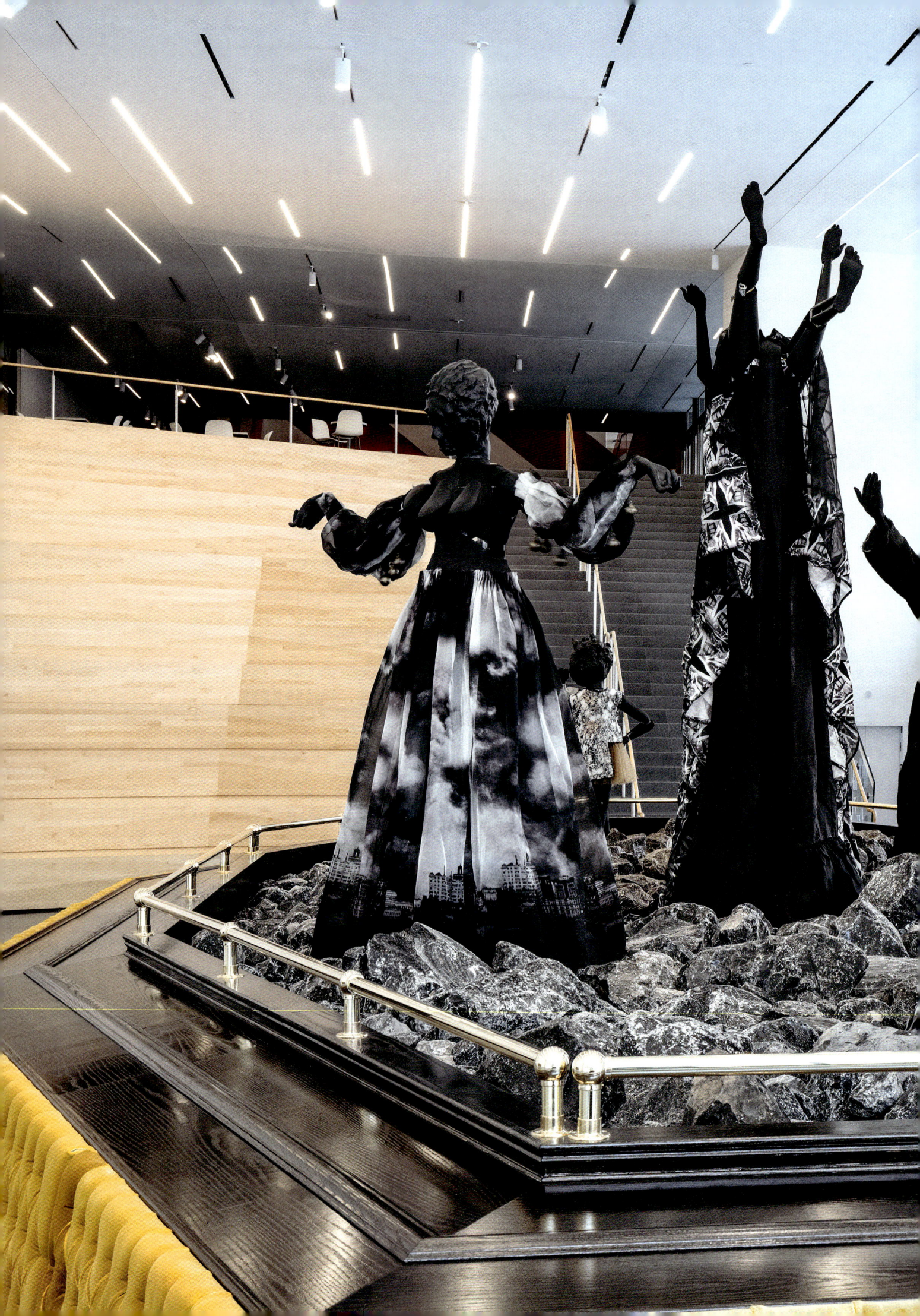

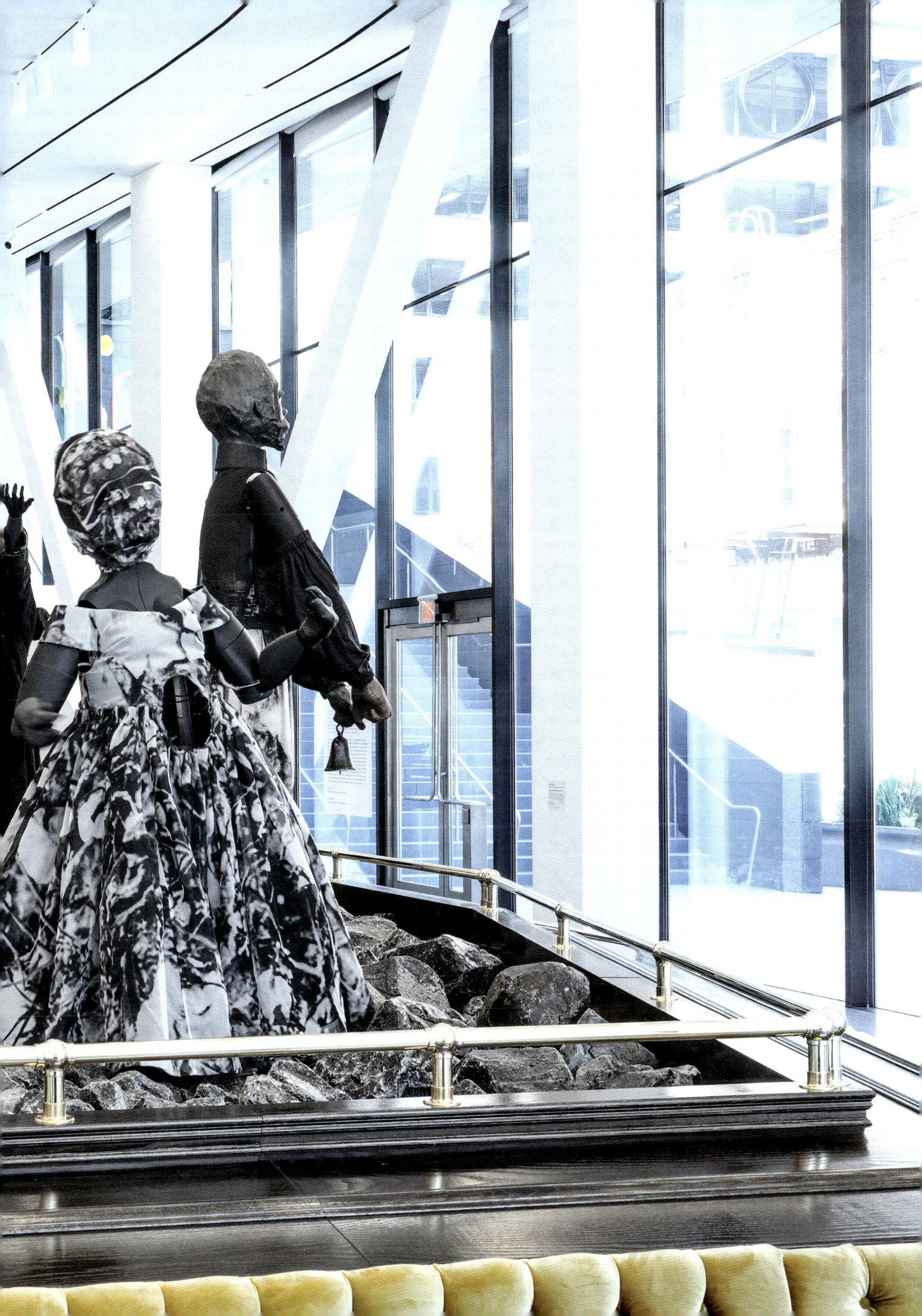

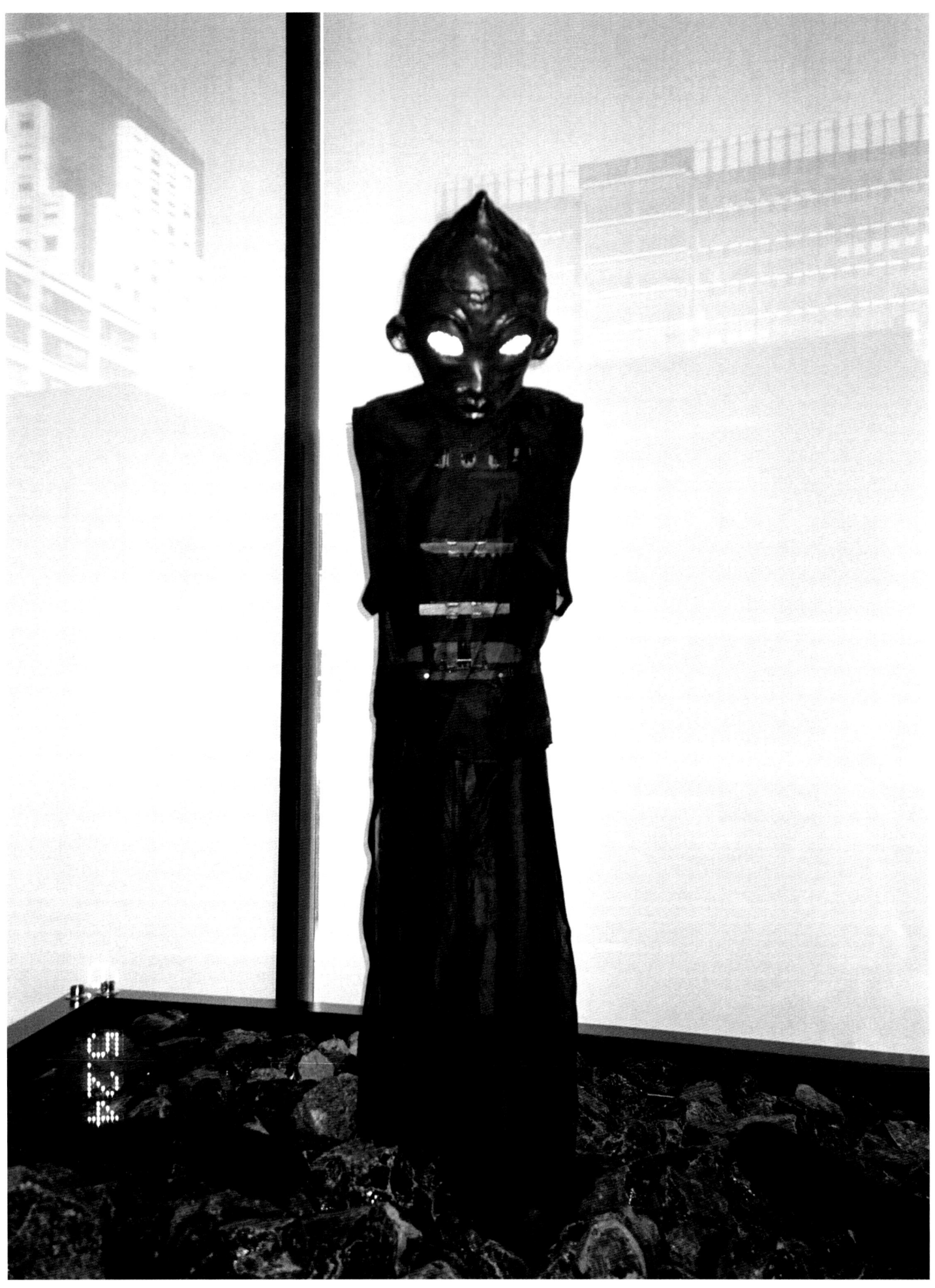

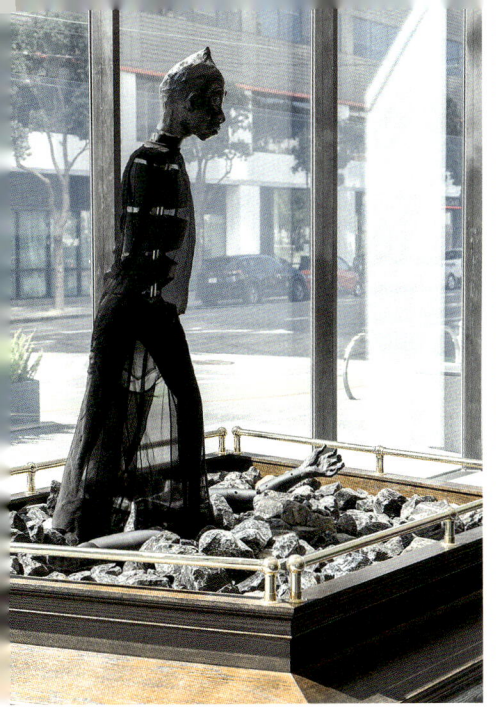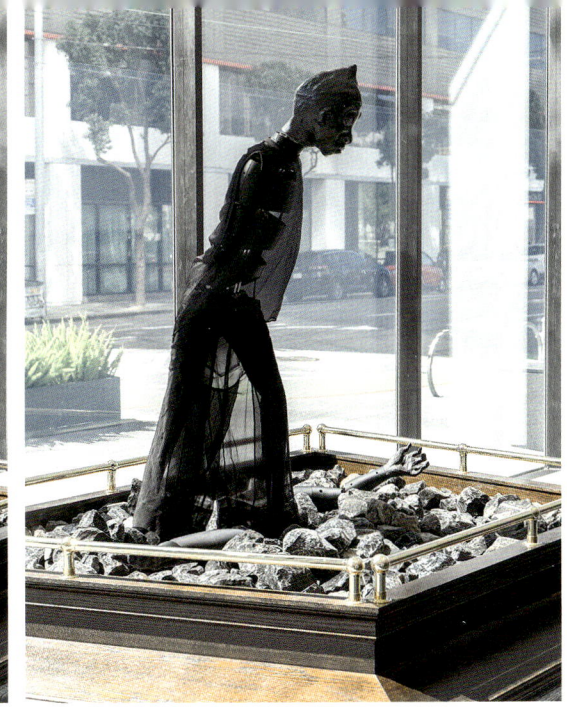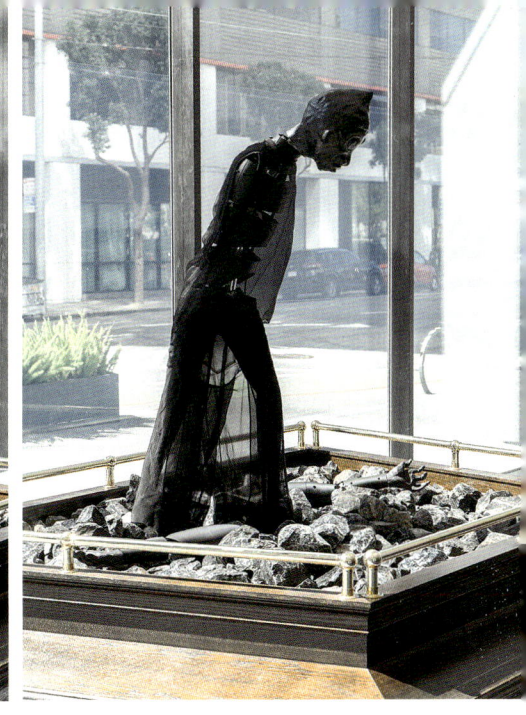
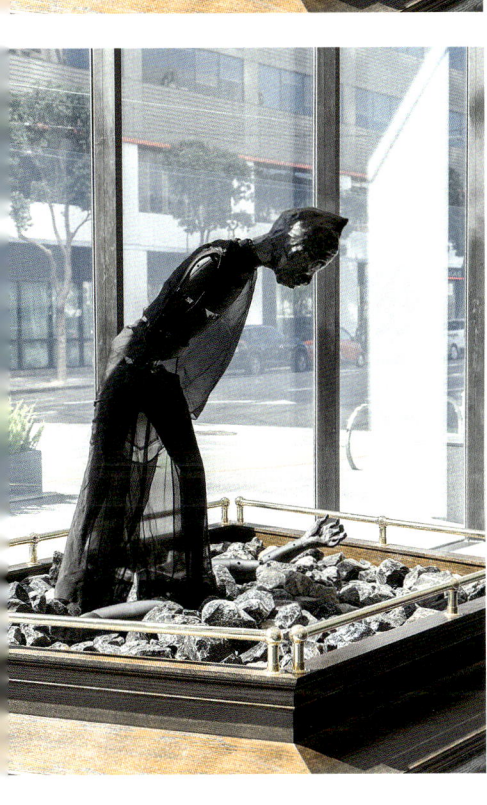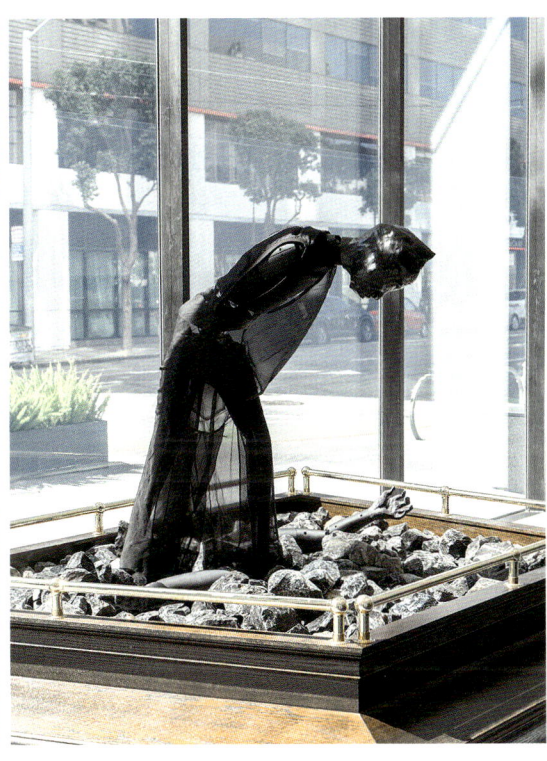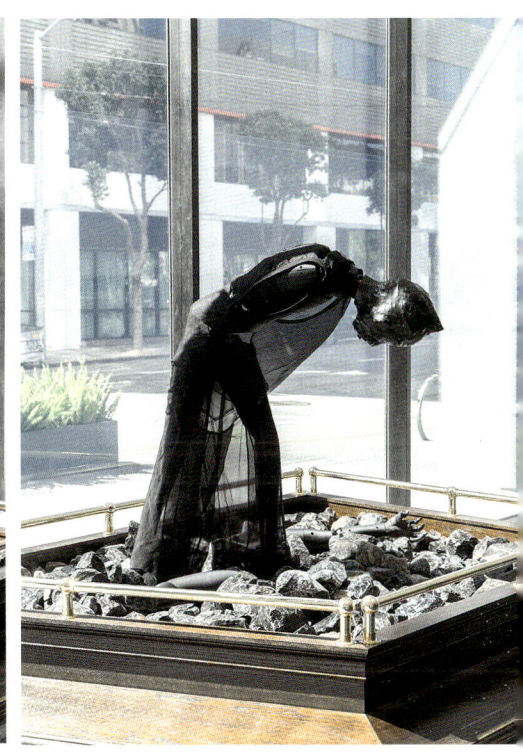
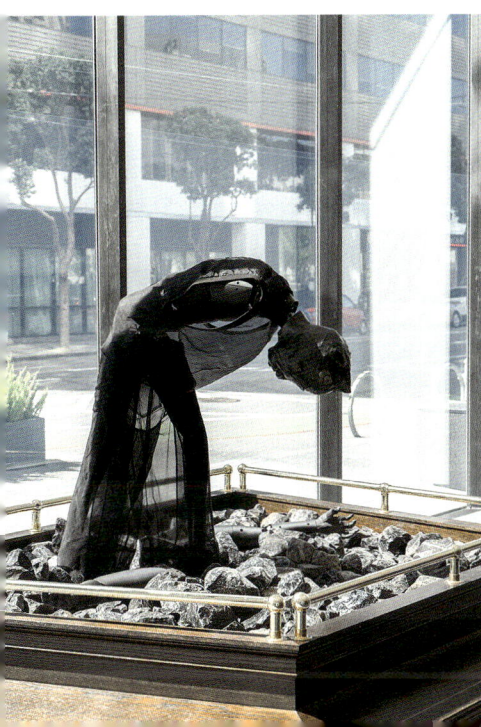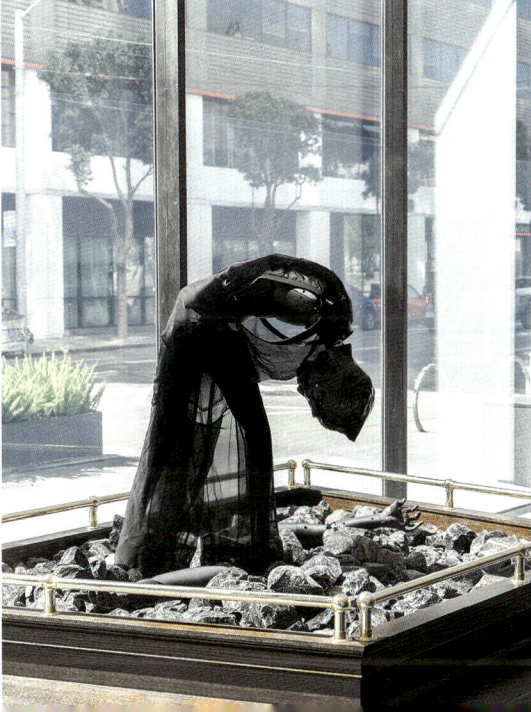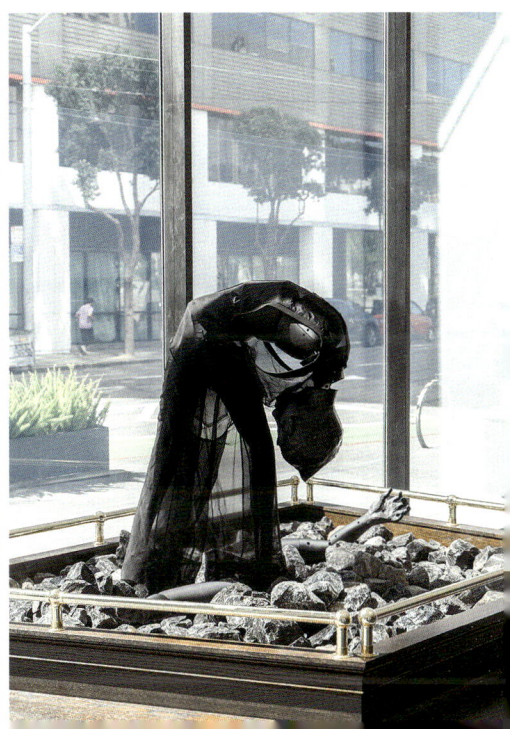

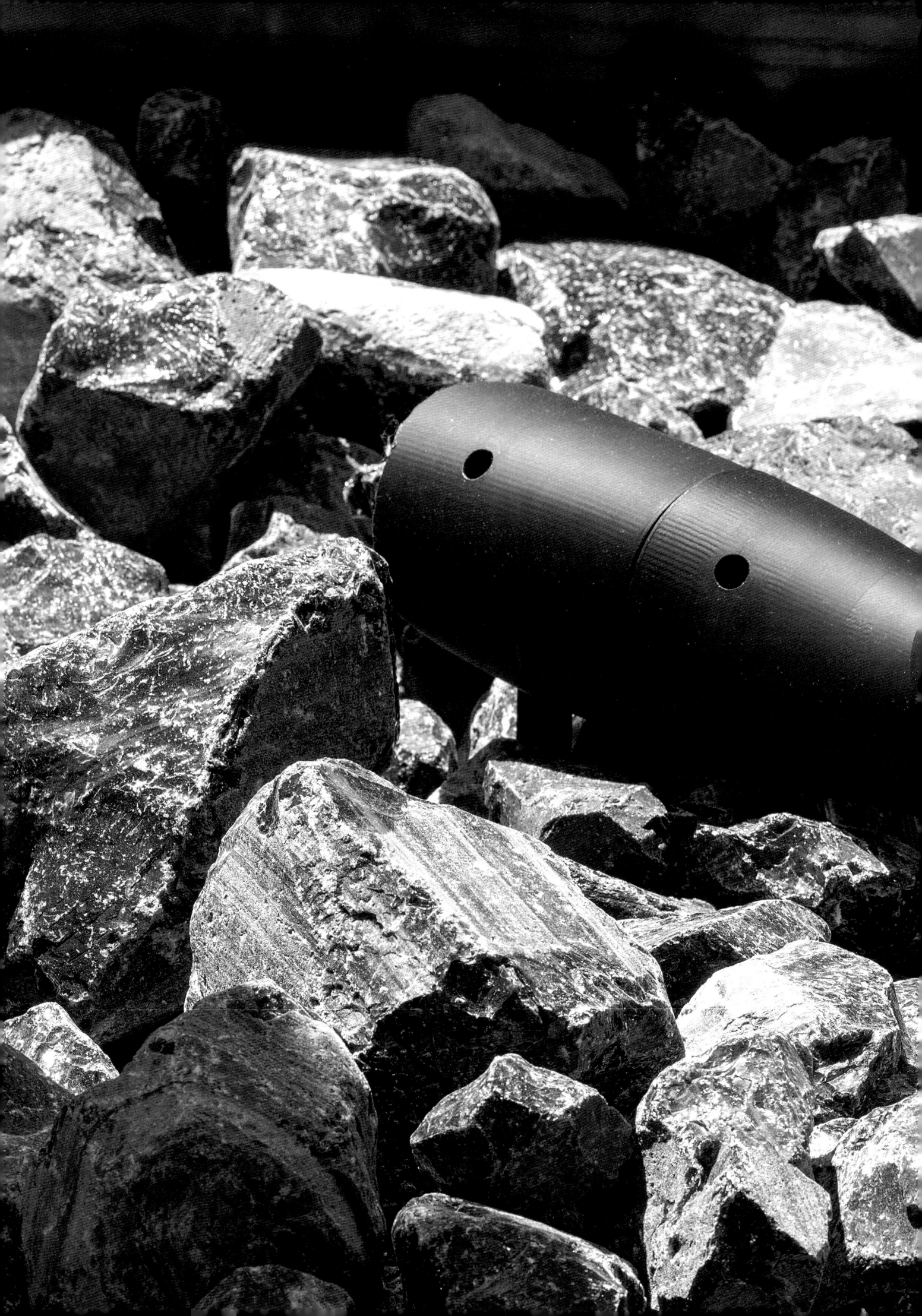

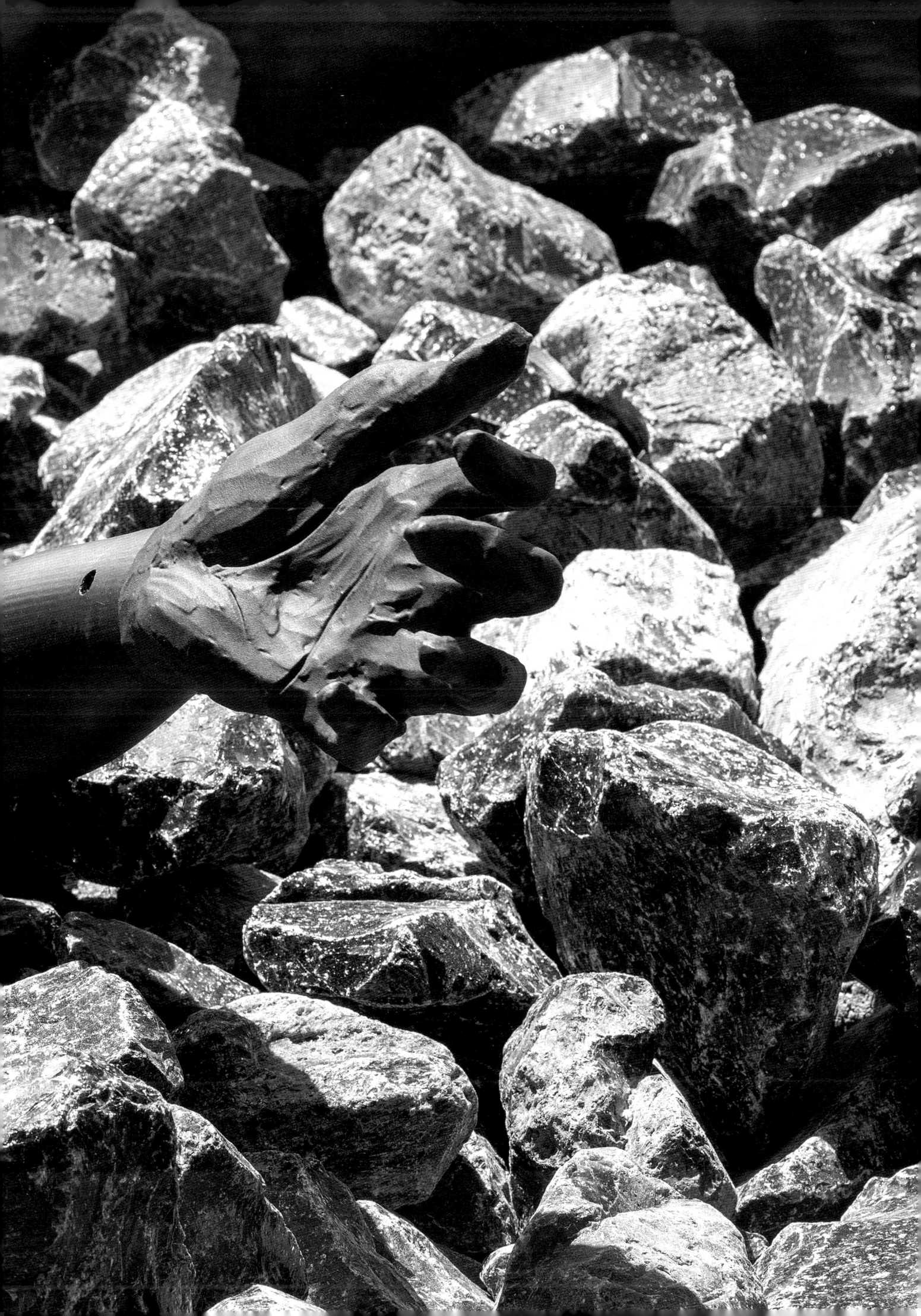

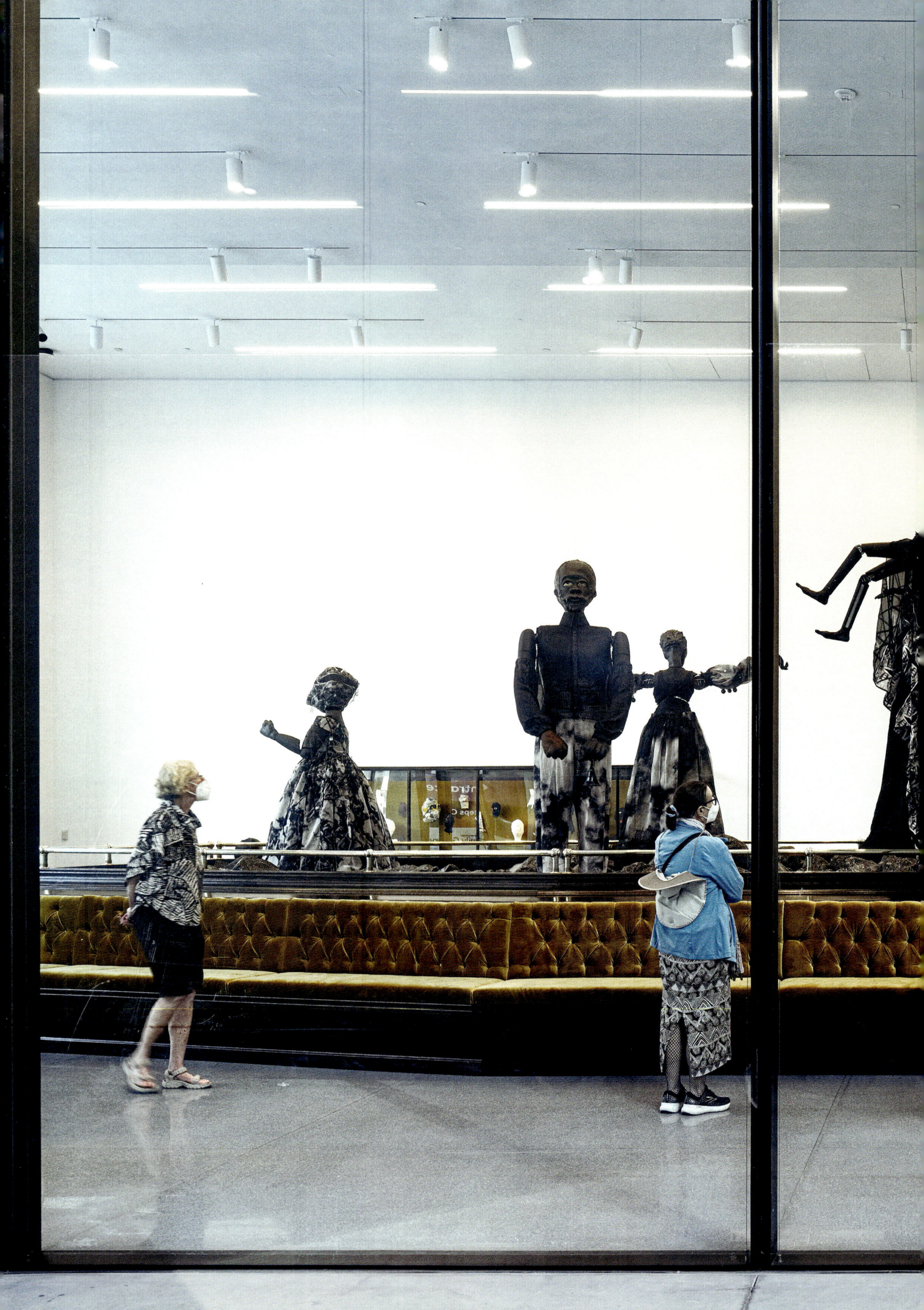

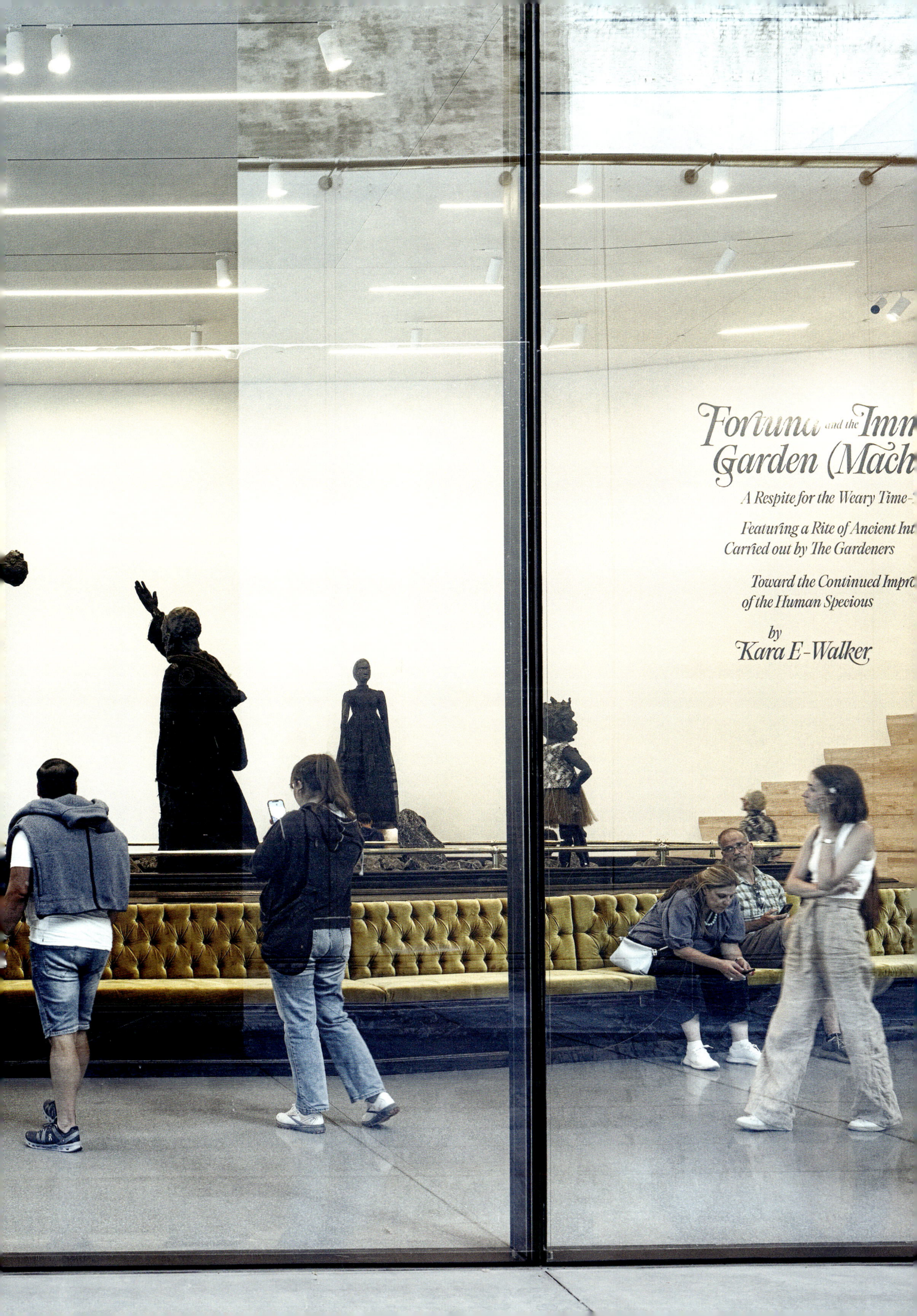

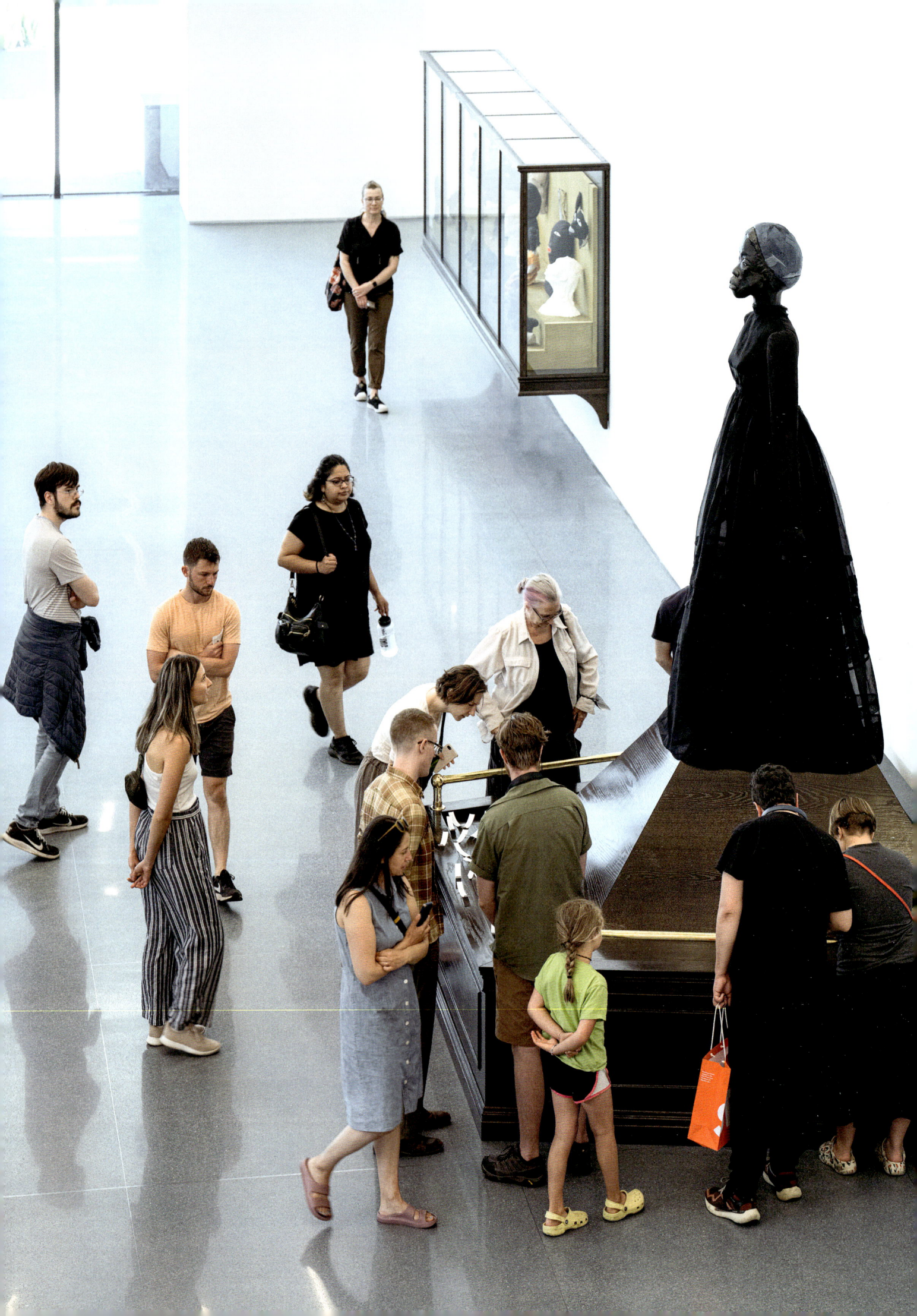

AFTERWORD
Christopher Bedford
Helen and Charles Schwab Director, San Francisco Museum of Modern Art

In an interview published on the occasion of the 1997 SFMOMA exhibition *Kara Walker: Upon My Many Masters—An Outline*, the artist, discussing an early major transition in her art, said, "I figured that if I succeeded in one radical transformation, then I could do anything." These words have proved prescient. Over and over during her exceptional career, Walker has transformed her artistic practice in astonishing ways. In the beginning stages of discussing with her a commission for our Roberts Family Gallery, her ideas seemed to me completely unfamiliar and truly singular, as if the work she was conceiving would take us somewhere uncharted—and indeed it has. At a time when imagining new futures is more critical than ever, it has been exhilarating to present *Fortuna and the Immortality Garden (Machine)*, a work of art that is bracingly relevant to our present moment and resonant with a spirit both of reckoning and of hope. And while it represents a continuation and deepening of many of the themes Walker has examined throughout thirty years of art making, it is also wholly new.

Her 1997 show at SFMOMA—part of the museum's ongoing *New Work* series—marked Walker's first solo museum exhibition on the West Coast. Since then, SFMOMA has included Walker's art in various group exhibitions and acquired it for the collection, including the monumental cut-paper work *No mere words can Adequately reflect the Remorse this Negress feels at having been Cast into such a lowly state by her former Masters and so it is with a Humble heart that she brings about their physical Ruin and earthly Demise* (1999); several remarkable works on paper; and a maquette of *The Katastwóf Karavan* (2017), the steam calliope Walker created for the triennial Prospect.4 in New Orleans. In 2018 SFMOMA awarded Walker our Contemporary Vision Award, which celebrates creators, innovators, and change-makers whose work foregrounds contemporary art as a vital part of public life.

We are immensely proud to present *Fortuna and the Immortality Garden (Machine)* in the Roberts Family Gallery, which is free to the public and visible from Howard Street. It is the first presentation in this space that takes full advantage of—and that fully activates—its purpose-based design. It is also the first work commissioned for this gallery.

I express my gratitude to Kara Walker for entrusting SFMOMA with the stewardship of *Fortuna and the Immortality Garden (Machine)*, her most ambitious installation to date. Curator and head of contemporary art Eungie Joo, who has nurtured an enduring friendship and collaboration with Walker for more than twenty-five years, ably took the lead in bringing this commission to the museum, supporting its development over the course of the past several years, and realizing it in stunning fashion. I am keenly grateful to Joo for her brilliant work on this project, and to curatorial associate Alison Guh for her dedication throughout its evolution. I add my thanks to Walker's production team and to the many SFMOMA staff members who contributed their expertise, as outlined on pages 123–25.

Many of our nearest and dearest philanthropists generously supported *Fortuna and the Immortality Garden (Machine)*. Major support was provided by Roberta and Steve Denning Commissioning Endowed Fund and Sir Deryck and Lady Va Maughan. Significant support was provided by Jim Breyer, Mary Jane Elmore, Agnes Gund, Pamela J. Joyner and Alfred J. Giuffrida, Jessica Moment, Diana Nelson and John Atwater Commissioning Fund, Deborah and Kenneth Novack, Sonja Hoel Perkins and Jonathan Perkins, SFMOMA Contemporaries, and Lydia Shorenstein. Meaningful support was provided by Alka and Ravin Agrawal, Ethan Beard and Wayee Chu, Agnes Cowles Bourne Bay Area Contemporary Arts Exhibition Fund, Davis/Dauray Family Fund, Patricia W. Fitzpatrick Commissioning Endowed Fund, Girlfriend Fund, Sheri and Paul Siegel Exhibition Fund, Sikkema Jenkins & Co., and Denise Littlefield Sobel Commissioning Endowed Fund. This project was also supported in part by the National Endowment for the Arts. This publication was furthermore supported by grants from the Jay DeFeo Foundation and Miyoung Lee.

Art history is written by individuals. I have long believed that there is an art history before Kara Walker and an art history after Kara Walker, and they are in no way the same. I extend my most profound thanks to the artist for her virtuosity and for the honor of sharing *Fortuna and the Immortality Garden (Machine)* with our audiences.

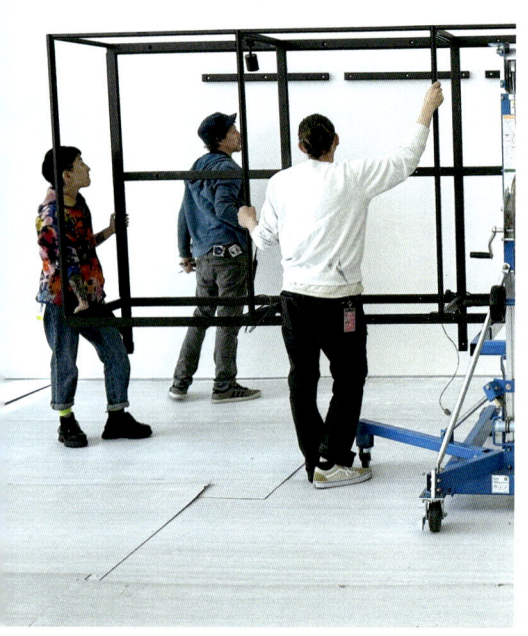
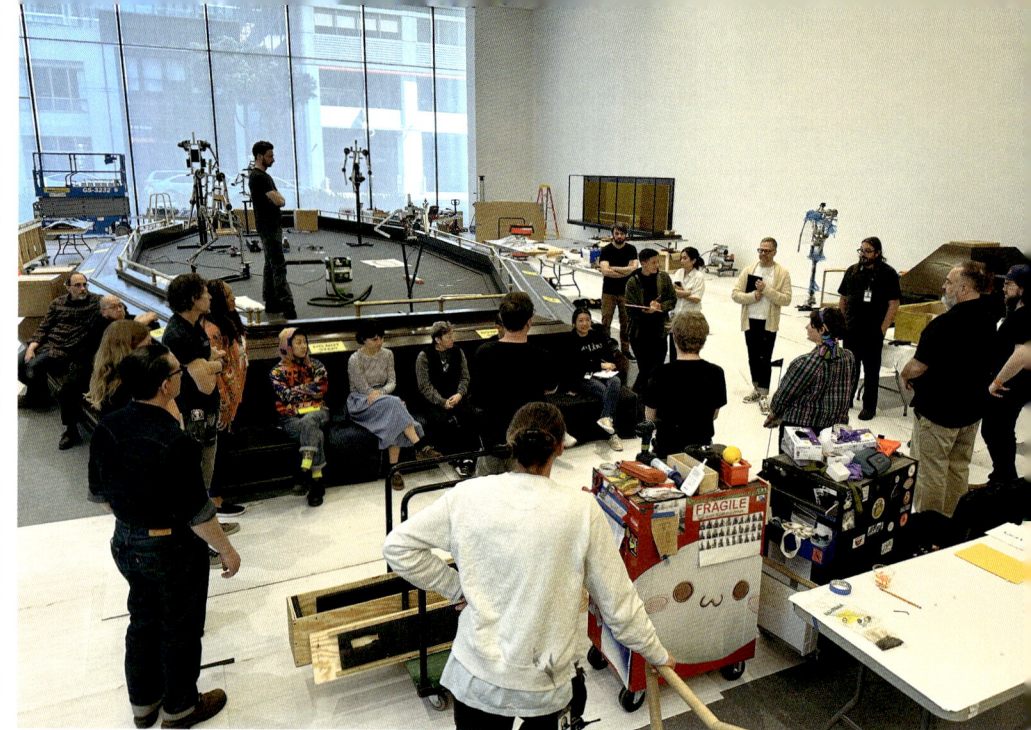
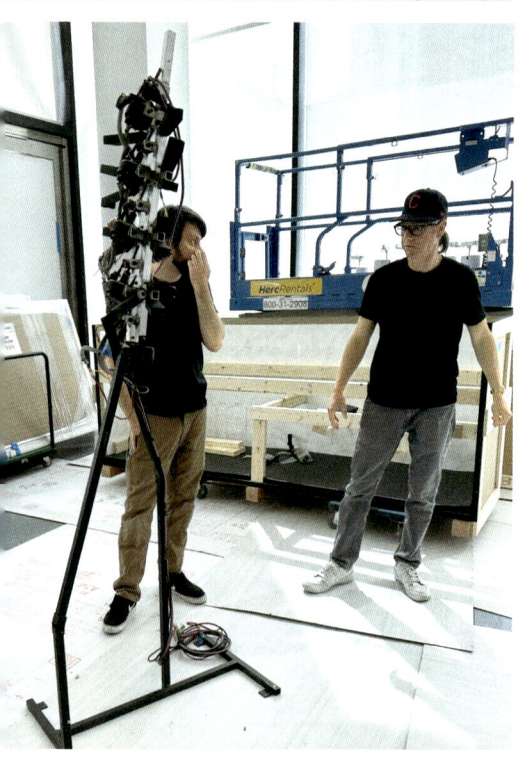
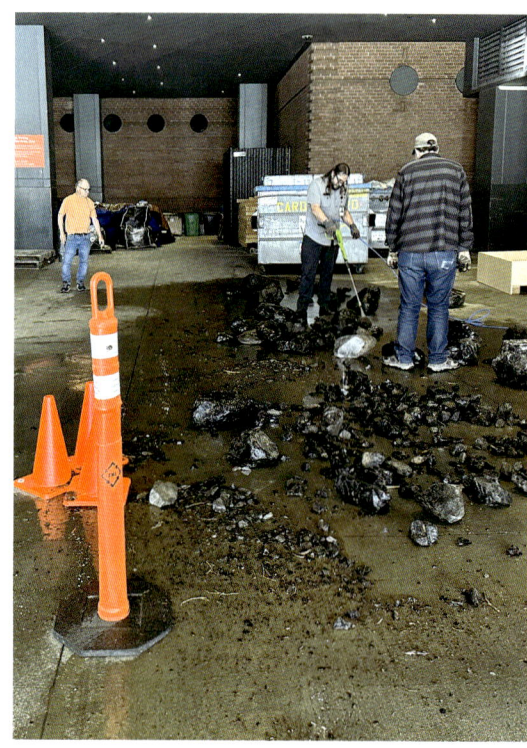
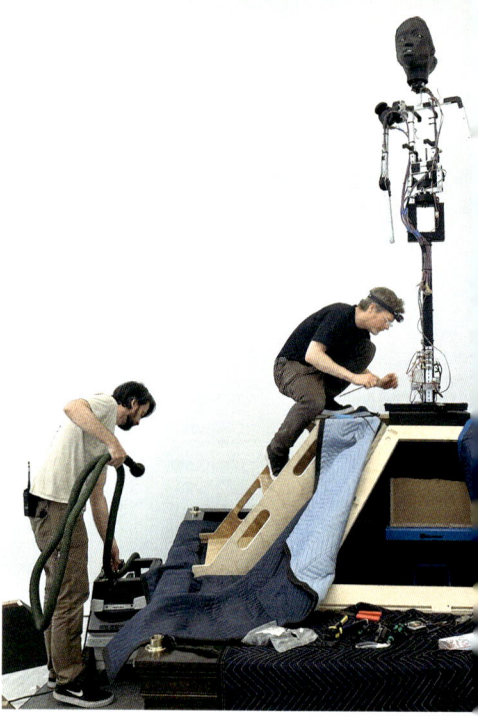
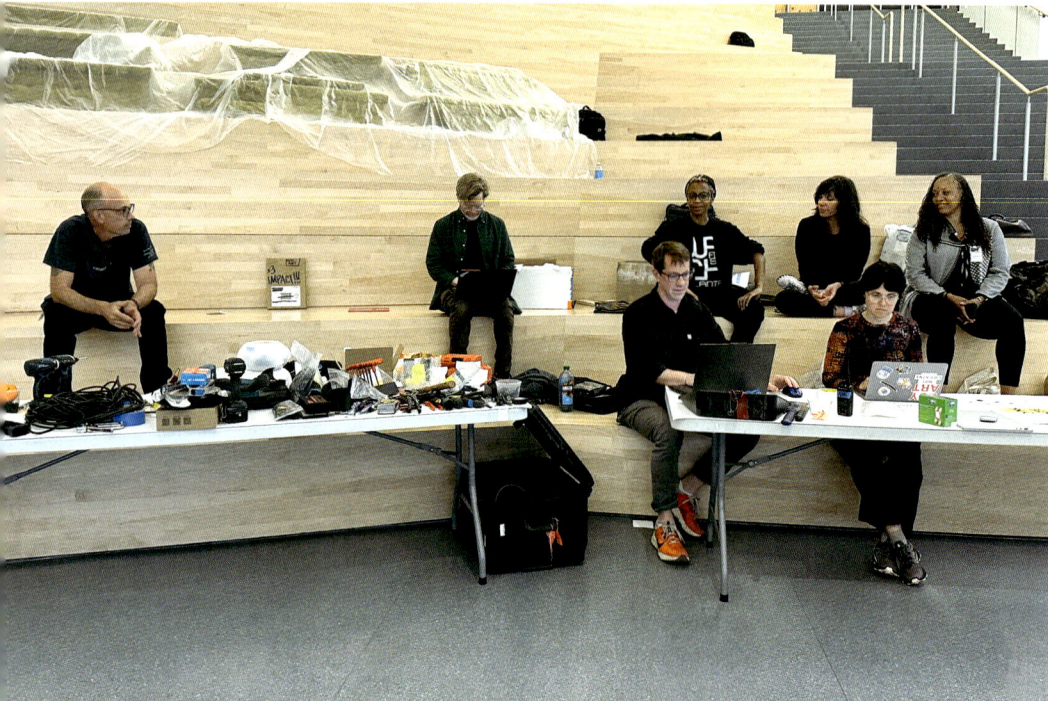
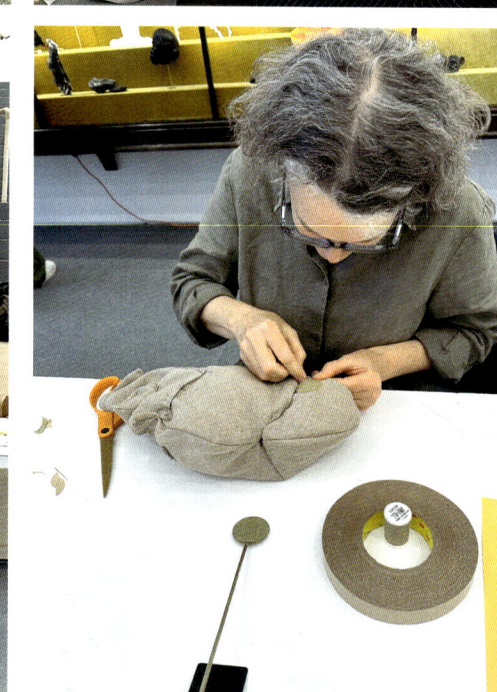

ACKNOWLEDGMENTS
Eungie Joo
Curator and Head of Contemporary Art, San Francisco Museum of Modern Art

Since I first approached Kara Walker about creating new work for SFMOMA, *Fortuna and the Immortality Garden (Machine)* has flirted with many forms, from a staged opera or its detritus to a graveyard of monumental bronze sculptures to a topographic landscape. Shaped by the intervening years of the COVID-19 pandemic with our deep isolation and heightened dependence on technology, *Fortuna and the Immortality Garden (Machine)* emerges as memorial, spectacle, and loving offering of healing—an entrancing choreography of automatons mining an energy field of gleaming black obsidian. On behalf of SFMOMA, I thank Walker for the trust she has shown in creating this profound work for our institution—arguably her most significant installation to date and the first site-specific commission for SFMOMA's Roberts Family Gallery. My appreciation goes to Christopher Bedford, Helen and Charles Schwab Director, for his sincere enthusiasm for Walker's practice and for his boundless support of this commission since starting at the museum in 2022. He recognizes all our generous funders in his afterword on page 121, but let me also express my gratitude to the many sponsors of this ambitious work and to SFMOMA's Board of Trustees for their ongoing support of the art of our time.

Special recognition is due to Meg Malloy and the entire team at Sikkema Jenkins & Co., who have generously supported Walker's work, the present exhibition, and the production of this publication at every stage, and in the midst of great tragedy. Brent Sikkema (1948–2024) was Walker's extraordinary champion and confidant for three decades, and their commitment to each other is embedded in Walker's work. Thank you, Brent.

At the museum, we are also indebted to Walker for her partnership in developing this publication, including the original text "I Am Not Your Robot," as well as for her elegant candor in our conversation published in these pages. Thanks to David A. M. Goldberg for transforming his dissertation research into the powerful essay included here, to Donna Haraway for granting us permission to reproduce an excerpt from her groundbreaking essay "A Cyborg Manifesto," and to Damani McNeil for his experimental short fiction text. This publication is richly illustrated with drawings by Walker, pages from Gary Graham's notebooks, and photography by Ari Marcopoulos and Fredrik Nilsen Studio—crucial documentation of *Fortuna and the Immortality Garden (Machine)* from its earliest stages through its final installation and experience by the public. Elizabeth Karp-Evans has taken these elements and designed a beautiful volume that immortalizes the commission; my thanks to her and Adam Turnbull at Pacific studio. We are also grateful to Julie Allred at BW&A Books for serving as production designer. Michelle Komie at Princeton University Press was an enthusiastic champion of this publication from its conception. Michelle Piranio is a remarkable editor and friend, and there is no one whom I trust more to unclutter ideas while retaining a writer's voice. Thank you for your careful editing of the exhibition and publication texts. To Kari Dahlgren, SFMOMA's fearless director of publications, who skillfully managed every aspect of this book's ambition and production—deep appreciation for your partnership and guidance in realizing this affordable but mighty publication.

I extend heartfelt thanks to my colleagues across the curatorial division—especially chief curator Janet Bishop for her unwavering support of this project over its years of development; curatorial associate Alison Guh for her work throughout the exhibition development, installation, and publication; and division administrator Jacqueline Belloso and administrative assistant Corinne Ladner for their support of travel logistics and the opening program. Thanks also to Jovanna Venegas, former associate curator, for her contributions at the early stages of the exhibition's development.

The design, fabrication, and installation of *Fortuna and the Immortality Garden (Machine)* was a monumental collaboration between the artist, her studio, numerous collaborators, and a broad team at SFMOMA. At Kara Walker Studio, we are beholden to registrar Allison Calhoun for her dedication to the publication, research, and installation; digital technician Mike Koller, who worked closely with Walker on the design of the installation; operations manager Petra Schmidt, who oversaw the production management of the work as well as partnering on logistics; and in-house fabricator

Justice Thomas, who produced all the plaster casts from Walker's air-dried clay busts and helped transform studio experiments into an incredible display. We owe an immense debt of gratitude to *Fortuna and the Immortality Garden (Machine)*'s technical lead, Noah Feehan, who spearheaded the technical development of the exhibition, as well as to the design and engineering firm Hypersonic. Led by Bill Washabaugh, the Hypersonic team of Ashwin Barama, Julia Daser, Alex Garcia, David Gould, and Mischa Langley designed and fabricated the exhibition's robotics. Sincere thanks to couturier Gary Graham, who designed the intricate costumes and haunting custom fabrics that adorn the automatons. I also extend our appreciation to New Project for fabricating the colossal exhibition furniture, especially their team members Luke Lynch and Kalle Miller, who came to install the pedestals at SFMOMA. Stitchroom upholstered the cushions surrounding the central diorama with fabric generously donated by Kvadrat; thanks go to the wonderful Julia Rodrigues for assisting us with this donation, and the New York team of Karina Frederiksen, Josefine Milora, Julia Szpunar, and Michelle Walker for working directly with Kara Walker Studio to ensure the timely shipment of samples and matching bolts of textiles. Susan Sueiro and Arpad Molnar of Obsidian Wine Co. were great partners for the imagination, ultimately providing their beautiful wine for our dinner and fundraising event as well as the more than seventeen tons of obsidian that populate Fortuna's Garden. We are grateful to Walker's dear friends Melinda Price and Simon Avery of Peace & Plenty Farm, who arranged the visit to Obsidian Ridge that piqued her interest in the healing properties of obsidian. We also recognize Broderick General Engineering, who excavated the raw material.

Installing a project of this scale, complexity, and ambition was a herculean task, involving everything from assembling, hand-dressing, and troubleshooting temperamental, custom-built automatons to handwashing thirty-five thousand pounds of raw obsidian mined from Lake County, California. Working with SFMOMA installation leads Alexander Cheves and Kimberly Walton was an absolute pleasure. They came to the project with skills, patience, and humor, nimbly leading their team of dedicated preparators, including Joseph Blake, Srimongkol (Jack) Darawali, Ximaps Dong, Bink Galbraith, Adam Henderson, Nahkoura Mahnassi, Martin Malvar, Neil Miller, Dylan Roberts, Rico Solinas, Brooke Valentine, and Mia Vienna. Alex Dangles, our technical lead, studied all the back-end programing and systems during the installation, and he continues to maintain and troubleshoot this complex project with the collections technical team of Joshua Churchill, John Davis, Steve Dye, Derek Gedalecia, Sean Horchy, Laura Kruize, Papatson Suphavai, Syl Sutton, and Jesse Walton. Meaningful thanks to Michelle Barger, Natalya Swanson, and Chantal Willi for their active participation in finalizing the costuming and their ongoing work maintaining these highly complex works. In partnership with Kevin Binkert, these teams continue to learn about the mechanics of maintaining the work to ensure that visitors experience *Fortuna and the Immortality Garden (Machine)* to its full intent for many months ahead.

Transporting and receiving a work of this scale required many hours of keen oversight and proactive planning by two remarkable registrars, Anna Lau and Jennifer Hing. Our construction and facilities teams comprising Diana Conzett Kuroda, David Dial, Brandon Larson, Ruben Oregon, and Brian Weinstein were critical partners in ensuring that the Roberts Family Gallery was ready to house this commission. No task was beyond the expert problem solving and coordination of our exhibition project managers Jillian Aubrey, who guided the project from its inception, and Angelo Hallinan, who joined the museum this year and took over with great aptitude and a priceless positive attitude. Sincere thanks to them, and to David Funk, director of exhibitions and program management; Mei Li, assistant general counsel; Dee Minnite, chief collections, exhibitions, and design officer; and Adine Varah, general counsel, each of whom worked closely with our project managers to negotiate complex contracts and budgets to realize this exhibition.

SFMOMA's design studio was integral to realizing the visual identity of the exhibition. Caroline Holley, senior graphic designer, produced a dynamic graphic identity for the exhibition in partnership with Pacific, and brought in the sign painters New Bohemia to paint the title signage above the Roberts Family Gallery's iconic roman steps. Additional thanks to Bosco Hernández, design director, and Sarah Choi, lead senior exhibition designer, for their contributions from the earliest planning to the final elements of opening to the public. I also thank Tobey Martin, who designed and produced the merchandise for the exhibition in collaboration with Walker and Ari Marcopoulos.

This exhibition was and continues to be an immense collaborative effort from countless others across SFMOMA. In philanthropy, I extend my gratitude to Samantha Leo and her staff, with special acknowledgment of Alison Bowman, Laura Cunniff, and Richard Havens for leading the fundraising efforts. Under the leadership of Sheila Shin, the museum's marketing and communications team has worked to promote this exhibition across all channels. Thanks to director of communications Clara Hatcher Baruth, who partnered with Alina Sumajin from PAVE Communications & Consulting to craft the communications strategy for this exhibition, and to our interpretive media team, Erica Gangsei and Santino Gonzales, who produced a vibrant short film about *Fortuna and the Immortality Garden (Machine)*. I additionally extend appreciation to Claire Bradley, Cristina Chan, Anne-Marie Conde, Cassie Eng, Hayley Goebel, Colin Howard, Sriba Kwadjovie Quintana, Julie Lamb, Alexandra Nguy, Don Ross, David Rozelle, and Andrea Wang for their documentation and promotion of this exhibition on all platforms. Sincere thanks to Brianna Jilson, Nicole Meshack, and the visitor experience team, as well as to Derrick Bowman, Walter Coupland, and the security team for your ongoing support on this project. Walter Logue and Tim Tengonciang in operations and Anna Tang and Nahshon Clark in finance also provided crucial support.

Fortuna and the Immortality Garden (Machine) opened to the public on July 1, 2024, with more than six hundred community members, friends, and loved ones in attendance. Sincere thanks to Gamynne Guillotte, Tomoko Kanamitsu, Kathleen Maguire, Océane Qiu, and their teams for realizing a memorable celebration, which in the spirit of the exhibition was free and open to the public. Obsidian Wine Co., Sikkema Jenkins & Co., and Sprüth Magers Gallery graciously supported the opening dinner.

I first came to know Walker's practice in 1995, when my brother, Michael Joo, who had just participated in a group exhibition with her in Paris, took me to see her show at Wooster Gardens. Introduction to her art reignited my interest in issues of representation and race and shifted the focus of my graduate studies. Walker's work became a key part of my dissertation research, and its impact on my practice as a curator cannot be overstated. We first worked together when she participated in Richard Flood's *no place (like home)* at Walker Art Center in 1997. She had not yet gone public with her pregnancy, and I was enlisted to keep her in tuna sandwiches and music while she installed her masterful cyclorama, *Slavery! Slavery! Presenting a GRAND and LIFELIKE Panoramic Journey into Picturesque Southern Slavery or "Life at 'Ol' Virginny's Hole' (sketches from Plantation Life)" See the Peculiar Institution as never before! All cut from black paper by the able hand of Kara Elizabeth Walker, an Emancipated Negress and leader in her Cause* (1997). In the intervening years, she and I have been fortunate to have several opportunities to work together on exhibitions, performances, talks, and publications in Los Angeles, New York, and San Francisco. Perhaps most significantly, we have accompanied each other on the complex and beautiful journey of this life, and I have benefited greatly from her care and insight.

Thank you, Kara, for sharing your labor, grief, hope, and love with us.

DAVID A. M. GOLDBERG is a Black San Franciscan who came of age in the era of the Commodore 64, 1200-baud online culture, and the birth of hiphop. He uses a lifelong interest in art, culture, and technology to transform the means by which people access, assess, and organize knowledge. Goldberg's independent writing and research map intersections of art, race, technology, and history with a focus on generative AI, collective intelligence, and digital epistemologies. Professionally, he is a product designer for interactive and gaming content that is grounded in and informed by the authentic experiences and desires of underrepresented folks. He is a trained programmer, a "first wave" (1998–2001) Afrofuturist, and a cofounder of betalounge.com, one of the first music streaming platforms. He holds degrees in computer systems engineering (Howard University) and visual criticism (California College of the Arts), and a PhD in American studies (University of Hawai'i at Mānoa).

DONNA J. HARAWAY is distinguished professor emerita in the History of Consciousness Department at the University of California Santa Cruz. She earned her PhD in biology at Yale in 1972, and her writing and speaking encompass science and technology studies, feminist theory, and multispecies studies. Attending to the intersection of biology with culture and politics, Haraway's work explores the string figures composed by science fact, science fiction, speculative feminism, speculative fabulation, science and technology studies, and multispecies worlding. Her numerous books include *Staying with the Trouble*: *Making Kin in the Chthulucene* (2016); *Manifestly Haraway* (2016); *When Species Meet* (2008); *The Haraway Reader* (2004); *The Companion Species Manifesto* (2003); and *Simians, Cyborgs, and Women* (1991), among others, and she coedited with Adele Clark *Making Kin Not Population* (2018). She was the subject of Fabrizio Terranova's feature-length film *Donna Haraway: Story Telling for Earthly Survival* (2016), and participated, along with philosopher Vinciane Despret, in Diana Toucedo's visual essay *Camille & Ulysse* (2021).

EUNGIE JOO is curator and head of contemporary art at San Francisco Museum of Modern Art. She was previously Keith Haring Director and Curator of Education and Public Programs at the New Museum and founding director and curator of The Gallery at the Roy and Edna Disney/CalArts Theater (REDCAT). Joo has published essays on the practices of Mark Bradford, Margaret Kilgallen, Tanya Lukin Linklater, Cinthia Marcelle, Tuan Andrew Nguyen, Adrián Villar Rojas, and Apichatpong Weerasethakul, among others. She has served as a curatorial advisor to numerous biennial and triennial exhibitions; artistic director of the 5th Anyang Public Art Project/APAP 5 (2016); curator of Sharjah Biennial 12: *The past, the present, the possible* (2015); curator of the 2012 New Museum Generational Triennial: *The Ungovernables*; and commissioner of the Korean Pavilion at the 53rd Venice Biennale, where she presented *Condensation: Haegue Yang* (2009). She earned her PhD in ethnic studies from the University of California, Berkeley.

DAMANI MCNEIL is a writer and editor from Berkeley, California. Black history and liberation are at the forefront of his writing practice—whether in the form of cultural commentary or research on housing justice—which he views as both an opportunity for the production of radical educational resources and a route to producing a more honest historical archive, curated by and for our community. McNeil studied Africana studies and politics at Oberlin College, where he edited the Arts and Culture section of the *Oberlin Grape*, writing and editing commentary on a range of auditory and visual art. His research, editing, and writing pursuits center on the intersections of music, sports, diaspora, and domestic affairs. His essay "Hoop and Black Imagination" was published in photographer Ari Marcopoulos's book *Conrad McRae Youth League Tournament* (2020). McNeil lives and works in the Outer Sunset district of San Francisco, coordinating events and nurturing a burgeoning literary press at Black Bird Bookstore.

Fortuna and the Immortality Garden (Machine) (2024) was commissioned by the San Francisco Museum of Modern Art. All images of and studies for the work in progress and as installed are © Kara Walker and courtesy the artist, Sikkema Jenkins & Co., and Sprüth Magers.

Work in progress, 2023–24
Cover and pages 6, 23 (bottom), 30, 32–33, 39, 42–43, 45–49, 51, 57, 64–73, 75, 77, photos: Ari Marcopoulos

Studies, 2023–24
Pages 2–3, 13–15, 17, 19–22, 23 (top), 24–25, 26, 27, 36, 40

Installation views, San Francisco Museum of Modern Art, 2024
Pages 10–11, 82–92, 93 (top), 94–96, 98–104, 106–13, 115–20, photos: Fredrik Nilsen Studio; pages 93 (bottom), 97, 105, 114, photos: Ari Marcopoulos; page 122: photo: Eungie Joo

Page 29, photo: Kara Walker Studio

Page 35, © 1998 Center for Creative Photography, Arizona Board of Regents

Page 41, photo: John Greenberg

Page 44, images courtesy Noah Feehan

Pages 58–63, images courtesy Gary Graham

Page 80, photo © Eugene Richards

Inside front cover: Arnold Genthe, *Untitled*, 1906, printed later. Gelatin silver print. 10 × 8 in. (25.4 × 20.3 cm). San Francisco Museum of Modern Art, 2002.145

Inside back cover: Arnold Genthe, *Untitled*, 1906, printed later. Gelatin silver print. 10 × 8 in. (25.4 × 20.3 cm). San Francisco Museum of Modern Art, 2002.144

This book is published on the occasion of the exhibition *Fortuna and the Immortality Garden (Machine) / A Respite for the Weary Time-Traveler. / Featuring a Rite of Ancient Intelligence Carried out by The Gardeners / Toward the Continued Improvement of the Human Specious / by / Kara E-Walker*, commissioned by the San Francisco Museum of Modern Art.

San Francisco Museum of Modern Art
July 1, 2024, to spring 2026

Major support for *Fortuna and the Immortality Garden (Machine)* is provided by Roberta and Steve Denning Commissioning Endowed Fund and Sir Deryck and Lady Va Maughan.

Significant support is provided by Jim Breyer, Mary Jane Elmore, Agnes Gund, Pamela J. Joyner and Alfred J. Giuffrida, Jessica Moment, Diana Nelson and John Atwater Commissioning Fund, Deborah and Kenneth Novack, Sonja Hoel Perkins and Jonathan Perkins, SFMOMA Contemporaries, and Lydia Shorenstein.

Meaningful support is provided by Alka and Ravin Agrawal, Ethan Beard and Wayee Chu, Agnes Cowles Bourne Bay Area Contemporary Arts Exhibition Fund, Davis/Dauray Family Fund, Patricia W. Fitzpatrick Commissioning Endowed Fund, Girlfriend Fund, Sheri and Paul Siegel Exhibition Fund, Sikkema Jenkins & Co., and Denise Littlefield Sobel Commissioning Endowed Fund.

SIKKEMA JENKINS&CO.

This project is supported in part by the National Endowment for the Arts

NATIONAL ENDOWMENT for the ARTS
arts.gov

San Francisco Museum of Modern Art
151 Third Street
San Francisco, CA 94103
sfmoma.org

Published in association with
Princeton University Press, Princeton and Oxford

41 William Street
Princeton, NJ 08540
USA

99 Banbury Road
Oxford OX2 6JX
UK

press.princeton.edu

This book was produced by the publications department at the San Francisco Museum of Modern Art (Kari Dahlgren, director of publications; Amanda Glesmann, managing editor; Clare Jacobson, editor; and Jessica Sevey, assistant editor).

Publication manager: Kari Dahlgren
Editor: Michelle Piranio
Designer: Elizabeth Karp-Evans, Pacific
Production design and typesetting: Julie Allred, BW&A Books
Proofreader: Bruno George

Color separations by Prographics, Rockford, Illinois
Printed by Point B Solutions, Minneapolis
Set in Editorial Old, Times Ten, and Acumin Variable
Printed on Sappi Opus Sheets Matte and Mohawk Superfine Eggshell

Library of Congress Control Number: 2024944698

ISBN: 978-0-691-27140-8

British Library Cataloging-in-Publication Data is available

10 9 8 7 6 5 4 3 2 1